PENGUIN BOOKS

LURE AND LOATHING

Gerald Early is the Director of the Department of African-American Studies at Washington University in St. Louis. He has written a book on Countee Cullen and edited *Speech and Power*, an anthology of African-American essays. He is also the author of *Tuxedo Junction*, a collection of essays on American culture, and *The Culture of Bruising: Essays on Prizefighting*. He is the recipient of a Whiting Writers' Award and a General Electric Foundation Award.

LURE
and
LOATHING

Essays on Race,

Identity, and the

Ambivalence of

Assimilation

Edited and With an Introduction by

Gerald Early

PENGUIN BOOKS

PENGUIN BOOKS

Published by the Penguin Group

Penguin Books USA Inc., 375 Hudson Street, New York, New York 10014, U.S.A.

Penguin Books Ltd, 27 Wrights Lane, London W8 5TZ, England

Penguin Books Australia Ltd, Ringwood, Victoria, Australia

Penguin Books Canada Ltd, 10 Alcorn Avenue, Toronto, Ontario, Canada M4V 3B2

Penguin Books (N.Z.) Ltd, 182–190 Wairau Road, Auckland 10, New Zealand

Penguin Books Ltd, Registered Offices: Harmondsworth, Middlesex, England

First published in the United States of America by Allen Lane The Penguin Press, an imprint of
Viking Penguin, a division of Penguin Books USA Inc., 1993
Published in Penguin Books 1994

1 3 5 7 9 10 8 6 4 2

THE LIBRARY OF CONGRESS HAS CATALOGUED THE HARDCOVER AS FOLLOWS:

Lure and loathing: essays on race, identity, and the ambivalence of assimilation/edited
with an introduction by Gerald Early.
p. cm.
ISBN 0-713-99101-1 (hc.)
ISBN 0 14 01.5937 1 (pbk.)
1. Afro-Americans—Race identity. 2. Afro-Americans—Cultural assimilation. I. Early, Gerald Lyn.
E185.625.L87   1993
305.896'073—dc20   92–50353

Printed in the United States of America
Set in Garamond No. 3
Designed by J. Metsch

Acknowledgments

I would like to thank members of the African and Afro-American Studies staff at Washington University, particularly Adele Tuchler and Raye Riggins, who provided much assistance at various stages of this project. I would also like to thank my wife, Ida, who read portions of the manuscript and made important suggestions and corrections. Finally, I would like to thank especially JoAnn Collins whose efforts on behalf of this project were of such magnitude that I do not think it would have been completed without her.

Contents

Contents

Introduction

Gerald Early

*And the chief captain answered. With a great sum obtained
I this freedom.
And Paul said, But I was free-born.*

—Acts 22:28

1. In the Beginning

As a child, whenever I was apt to become a bit too recalcitrant or
downright rebellious, refusing to do something my mother, in her
wisdom, thought it to be in my best interest to do, I would, when
scolded, reply sullenly, "Well, you know, mom, it's a free country."
And she would inevitably say, "I got news for you: That's the biggest
lie that's ever been told. Nothing's free."

The skepticism my mother displayed was far from surprising if also
a sort of unrelenting beam of hardihood bordering on sheer hardness.
But it was a skepticism only partly explained by blackness, although
my mother wears her blackness proudly enough, an unrepentant race
woman if ever there was one. It was born of an inexorable loathing of

any sense of the romantic: a widow at a very young age, a mother of three, a woman of limited formal education, I can think of no one more driven by "ought" than she was and no one more consumed by "must." For my mother, there truly was no freedom, only the necessary pursuit of the piety of duty; all the rest of life was chaos and the raging sea. This, of course, I did not understand as a child, this skepticism not entirely originating in race but of which race, in the end, becomes the only satisfactory explanation.

I have spent many contemplative moments in my adult life thinking about those two very contradictory assertions: America is a free country and nothing's free, of my mother's being caught between the inevitability, the enslavement, of duty and a piety that has no meaning unless one *chooses*, consciously and freely, to perform the duty. I have come to the conclusion that they are both true—America is a free country and nothing is or has ever been free—and that they are particularly apt polar summaries of the paradoxical circumstances of the African American.

2. *What It Means to Be an American of African Descent*

A few years ago I was surprised by a group of black students who walked into my office after my black American literature class had ended. I had just dropped off my class materials and I was about to go to lunch. A spokesman for this decidedly and ominously disgruntled group said that the students were not happy with the way I was teaching the course. "You are not teaching it in a way that is relevant to black students," I was told. "You are not teaching the course in an Afro-centric way. You are teaching this course like a white man." That I was surprised and, indeed, chagrined by this confrontation almost goes without saying. It was the end of class, I was tired, I was drained, I was hungry. And I did not feel like dealing with a group of students who wanted to choose this rather inopportune time to be "black" and polemical and who had never heard of, say, Hubert H. Harrison or could barely struggle through Du Bois's *Dusk of Dawn*. I wanted to say dismissively, "Come back and talk to me five years from now, after you have read about 150 books and have seen a bit more of life." But I decided to answer them by being teacherly in a sort of arch, Olympian way.

In my response to their complaint, I reminded them of several points: first, that I had no interest in teaching ethnic self-esteem and that if they desired that then they should not only leave my courses, they should leave college altogether and join some community organization or psychology group that promoted that cause. Second, I told them that it was impossible to understand black American literature without having some basic understanding of white American literature, which most of them, alas, did not possess. Many, if not most, black writers, I reminded them, had white models as sources of inspiration and imitation. I told them that a thorough understanding of the novels of William Faulkner would open the door to the novels of Toni Morrison. Read Theodore Dreiser, and Richard Wright becomes part of a tradition that is readily accessible. Peruse novels by Joyce, Conrad, and Melville, and Ralph Ellison's *Invisible Man* and *Shadow and Act* will no longer mystify. Third, I asked them how they would classify novels like Willard Motley's *Knock on Any Door*, Chester Himes's *Cast the First Stone*, Richard Wright's *Savage Holiday*, James Baldwin's *Giovanni's Room*, and other such books by black authors that feature white characters exclusively. It was not a good idea, I asserted, to place a black writer too tightly in the box of race. Most of them were and are fighting, in fact, to escape just such a restricted view of their work. The students found this response unsatisfactory.

In retrospect, I think the students had some cause to be dissatisfied with my response, reasonable and responsible though it was. First, there is a disingenuous aspect to it: black writers may, after all, have white models but many also have black models as well, both African and African American. Moreover, even if they did not in any circumstances ever have black models, they surely write books as a kind of ongoing dialogue with other books by blacks. The fact that I did not mention a point that would have needlessly complicated my argument is an understandable expedient that did not unduly distort my claims. My answer remains fundamentally correct.

But that is its most glaring shortcoming: that while it fairly drips with a certain earnest, if mockingly self-defensive, professionalism, it lacks patience, shielding itself by being instructively correct. I know that these black students, like most other undergraduates, do not come to literature classes to learn how and why writers write books but to see how and why a book speaks to them. They approach literature from an audience-oriented perspective, not much oriented toward the writer or the writerly process at all.

But the fact that I might be criticized for not exhibiting a bit more understanding of their needs as readers of literature does not explain why I was particularly disturbed by these black students. After all, in this regard I would have been as likely to give some such professional answer to white students who might have confronted me about teaching *The Scarlet Letter* or *Huckleberry Finn* or *Love Medicine* in an irrelevant way, especially if I was approached after a particularly tiring class session.

I was not in the end merely disturbed because they were carping students, who are generally unhappy when forced to see literature beyond the immediate feeding of the maw of autobiographical absorption. I was disturbed because they were black students and I am, alas, a black professor existing in a world—the academy being not a retreat from but in fact a reification of it—where the color of my skin and theirs means everything, in fact, explains in many painfully conspicuous ways why we are even there, providing in our manifold and great condescension the local color that most graphically illustrates the diversity of which we are both the cause and the effect, the subject and the object. I think the black professor and the black student at the white university sometimes confront each other over a gulf of precarious achievement and prosaic aspiration which can be bridged neither by revelation nor, certainly, by relief, but, in fact, only by a kind of pressurized disappointment: each thinking that he deserves a better fate than the other he faces while understanding that he has no fate other than what he faces in this moment of unveiling, as it were. Each is buoyed and embittered by the realization not that they are each other's salvation but what a paltry thing, finally, salvation for the black in an integrated world really amounts to if it is nothing more than the salvation one might be expected to have in a segregated world: a younger black and an older black approach each other and say, in effect, "Who are you?" and, in Du Boisian eloquence, "How does it feel to be a problem?" All of this has a comforting familiarity while seeming a predestined imprisonment.

I have thought a great deal over these ensuing years about what the students said, about the wickedly epistemological suggestions about my identity rooted in their complaint: what is white male pedagogy in the absence of a white male? In the absence of my being somehow "black" in a sense that these students could understand, had I through a default become white? Was whiteness simply the absence of blackness? Was I being condemned for being overly intellectual (which was their complaint), and, therefore, irrelevant on the grounds of bad politics (my intellectuality being too "Eurocentric," as it were), or simply for being boring? Or is "Eurocentricism" in a black person ipso facto a crushing form of boredom?

The idea that pedagogy should be judged according to race is absurd on its face, but the fact that they saw their relationship with me and with the school itself in those terms should have given me greater pause than it did. I chose to respond, much in the nature of God to Job, by saying, in effect, "I am the teacher and you are the student. So be it." I simply demonstrated in my answer that I was smarter than they were, which they already knew before they came to me. In fact, it is undoubtedly the reason they did come: because they wanted me to be smarter than they were, but in a different way.

What they wanted was for me to be different in a way that would illuminate the nature of their own difference, which they felt each day on the campus in the most acute and self-consciously agonizing ways. But to have a black professor who seemed no different from a white one was to say, in effect, that there was little point in taking my course, explicitly a racial one, since a white professor would be telling them virtually the same thing about the material. (In my defense, I must say that I sometimes pointed out aspects of the material that *I know* virtually no white professor would think of, but this was not simply because I am black in a generic sense but because I am a particular black *individual*. So virtually no other *black* professor would have pointed out those aspects *in the same way* that I did. I tried to be clever and, I suppose, for some black students I was too clever by half. What many of the black students wanted was for me to be more blatantly demagogic, at times, to make the white students in class feel as uncomfortable as they themselves felt when they were in classes with white professors who were dealing with white or European material. I failed the black students in one extremely important regard, in their view: I did not make them feel sufficiently superior.)

Ultimately, from their vantage point, there was little point in having me at the school at all, since I could only confirm the very fact that they wished to be denied, which is why they came to me in the first place: that blackness was not much different from whiteness. For those black students confronted me with the conundrum of blackness as theodicy: that is, in their Afrocentricism (which in its millennialistic fervor asks nothing more than this), those black students wished to know why God would give to them, to us, such a history of suffering and degradation, such a burden of warped consciousness, if blackness did not mean something, nay, everything in the beginning and the end. Were not the whites guilty of all pain, error, and evil that blacks have ever suffered in their history, as David Walker so eloquently cried in his 1828 manifesto, *The Appeal?* And, therefore, did not the meaning of the world come down to this black and white as a providential unfolding of the redemption of the blacks if, indeed, any of this is to mean anything at all? And I gave them the wrong answer, entirely and intentionally, in the irony of inadvertence, missing the point of the questions.

I should have answered, paraphrasing the unlettered workman in William James's "The Gospel of Relaxation": "There is very little difference between black Americans and white Americans when you go to the bottom of it. But what little there is, is very important."

3. The Du Boisian Dilemma

. . . his own soul rose before him, and he saw himself—darkly as through a veil.

—W. E. B. Du Bois, *The Souls of Black Folk*

One of the most famous quotations in American literature, and probably the most famous in all African American literature, is from W. E. B. Du Bois's opening chapter of his landmark 1903 book, *The Souls of Black Folk*:

> After the Egyptian and Indian, the Greek and Roman, the Teuton and Mongolian, the Negro is a sort of seventh son, born with a veil, and gifted with second-sight in this American world—a world which yields him no true self-consciousness, but only lets him see himself through the revelation of the other world. It is a peculiar sensation, this double-consciousness, this sense of always looking at one's self through the eyes of others, of measuring one's soul by the tape of a world that looks on in amused contempt

and pity. One ever feels his twoness—an American, a Negro; two souls, two thoughts, two unreconciled strivings; two warring ideals in one dark body, whose dogged strength alone keeps it from being torn asunder.

The history of the American Negro is the history of this strife—this longing to attain self-conscious manhood, to merge his double self into a better and truer self.

Although this passage is endlessly quoted, have we ever been sure what it means? What is Du Bois talking about when he speaks of this "double-consciousness"? What does he mean by "true self-consciousness"? This would imply that the Negro might possibly be a victim of false self-consciousness. Are "true self-consciousness" and "self-conscious manhood" the same thing, and what are the gender implications in the latter expression, which would seem to identify the dilemma of the Negro with that of the oppressed male only? How can it be that the Negro has been gifted with second-sight yet born with a veil, which seems a contradiction? In African American folklore (and European folklore as well), of course, it is not a contradiction to be born with a caul (literally a veil over one's face) and be considered a person gifted with supernatural powers or at least supernatural insight. Of course, the idea of the Negro's being the seventh son among the racial/national groups of the world is charged with some supernatural suggestiveness. But how can one be born with a gift of second-sight and yet have no true self-consciousness? Does Du Bois mean even a lack of self-consciousness about the nature of one's second-sight? And how is this "double-consciousness" of which he speaks related to "true self-consciousness"? Presumably, the two consciousnesses are an American consciousness and a black or racial consciousness but why do neither of these consciousness or both together yield a true self-consciousness even if they cannot be merged? Finally, does Du Bois mean that the Negro's consciousness of his own Negroness amounts to a race or racial consciousness, and what is racial consciousness?

Would it be more than a mere political consciousness or awareness of what one's race means in America as a social and political construct? Would it not have been more accurate, certainly more mythologically compelling, in the opening sentence for Du Bois to have used the word "African" instead of "Negro"? And is there a difference between "the Negro" and "the American Negro"? In short, how does consciousness relate to ethnicity and race? Obviously, Du Bois, through the use of words like "self-consciousness," "soul," "ideals," "manhood," and "blood" means something that is more than political. In fact, the words seem to be suggesting something spiritual, psychological, and biological in one fell swoop, and perhaps it is the conflating of these concepts that makes the passage so difficult to analyze. Yet, because they are words that we toss around quite a bit in discussions concerning the meaning of race, nationality, and being, the passage sounds and seems very accessible.

The first chapter of *The Souls of Black Folk* originally appeared as an essay in the August 1897 issue of the *Atlantic Monthly*, both versions bearing the same title, "Of Our Spiritual Strivings." As Thomas C. Holt pointed out in an article in the June 1990 number of *American Quarterly*, Du Bois had been thinking about double-consciousness and the black American's sense of alienation for some time. In an earlier version of the chapter delivered as a paper at the American Negro Academy in March 1897, Du Bois wrote:

No Negro who has given earnest thought to the situation of his people in America has failed, at some time in life, to find himself at these crossroads, has failed to ask himself at some time: what, after all, am I? Am I an American or am I a Negro? Can I be both? Or is it my duty to cease to be a Negro as soon as possible and be an American? If I strive as a Negro, am I not perpetuating the very cleft that threatens and separates black and white America? Is not my only possible practical aim the subduction of all that is Negro in me to the American? Does my black blood place

upon me any more obligation to assert my nationality than German, or Irish, or Italian blood would?

What this passage and the famous quotation from *The Souls of Black
Folk* reveal is twofold: first, that Du Bois saw blacks as being caught,
Hamlet-like, between the issue of a nationalistic and an assimilated
collective identity. In other words, blacks were caught, to use the
concept of Du Bois's Harvard teacher William James, in the famous
essay "The Will to Believe," published a year before the Du Bois essay,
between two live, forced options. To be an assimilated American and
to be an unassimilated Negro were both real and, more importantly,
equally or near equally appealing choices. This leads to the second
revelation in the two Du Bois statements: as the choices involved the
sanction and action of the will, not necessarily of the mind, the choices
were ultimately not just between two modes of perception but between
two modes of sentiment—Du Bois was a Victorian, after all—which
provided, either way, a format for action. Indeed, the best way to
understand the famous "double-consciousness" passage is not as the
expression of a unified idea but rather as an expression of a series of
sentiments that are, more or less, rhetorically connected. The passage
is clearly suggesting, as Holt asserts, that race and racial identity have
all the qualities of a sentiment: "contingent, contested, and historical."

Dickson D. Bruce, Jr., in the June 1992 number of *American Literature*, discusses the sources and origins for the idea of "double-
consciousness." It seems in the main that the sources are two: American
transcendentalist thought as Emerson, for instance, used the term in
an 1843 essay entitled, appropriately, "The Transcendentalist," referring to "the understanding" and "the soul" and the alternation in life
between moments of epiphany and, as Bruce puts it, "the social forces
inhibiting genuine self-realization." Philosophically, the term "double-
consciousness" is related to Romanticism, and Bruce suggests that Du
Bois was trying to elevate the idea of the Negro or African as pure
spirituality (or pure idealism, which is, philosophically, what drives

the Afrocentrics' idea of Africa's being in the mind, a location for them identical to the European Romantic's nature) by tying it to an obvious transcendentalist term; reinforcing, in one concept, not only the gift that the African had to offer to a materialistic white America but the feasibility and desirability of being African as a real option to being American or European.

The second source for double-consciousness is nineteenth-century psychology. It was a medical term describing what can be called "a split personality." Bruce suggests that Du Bois learned about this meaning of the term from William James during the former's Harvard days. But the double consciousness that is described medically is not quite the same as Du Bois's, for in the first instance the patient has two distinct personalities and is unaware of one when he or she is engaged by the other. The misery of the patient is, therefore, not having a consistent personality, not the matter of consciously knowing the temptations of both. For the Negro, as Du Bois made clear, the problem is not only knowing both personalities as American and as Negro as distinct options, that is, not simply knowing *that* both exist but consciously knowing *what* both are. It was the sense of intellectual intrigue surrounding Du Bois's famous statement—so classic in its formulation yet so baroque in its meaning, so like a blues in its fatalistic either/or yet so like a fugue in its fabricated labyrinths of invention —that led to this book.

The premise of this collection is really quite simple: nearly two dozen black intellectuals and writers were invited to write essays on assimilation, race, and identity. Nikki Giovanni, Stanley Crouch, Alton Pollard, Henry Louis Gates, C. Eric Lincoln, Wanda Coleman, Kristin Hunter Lattany, Toni Cade Bambara, Glenn Loury, Kenneth Manning, Ella P. Mitchell, Stephen Carter, James McPherson, Robert Staples, Itaberi Nieri, Reginald McKnight, Molefi Kete Asante, Anthony Walton, Wilson J. Moses, and Darlene Clark Hine, all accepted the challenge. They were given the famous Du Bois quotation as a kind of point of departure, something to get the brain cells working.

Then they were free to respond to Du Bois's quotation any way they wished to or not at all. They were free to write in any manner they wished. Some—such as Giovanni and Coleman, in keeping with being poets—wrote more fancifully; others—such as Staples and Lincoln—wrote more straightforwardly, in an expository way. Many of the essays are expansively autobiographical. All are serious meditations by black people who are, in one way or another, deeply troubled by the America in which they live. Some of the writers are identified with particular ideological positions: Asante is Afrocentric; Loury is considered a conservative; Crouch a neo-conservative; Giovanni a 1960s radical. But none of the essays here are particularly ideologically driven or particularly prescriptive. They are all thoughtful, cover a wide area of discussion, and merit considerable attention from that quarter of the public for whom this question of race and identity is important, a quarter I would think to be substantial. We can only wonder how Du Bois himself would feel if he could read these essays and contemplate how blacks at the turn of a new century are thinking about their situation. Attend.

4. At The End

One sunny, warm afternoon several weeks ago, I was playing catch with my youngest daughter as we talked about one thing and another. Finally, the conversation drifted to the topic of her friends. She had just had two girlfriends spend the weekend, and I suppose that explains why the topic of her friendships was even on my mind.

"I was wondering, Rosalind," I said, pitching the tennis ball back to her, "do you have any black friends? I mean, the only kids that come around our house are white."

"I know black kids at school," Rosalind said, throwing the ball back to me.

"Well, why don't you bring some of them home for supper or something?" I asked, missing her grounder.

"I don't like them as much as I like the kids I bring home," she said, making a one-handed catch that demanded applause.

"Well, you know, you ought to have a variety of friends. And you know you are black and you really ought to have some black friends," I said, cleanly catching Rosalind's grounder in my Darryl Strawberry glove.

"Why? Why do I have to have black friends? Just because I'm black? Don't I have the right to have any friends I want?" she asked, catching the ball one-handed again.

"Sure," I said, a little uncertain as to how to proceed. "But, you know, you wouldn't want to have a reputation among the blacks for being an, errr, Oreo, an Uncle Tom, or something like that." I think I was feeling very guilty at that moment about rearing black children in a white neighborhood, about having this awkward conversation with my child about something that discomforted me far more than it did her.

"Do you mean oriole like the bird?" she asked.

"You know what I mean," I said. "I'm sure you've heard the black kids use that term around school."

"I'm all right with the black kids," she said, catching another one with her bare hand.

"But," I continued with some noticeable tone of desperation. "I just don't want you to be unhappy. I mean, you could pay a price later on, when you're older, for having a white social life." But what I really was thinking about was not her at the moment but myself. The story of Joseph in the Old Testament is so much a metaphor for blacks in America but yet, except here and there, as in Toni Morrison's *Song of Solomon*, that tale has never caught on as the paradigm of black people's experience in America. Not like the Moses myth. Perhaps because we know the Joseph story really did not happen but something like the Moses story did. Joseph assimilated and Moses did not. Perhaps that is why the Joseph story has never caught on, never fired the collective African American mind the way Moses has. I thought of Joseph and how we need our children to carry forth our bones. Who will carry my bones home, if, when they are thrown in this American earth it is discovered, truly, that they cannot rest there? But there is only Rosalind, and here is my home. And how will this daughter see the little there is that makes us different from the whites and will she see that little difference in my bones?

"I wouldn't want you to pay later on," I repeated.

"Well, Daddy," she said, as she threw a grounder that even with my fancy Darryl Strawberry glove I could not possibly reach, "as you always like to say, nothing is free."

Gerald Early
July 25, 1992

LURE AND LOATHING

Free at Last?
A Personal Perspective
on Race and Identity
in America

Glenn C. Loury

> **Then Peter opened his mouth and said, Of a truth I perceive
> that God is no respecter of persons: But in every nation he that
> feareth him, and worketh righteousness, is accepted with him.**
>
> Acts 10:34–35.

A formative experience of my growing-up on the South Side of Chicago
in the 1960s occurred during one of those heated, earnest political
rallies so typical of the period. I was about eighteen at the time.
Woody, who had been my best friend since Little League, suggested
that we attend. Being political neophytes, neither of us knew many
of the participants. The rally was called to galvanize our community's
response to some pending infringement by the white power structure,
the exact nature of which I no longer remember. But I can still vividly
recall how very agitated about it we all were, determined to fight the

Glenn C. Loury is Professor of Economics at Boston University and has been an advisor
and consultant with state and federal government agencies and private business organizations. His essays and commentaries have been featured in *The New York Times, The Wall
Street Journal, The Public Interest, Commentary, The New Republic,* and many other publications.

1

GLENN C. LOURY

good fight, even to the point of being arrested if it came to that. Judging by his demeanor, Woody was among the most zealous of those present.

Despite this zeal, it took courage for Woody to attend that meeting. Though he often proclaimed his blackness, and though he had a Negro grandparent on each side of his family, he nevertheless looked to all the world like your typical white boy. Everyone, on first meeting him, assumed as much. I did, too, when we began to play together nearly a decade earlier, just after I had moved into the middle-class neighborhood called Park Manor, where Woody's family had been living for some time.

There were a number of white families on our block when we first arrived; within a couple of years they had all been replaced by aspiring black families like our own. I often wondered why Woody's parents never moved. Then I overheard his mother declare to one of her new neighbors, "We just wouldn't run from our own kind," a comment that befuddled me at the time. Somewhat later, while we were watching the movie *Imitation of Life* on television, my mother explained how someone could be black though he or she looked white. She told me about people like that in our own family—second cousins living in a fashionable suburb on whom one would never dare simply to drop in, because they were "passing for white." This was my earliest glimpse of the truth that racial identity in America is inherently a social and cultural, not simply a biological construct—that it necessarily involves an irreducible element of choice.

From the moment I learned of it I was at once intrigued and troubled by this idea of passing. I enjoyed imagining my racial brethren surreptitiously infiltrating the citadels of white exclusivity. It allowed me to believe that, despite appearances and the white man's best efforts to the contrary, we blacks were nevertheless present, if unannounced, *everywhere* in American society. But I was disturbed by an evident implication of the practice of passing—that denial of one's genuine self is a necessary concomitant of a black person's making it in this society. What "passing" seemed to say about the world was that if one were both black and ambitious it was necessary to choose between racial authenticity and personal success. Also, and ironically, it seemed grossly unfair to my adolescent mind that, however problematic it might be, this passing option was, because of my relatively dark complexion, not available to me!

It dawned on me after this conversation with my mother that Woody's parents must have been passing for white in preintegration Park Manor. The neighborhood's changing racial composition had confronted them with a moment of truth. They had elected to stay and to raise their children among "their own kind." This was a fateful decision for Woody, who, as he matured, became determined not simply to live among blacks but, perhaps in atonement for his parents' sins, unambiguously to become one. The young men in the neighborhood did not make this easy. Many delighted in picking fights with him, teasing him about being a "white boy," and refusing to credit his insistent, often repeated claim: "I'm a brother, too!"

The fact that some of his relatives were passing made Woody's racial-identity claims more urgent for him, but less compelling to others. He desperately wanted to be black, but his peers in the neighborhood would not let him. Because he had the option to be white—an option he radically rejected at the time—those without the option could not accept his claim to a shared racial experience. I knew Woody well. We became good friends, and I wanted to accept him on his own terms. But even I found myself doubting that he fully grasped the pain, frustration, anger, and self-doubt many of us felt upon encountering the intractability of American racism. However much he sympathized with our plight, he seemed to experience it only vicariously.

So there we were, at this boisterous, angry political rally. A critical moment came when the leaders interrupted their speech making to solicit input from "the people." Woody had an idea, and enthusiastically raised his voice above the murmur to be heard. He was cut short before finishing his first sentence by one of the dashiki-clad brothers-in-charge, who demanded to know how a "white boy" got the authority to have an opinion about what black people should be doing. That was one of our problems, the brother said, we were always letting white people "peep our hole card," while we were never privy to their deliberations in the same way.

A silence then fell over the room. The indignant brother asked if anyone could "vouch for this white boy." More excruciating silence ensued. Now was *my* moment of truth; Woody turned plaintively toward me, but I would not meet his eyes. To my eternal disgrace, I refused to speak up for him. He was asked to leave the meeting, and did so without uttering a word in his own defense. Subsequently, neither of us could bear to discuss the incident. I offered no apology or explanation, and he asked for none. However, though we continued to be friendly, our relationship was forever changed. I was never again to hear Woody exclaim: "I'm a brother, too."

I recall this story about Woody because his dilemma, and mine, tell us something important about race and personal identity in American society. His situation was made so difficult by the fact that he embraced a self-definition dramatically inconsistent with the identity reflexively and stubbornly imputed to him by others. This lack of social confirmation for his subjective sense of self left him uncertain, at a deep level, about who he really was. Ultimately there seemed to be no way for him to avoid living fraudulently—either as a black passing for white, or as a white trying (too hard) to be black. As his close friend and frequent companion I had become familiar with, and occasionally shared in, the pitfalls of this situation. People would assume when they saw us together both that he was white, and that I was "the kind of Negro who hangs out with white boys." I resented that assumption.

Since then, as a black intellectual making my living in the academic establishment during a period of growing racial conflict in our society, I have often experienced this dissonance between my self-concept and the socially imputed definition of who I am supposed to be. I have had to confront the problem of balancing my desire not to disappoint the expectations of others—both whites and blacks, but more especially blacks—with my conviction that one should strive to live life with integrity. This does not make me a heroic figure; I eschew the libertarian ideologue's rhetoric about the glorious individual who, though put upon by society, blazes his own path. I acknowledge that this opposition between individual and society is ambiguous, in view of the fact that the self is inevitably shaped by the objective world, and by other selves. I know that what one is being faithful to when resisting the temptation to conform to others' expectations by "living life with integrity" is always a socially determined, if subjectively experienced, vision of the self.

Still, I see this incident of a quarter-century ago as a kind of private metaphor for the ongoing problem of living in good faith, particularly as it relates to my personal identity as a black American. I have since lost contact with Woody. I suspect that, having tired of his struggle against society's presumptions about him, he is now passing. But that moment of truth in that South Side church basement, and my failure in the face of it, have helped me understand the depth of my own need to be seen by others as "black enough."

Upon reflection, my refusal to stand up for Woody exposed the tenuous quality of my personal sense of racial authenticity. The fact is, I willingly betrayed someone I had known for a decade, since we began to play stickball together in the alley that ran between our homes, a person whom I loved and who loved me, in order to avoid the risk of being rejected by strangers. In a way, at that moment and often again later in my life, I was "passing" too—hoping to be mistaken for something I was not. I had feared that to proclaim before the black radicals in the audience that this "white boy" at my side was in fact our "brother" would have compromised my own chance of being received among them as a genuine colleague, too. Who, after all, was there to vouch for me, had I been dismissed by one of the "brothers" as an Uncle Tom?

This was not an unfounded concern, for at that meeting, as at so many others of the period, people with insufficiently militant views were berated as self-hating, shuffle-along, "house nigger" types, complicit with whites in the perpetuation of racial oppression. Then, as now, blacks who befriended (or, heaven forbid, married) whites, who dressed or talked or wore their hair a certain way, who listened to certain kinds of music, read certain books, or expressed certain opinions were laughed at, ostracized and generally demeaned as inauthentic by other, more righteous (as in "self-righteous") blacks. The indignant brother who challenged Woody's right to speak at that rally was not merely imposing a racial test (only blacks are welcome here), he was mainly applying a loyalty test (are you truly with us or against us?) and this was a test that anyone present could fail through a lack of conformity to the collective definition of what it meant to be genuinely black. I feared that speaking up for Woody would have marked me as a disloyal Tom among the blacker-than-thou crowd. This was a fate, in those years, the thought of which I could not bear.

I now understand how this desire to be regarded as genuinely black, to be seen as a "regular brother," has dramatically altered my life. It narrowed the range of my earliest intellectual pursuits, distorted my relationships with other people, censored my political thought and expression, informed the way I dressed and spoke, and shaped my cultural interests. Some of this was inevitable and not all of it was bad, but in my experience the need to be affirmed by one's racial peers can take on a pathological dimension. Growing into intellectual maturity has been, for me, largely a process of becoming free of the need to have my choices validated by "the brothers." After many years I have come to understand that until I became willing to risk the derision of the crowd I had no chance to discover the most important truths about myself or about life—to know and accept my "calling," to perceive what I really value, what goals are most worth striving toward. In a perverse extension of the lesson from *Imitation of Life*, I have learned that one does not have to live surreptitiously as a Negro among whites in order to be engaged in a denial of one's genuine self for the sake of gaining social acceptance. This is a price that blacks often demand of each other as well.

I used to think about the irony in the idea of some blacks seeking to excommunicate others for crimes against the race, given that the external factors that affect us all are unaffected by the distinctions that so exercised the blacker-than-thou crowd. I would relish the seeming contradiction: I was still a "nigger" to the working-class toughs waiting to punish with their fists my trespass onto their white turf, yet I could not be a "brother" to the middle-class radicals with whom I shared so much history and circumstance. My racial identity in the larger white society was in no way conditional upon the espousal of particular beliefs or values (whatever my political views or cultural interests, I would always be black in white America), yet my standing among other blacks could be made conditional upon my fidelity to the prevailing party line of the moment. I would ponder this paradox, chafing at the restraint of an imposed racial uniformity, bemoaning the unfairness that I should have to face a threat of potential ostracism as punishment for the sin of being truthful to myself. In short, I would wallow in self-pity, which is always a waste of time. These days I am less given to, if not entirely free of, such inclinations.

Underlying my obsession with this paradox was a premise which I now believe to be mistaken—that being an authentic black person involves in some elemental way seeing oneself as an object of mistreatment by white people, while participating in a collective consciousness of that mistreatment with other black people. As long as I believed that my personal identity as a black American was necessarily connected to our country's history of racial violation, and derived much of its content from my sharing with other blacks in a recollection of and struggle against this violation, I was destined to be in a bind. For, as my evolving understanding of our history began to clash with the black consensus, and my definition of the struggle took on a different, more conservative form from that popular among other black intellectuals, I found myself cut off from the group, my racial bona fides in question. I was therefore forced to choose between my intellectual integrity and my access to that collective consciousness of racial violation and shared experience of struggle which I saw as essential to my black identity. Like Woody, lacking social confirmation of my subjective sense of self, I was left uncertain about who I really was.

I no longer believe that the camaraderie engendered among blacks by our collective experience of racism constitutes an adequate basis for any person's self-definition. Even if I restrict attention to the question "Who am I as a black American at the end of the twentieth century?," these considerations of historical victimization and struggle against injustice do not take me very far toward finding an answer. I am made "black" only in the most superficial way by virtue of being the object of a white racist's hate. The empathetic exchange of survivors' tales among "brothers," even the collective struggle against the clear wrong of racism, does not provide a tapestry sufficiently rich to give meaning and definition to the totality of my life. I am so much 'more than the one wronged, misunderstood, underestimated, derided, or ignored by whites. I am more than the one who has struggled against this oppression and indifference; more than a descendant of slaves now claiming freedom; more, that is, than either a "colored person" (as seen by the racist) or a "person of color" (as seen by the antiracist.)

Who am I, then? Foremost, I am a child of God, created in his image, imbued with his spirit, endowed with his gifts, set free by his grace. The most important challenges and opportunities that confront me derive not from my racial condition, but rather from my human condition. I am a husband, a father, a son, a teacher, an intellectual, a Christian, a citizen. In none of these roles is my race irrelevant, but neither can racial identity alone provide much guidance for my quest to adequately discharge these responsibilities. The particular features of my social condition, the external givens, merely set the stage of my life, they do not provide a script. That script must be internally generated, it must be a product of a reflective deliberation about the meaning of this existence for which no political or ethnic program could ever substitute.

Or, to shift the metaphor slightly, the socially contingent features of my situation—my racial heritage and family background, the prevailing attitudes about race and class of those with whom I share this society—these are the building blocks, the raw materials, out of which I must construct the edifice of my life. The expression of my individual personality is to be found in the blueprint that I employ to guide this project of construction. The problem of devising such a plan for one's life is a universal problem, which confronts all people, whatever their race, class, or ethnicity. By facing and solving this problem we grow as human beings, and give meaning and substance to our lives. In my view, a personal identity wholly dependent on racial contingency falls tragically short of its potential because it embraces too parochial a conception of what is possible, and of what is desirable.

Thus, and ironically, to the extent that we individual blacks see ourselves primarily through a racial lens, we sacrifice possibilities for the kind of personal development that would ultimately further our collective, racial interests. We cannot be truly free men and women while laboring under a definition of self derived from the perceptual view of our oppressor, confined to the contingent facts of our oppression. In *A Portrait of the Artist as a Young Man* James Joyce says of Irish nationalism: "When the soul of a man is born in this country there are nets flung at it to hold it back from flight. You talk to me of nationality, language, religion. I shall try to fly by these nets. . . . Do you know what Ireland is? . . . Ireland is the old sow that eats her farrow." It seems to me that, too often, a search for some mythic authentic blackness works similarly to hold back young black souls from flight into the open skies of American society. Of course there is the constraint of racism also holding us back. But the trick, as Joyce knew, is to turn such "nets" into wings, and thus to fly by them. One cannot do that if one refuses to see that ultimately it is neither external constraint nor expanded opportunity but rather an indwelling spirit that makes this flight possible.

Last winter, on a clear, cold Sunday afternoon, my three-year-old son and I were walking in the woods near our New England home. We happened upon a small pond, which, having frozen solid, made an ideal skating rink. Dozens of men, ranging in age from late teens to early thirties were distributed across the ice in clusters of ten or so, playing, or preparing to play hockey. They glided over the pond's surface effortlessly, skillfully passing and defending, stopping and turning on a dime, moving with such power, speed, and grace that we were spellbound as we watched them. Little Glenn would occasionally squeal with delight as he marveled at one astounding feat after another, straining against my grip, which alone prevented him from running out onto the ice to join in the fun.

All of these men were white—every last one of them. Few took notice of us at the pond's edge, and those who did were not particularly generous with their smiles, or so, at least, it seemed to me. I sensed that we were interlopers, that if we had come with sticks and skates we would not necessarily have been welcome. But this may be wrong; I do not really know what they thought of our presence; no words were exchanged. I do know that my son very much enjoyed watching the game, and I thought to myself at the time that he would, someday too soon, come asking for a pair of skates, and for his dad to teach him how to use them. I found myself consciously dreading that day.

The thought of my son's playing hockey on that frozen pond did not sit well with me. I much preferred to think of him on a basketball court. Hockey, we all know, is a white man's game. Who was the last "brother" to play in the NHL? Of course, I immediately sensed that this thought was silly and illegitimate, and attempted to banish it from my mind. But it kept coming back. I could not avoid the feeling that something important was at stake here. So I decided to discuss it with my wife, Linda.

We had carefully considered the implications for our children of our decision to buy a house in a predominantly white suburb. We joined and became active in a church with many black families like our own, in part so that our boys would be provided with suitable racial peers. We are committed to ensuring that their proper education about black history and culture, including their family history, is not left to chance. We are ever vigilant concerning the effect on their developing psyches of racial messages that come across on television, in their books, at their nursery school, and so on. On all of this Linda and I are in full accord. But she thought my concerns about hockey were taking things a bit too far.

I now believe that she was right, and I think I have learned something important from our conversations about this issue. My aversion to the idea of my son's involvement in that Sunday-afternoon ritual we witnessed was rooted in my own sense of identity, as a black American man who grew up when and where I did, who has had the experiences I have had. Because *I* would not have felt comfortable there, I began to think that *he* should not want to be a part of that scene either. I was inclined to impose upon my son, in the name of preserving his authentic blackness, a limitation of his pursuits deriving from my life but not really relevant to his. It is as if I were to insist that he study Swahili instead of Swedish because I could not imagine myself being interested in speaking Swedish!

The fact is that, given the class background of our children and the community in which we have chosen to make our lives, it is inevitable that their racial sensibilities will be quite different from ours. Moreover, it is impossible to predict just what self-definition they will settle upon. This can be disquieting to contemplate for those of our generation concerned about retaining a "genuinely black" identity in the face of the social mobility we have experienced within our lifetimes. But it is not, I think, to be feared.

The alternative seems much more frightening to me—stifling the development of our children's personalities by imposing upon them an invented ethnicity. I have no doubt that my sons will be black men of the twenty-first century, but not by their singing of racial anthems peculiar to our time. Theirs will be a blackness constructed yet again, out of the external givens of their lives, not mine, shaped by a cultural inheritance that I am responsible to transmit but expressed in their own voices, animated by a Spirit whose basis lies deeper than the color of any man's skin, and whose source is "no respecter of persons."

Sushi and Grits:
Ethnic Identity and
Conflict in a Newly
Multicultural America

Itabari Njeri

At a camp in the woods of eastern Massachusetts, a woman stepped to the front of a room bathed in harsh fluorescent light and took the hand of Barbara Love. "So, tell us who you are," said Love. The woman shifted from side to side. She flashed a nervous smile. Knowing she was here to heal, knowing it was a setting of anonymity, knowing she had the complete, respectful attention of a community of people who—no matter their disparate origins—had lived some piece of her psychic terror, she spoke her name.

"Gloria.* I am of Creole ancestry, born in Louisiana." She was about forty-five, a handsome, statuesque woman with a hint of gold in a complexion that was brown like the crown of a well-baked biscuit. A college dean, she told the group she often mediates disputes involving

---

Itabari Njeri, a 1992 Pulitzer Prize finalist for distinguished criticism and Contributing Editor to *The Los Angeles Times Magazine*, specializes in interethnic relations and cultural diversity. During a twelve-year career, she has won numerous awards, including an Associated Press award for feature writing, the National Association of Black Journalists award for feature writing, and a National Endowment for Humanities Fellowship for Outstanding Journalists. Njeri—African, East Indian, English, and French—describes herself as a typical descendant of the African diaspora. Her memoir, *Every Good-bye Ain't Gone*, won the 1990 American Book Award.
* Some names and details have been changed to protect the anonymity of sources.

issues of "race"* and ethnicity on campus. "I," she said, "was the darkest one in my family. All my life I heard my grandparents, my cousins, my—everyone—whispering 'nigger-nigger-nigger-nigger. . . .' " The more she said it, the more it became an aspirate hiss—" 'nihhger-nihhger-nihhger . . . NIHHGGER!' " She laughed. *"Errrgggggg."* It was the sound of someone gargling with gravel. She shivered.

"When I had my first child, it was a beautiful mahogany-colored boy. He was so beautiful. *Errrgggggg."* She shook again. "Then I had my daughter." The woman moaned.

Love caressed her hand and smiled encouragingly. "Then you had a daughter," she said. They stood silent for seconds. All that was flesh and wood in the room seemed to breathe with them. Gloria looked at the gathering of Re-Evaluation Counselors—Puerto Ricans, Chinese Americans, Colombian Americans, Japanese Americans, and the seemingly endless variations on "Black." All of them were members of an international peer-counseling community spawned by the human po-

* Except in direct quotations, I will place the word "race" in quotes or italics to signal how problematic the use of this term is. As many social scientists have acknowledged for years, "race" is a pseudo-scientific category that has been used to justify the political subordination of non-White peoples based on superficial physical differences. "Race," of course, is a social construct of enormous political significance. But there is one race, *Homo sapiens*, and the physical variations that characterize the species do not amount to fundamental, qualitative differences, as the popular use of the term suggests.

The cultural and physical variations among humans are best contained within the concept of ethnicity, a term that can encompass shared genetic traits, culture, and history—real or perceived.

Further, no one's skin color, obviously, is literally black or white. Phenotype is not a definitive indicator of one's genetic background. Recognizing, however, that social identity in the United States is based primarily on this color divide, I acknowledge it, but treat *Black* and *White* as proper nouns. Throughout this essay I use *Black* to refer to so-called *Negroid* peoples in Africa or of African descent, treating it as a generic ethnic reference to people lumped together for political reasons though, indeed, linked by history, blood, and culture—no matter how distant or diluted. Similarly, I treat *White* as a proper noun, a generic ethnic reference to so-called *Caucasoid* peoples, especially Europeans, Euro-Americans, and others claiming pure European ancestry.

Both the accepted meanings attached to "race" and ethnicity in our current social lexicon and my challenges to them are imperfect descriptors. My hope is that, by challenging our *a priori* acceptance of "race," and the social classifications that result, I will prompt discussions of "race" as a concept, "racism" as an ideology, and the false reality they create in our daily lives.

tential movement, influenced by twelve-step programs such as Alcoholics Anonymous, and based on an understanding that the hurt child in all of us is usually the result of damage from physical injury, illness, or various forms of social oppression—classism, racism, sexism, adultism (the oppression of children). Further, RC assumes that unless we have a safe place to express the pain that results from these assaults to the psyche, the wounds fester, and can lead to rigid, irrational patterns of thought and behavior.

But here Gloria had the safety to speak.

She squealed, "Blue eyeeeees. My daughter, she was vanilla-colored, like ice-cream, with red hair and blue . . . eyes." She pulled her shoulders to her ears. "And I freaked out."

"Why?"

"Why? Why?" Her voice was singsong. "Because . . ." Then, from some boxed-up corner of her soul, she let loose a scream so primal it seemed to reach back thirty thousand years . . . pierced the room's thin, dry wall . . . echoed through the woods . . . shook the leaves and scarred the trees. "Because . . ."

And then this biscuit-brown woman revealed that she'd spent the past twenty-five years of her life in mortal fear that her vanilla-ice-cream-colored child would hate her, reject her because . . .

"I'm a nigger. Oh, God, because I'm Black, because I'm so Black. . . ." And then she screamed that ancient scream again and fell into moaning for what seemed an eternity by the unyielding knot in my gut. I heaved and thought of Jeffrey, my cousin. He looked like Ricky Nelson and always wanted to be the baddest nigger on the block.

Like me, he was African American and Caribbean American or, to break it down, African, French, English, Arawak, East Indian, and probably more—a typical New World Black. When he was being sent to prison, the judge, examining his record, called him a White man. My cousin protested and pointed to our brown-skin grandmother in the courtroom. "If she's Black, I'm Black, too." Then he demanded he be treated just like any other "Negro." The judged obliged, adding a year to his sentence.

Trying to prove how bad he was in the eyes of other Black men, my cousin bought into the street life, absorbing, as they had, an oppressor's definition of a Black male: a hustler—confusing patterns of survival for culture. And since Jeffrey was a Black man growing up in Harlem during the late fifties, he saw few options but the street life. But his looks made the price of admission exceedingly high.

When they found his body on a Harlem rooftop, bloated, bullet-pierced, it was because he'd spent his too-short life trying to prove how *bad* he was.

I cannot hear this golden-hued Creole woman's story without thinking of Jeffrey or his sister—pale, golden-haired, and hoping desperately that her next baby is *black-black-black*—wishing out loud that she could give her first child to somebody else to raise 'cause he's so *light-light-light*.

Caught in the shifting, irrational nuances of a seldom acknowledged but constantly reinforced color hierarchy, and the aesthetic preferences that accompany it, I know that moaning woman, in her capacity as dean and sometime mediator, has to deal with feelings of inadequacy and resentment based on the hue of her skin when dealing with other people of color. These feelings impede her effectiveness as a mediator and, in her larger community, a political activist. I believe it's one of many similar psychological factors that insidiously undermine attempts by Blacks, and other people of color, to achieve economic, political, and cultural self-determination. These psychological factors are rooted in our oppression by the dominant group in this society and its rationalizing ideology of White supremacy, which is used to mask and facilitate class exploitation of every ethnic group in this country.

What writer Alice Walker defined as *colorism*, the preferential or prejudicial treatment of same-*race* people based on skin color, continues to this day. And as she once wrote, unless we exorcise it "we cannot as a people progress. For colorism, like colonialism, sexism and racism, impedes us."

Just four years ago, two Euro-American social scientists documented that the social and economic gap between light- and dark-skinned African Americans is as significant as "one of the greatest socioeconomic cleavages in America," the chasm between the income and status of all Blacks and Whites. A dark-skinned Black earns seventy cents for every dollar a light-complexioned African American makes, according to the 1988 study conducted by Michael Hughes and Bradley R. Hertel, professors at Virginia Polytechnic Institute and State University in Virginia. Most telling, said the two social psychologists, are the percentages for Blacks and Whites that show who is employed in professional and managerial occupations—high-status jobs.

Almost 29 percent of all Whites hold such jobs, the study found, while Blacks hold only about 15 percent. That is nearly a two-to-one ratio. Ironically, the same ratio holds true for light-skinned Blacks— 27 percent of whom hold such jobs—compared with 15 percent of dark-skinned Blacks who were employed in these positions.

Significantly, when Hughes and Hertel compared their findings to studies done between 1950 and 1980 on the relationship between skin color and socioeconomic status, they concluded that nothing had "changed appreciably." The effect of "skin color on life chances of Black Americans was not eliminated by the Civil Rights and Black pride movements."

Understandably, African Americans are loath to acknowledge such disparities, even though we aren't to blame for them. It undermines the image of ethnic solidarity.

"It's absurd for any Black person to be talking about [color distinctions among African Americans] without talking about White supremacy," says Washington, D.C., psychiatrist Frances Cress Welsing, the controversial author of "The Cress Theory of Color Confrontation and Racism (White Supremacy)," which traces the roots of White racism to a fear of genetic annihilation of the planet's White minority.

"It is White people that keep saying and imposing that if you look like an African you should be at the bottom of the choice spectrum."

That is what Hughes and Hertel concluded from their study, too. They found that skin color, like gender, acts as a "diffuse status characteristic." For example, a man is believed more competent to pilot a plane than a woman "when in fact there is no evidence that gender has anything to do with ability," Hughes said.

Skin color works this way too, and that's how Whites respond to it. "We focused on Whites because White people are the ones who are generally responsible for making upper-level management and personnel decisions. They are more likely to decide whether people get through educational institutions." In short, they are the ones in power. And when they look at a darker-complexioned Black person, Hughes and Hertel believe, they think they are seeing someone "less competent"—someone less like them than a fairer-complexioned person.

White people may make these distinctions, African Americans argue, but most Blacks don't, they continually insist, reading from a script W. E. B. Du Bois might have written in the first quarter of this century.

In a 1921 attack on the Jamaican-born Black nationalist leader Marcus Garvey, Du Bois, writing in an issue of *The Crisis*, contended that "Garvey has sought to import to America and capitalize the antagonism between blacks and mulattoes in the West Indies. This has been the cause of the West Indian failures to gain headway against whites. Yet Garvey imports it into a land where it never had any substantial footing and where today, of all days, it is absolutely repudiated by every thinking Negro. . . . American Negroes recognize no color line in or out of the race, and they will in the end punish the man who attempts to establish it."

When I raise the painful issue of colorism, African Americans write angry letters, call in to radio shows or attack me in person, asserting I exaggerate the problem, the problem doesn't exist, or, conversely, accuse me of airing the "race's" dirty laundry.

Seventy-one years after Du Bois, essayist Stanley Crouch claims: "Hysterically overstated. If that were really true, most Afro-Americans

I know of couldn't even have Christmas dinner, 'cause they'd have too wide a range of people in the family. I mean the light-skinned ones would have to meet on Avenue L for light, and the dark-skinned ones would have to meet on Avenue D for dark."

While taking questions from listeners during one radio show, I was told, "You just raise this colorism stuff 'cause you're light with green eyes and wanna be White."

"Where did you get that impression?" I asked.

"I've seen you," the caller insisted, "on TV, in magazines."

"I'm looking at the sister," said the radio show's host, "and she looks like nothing you've described."

"I can tell from the passion in your voice that you've suffered a lot because of looking White," another caller told me. "But forgive, it'll be all right."

I have been called redbone a few times in my life. And once, from a distance, late at night, a Haitian cab driver said he almost mistook me for a White woman. (A bartender in a Tanzanian hotel actually believed I was White because I was so much lighter than he.) Those exceptions aside, no one in America has ever mistaken sapodilla-brown me (that's the color my Guyanese relatives call me) for anything but a New World Black.

I know the exact moment I was compelled to investigate the extent and impact of colorism among our people. It was 1976. I was not long out of college, living in Brooklyn, recovering from my travels as a backup singer with Major Harris of "Love Won't Let Me Wait" fame and reading Alice Walker's essay "If the Present Looks Like the Past, What Does the Future Look Like?" in *In Search of Our Mothers' Gardens*.

I wanted to know who these light-skinned Black women were that Walker wrote were insensitive to the pain of their darker-skinned sisters. As with many light-complexioned Blacks, the people in my family who looked closest to being White compensated by being aggressively Black.

But Walker wrote: "I think there is probably as much difference between the life of a black black woman and a 'high yellow' black woman as between a 'high yellow' woman and a white woman."

I put down the book and called the woman who had been my best friend since college, Celia. She was short, beautiful, charismatic, and a black-black Black woman. She was more than a dear friend. I called her Sister C.

When we hung up, I was numb. And for many days after, I would suddenly weep when alone, replaying her voice in my head. How could we have been so close and I not know how much she'd been hurt by people contemptuous of her for her color, her belligerently close-cropped hair, and the defiantly neon-bright colors she wore? And she was particularly bitter about her relatives, half of whom looked White, some of whom passed for White, and had practically disowned Celia and the other dark, poorer members of her family. Over the next decade I would watch Celia, with the help of friends but virtually none of her more affluent, fair-complexioned relatives, take care of two parents stricken with Alzheimer's and no money, nurse the children of several brothers who had been lost to the streets, put one parent in the grave, leave another in a nursing home, and finally die herself of cancer at the age of thirty-eight.

In 1988, two years before Celia's death, I remember telling a very dark-complexioned acquaintance—a fellow female journalist—how appalled I was at the pervasiveness of a problem I, too, had thought buried. She looked me up and down with silent contempt, examining pore by pore my face—a fraction past yellow, barely brown—and shot a blast of air through her nose that was half a chuckle, half a snort. "You just finding all this out?"

While all Blacks suffer discrimination in America, the darker one's skin the more one's humanity is ignored. "You know the Links," said E. B. Attah, a Nigerian-born sociologist who has taught at Atlanta University, referring to the elite Black social-service organization. "Well, I had a member of the Links showing me pictures of different chapters. When she encountered a dark-skinned woman in a picture she'd say: 'How did *she* get in there?'

"I'm very dark-skinned and anybody in this country who is dark-skinned can tell you about encountering situations of lighter-skinned people devaluing you as a human being because of your darkness."

About a year ago, I sat in an African American braiding parlor in Los Angeles having my hair done. Two men walked in and waited for a friend. "Did you see the guy Pam brought to the party last night?" one asked.

"I was too busy jammin'. What did he look like?"

The other man chuckled. "If you'd seen him, you'd remember. The nigger looked like eleven fifty-nine."

My mouth dropped and I lifted my bent head. "You mean a shade shya midnight?"

The guy laughed. "You got it, sister."

Said one twenty-three-year-old man I interviewed, after hearing him on a radio show: "I did say I want a fair-complected Black woman." Brown-skinned, which is what he described himself as being, "is all right." He just didn't want a woman who's too dark. And his parents didn't want him dating one either.

The one time he did bring home a dark-skinned girl, his mother took him aside and said: "Don't let it go too far. We don't want any dark people in our family." Both his parents are light brown, the man said.

"My sister has two beautiful light-skinned children," and that's what he wants too. "I don't want to marry a woman who's African dark, even if she's really nice. Uh uh. Nope. I'm going to be truthful. I don't want to walk into the room at night and be scared by just the whites of her eyes."

. . . nihhgger-nihhgger-nihhgger . . . and I freaked out . . . she screamed . . . primal . . . thirty-thousand years . . . scarring the trees . . . My name is Gloria. . . .

Against this historical landscape of psychological anguish, fortified daily by continued socioeconomic discrimination based on color and "race," comes a new generation of so-called multiracial Americans demanding that they be acknowledged as a distinct "racial" group. The concerns they raise are not new within communities of color. However, that their concerns are becoming part of a national debate relates to massive population shifts that may lead to a new majority in twenty-first-century America: people of color. Many demographers predict that Whites (I don't consider most Latinos White, given their largely mixed Indian, African, and European ancestry) may be a minority toward the end of the next century. Latino and Asian immigration, the higher birthrate among Latinos and Blacks and intermarriage among all groups are key factors in the rise of the multiethnic population.

Tagged an "emerging" population by social scientists, multiethnic Americans may be the most significant group to spring from a newly pluralistic America. Their demand for recognition is stimulating what I think will be a decades-long debate—one that may force all Americans to confront the myths that surround "race" and ethnicity in the United States.

High on the political agenda of many now-vocal multiethnic Americans is the demand for a new "multiracial" census category that specifically identifies ethnically and "racially" mixed citizens. The size of the "multiracial" population may be about five million—probably more than twice that number, say multiethnic activists. But the exact figures are unknown because the census requires people to either identify with one "race" or ethnic group or to check "other" when filling out data for the Census Bureau.

The ranks of multiethnic activists are being bolstered by their monoethnic kin—parents, grandparents, and spouses—who have helped form support groups in, among other places, Atlanta, Buffalo, Chicago, Houston, Los Angeles, Omaha, San Diego, Seattle, San Francisco, Pittsburgh, and Washington, D.C. Similar support groups are popping up on college campuses, particularly in California, a center of multicultural activism. While these activists failed to get a new multiethnic designation on the 1990 census, they are pushing to see one established for the year 2000.

In general, supporters of the category want recognition and political representation for people of mixed heritage. Opponents say minority groups would shrink if such a designation is allowed, leading to a loss of political representation and congressionally appropriated funds, based on the census count, used to remedy the effects of past and continuing discrimination.

These multiethnic Americans may be Mexican American and Italian American; Japanese American and Cherokee; Korean American, Armenian American, and Chinese. But the most problematic amalgams are those that include the genes of America's most stigmatized group: Negroes, Blacks, Afro-Americans, African Americans, African heritage people—a "spade" by any other name in the consciousness of still too many White Americans. The issue of a special census designation, and social recognition, is especially important to this group because of the way in which "race" has been traditionally defined in America for people of African descent: socially, any known or perceived African ancestry makes one Black—the one-drop-in-the-bucket theory of descent.

"If you consider yourself Black for political reasons, raise your hand," Charles Stewart said to a predominantly African American audience at a symposium I organized for the National Association of Black Journalists in 1990. "The overwhelming majority raised their hands," said Stewart, a Democratic Party activist in Los Angeles. "When I asked how many people here believe that they are of pure African descent, without any mixture, nobody raised their hands." The point, said Stewart, is this: "If you advocate a category that includes people who are *multiracial* to the detriment of their Black identification, you will replicate what you saw—an empty room. We cannot afford to have an empty room. We cannot afford to have a race empty of Black people—not so long as we are struggling against discrimination based on our identification as Black people."

But a woman I will call Anna Vale eschews the little-dab'll-do-you school of genetics. She is a Californian of Japanese, African American, and Native American descent. A voice from the sushi-and-grits generation, she represents the new kind of diversity challenging old "racial" conceptions. Her eyes scan me skeptically. She does not trust me. Though I have written often and sympathetically about the issues so-called "multiracial" Americans face and the problem of colorism, she fears that I, too, will "rape" her. That's what Black people have been doing to her all her life, she claims, committing political and psychological rape on her person. And I'll do it, too, she insists, by writing a piece that distorts the reality of Americans like her who assert their "biological truth" and seek an identity separate from Blacks.

"What I don't appreciate about the African American community," she tells me, "is this mentality of annexing anyone with one drop of African blood. . . . I don't know why African American people seem so obsessed with annexing other people." Yet, says Anna, when "multiracial" people want to voice their unique concerns—political support for Amer-Asian refugees, many of whom have African American fathers, funding for works of art that present the complex cultural views of, for instance, a Black-Korean American—they are told to "be quiet," and "just carry out the political and cultural agenda of African Americans."

As she sits in a Santa Monica café, Vale's delicate body belies the dragon within. "African Americans want us to be their political slaves," she says with the intensity of water at a low boil. "They are saying, 'Come join us.' But it's not because of some great brother or sister love—it's political. If their numbers decrease, their chance of getting public funds decrease—as well as political representation. To me, that's a totally unethical way of saying that you want people to be a member of your community. As far as I am concerned all slavery is over—whether it's physical slavery on the plantation or political slavery that gives one group, like African Americans, the audacity to say that they own people because they have one drop of African blood."

Of course, it was White slave owners in the antebellum South who perpetuated the little-dab'll-do-you rule. They wanted to make sure that Blacks of mixed heritage—usually the products of White masters' raping of enslaved Black women—had no special claim to freedom because their fathers were free. They inherited the status of their slave mothers and were categorized with "pure" Blacks to assure the perpetuation of the slave population. In the postslave era, the alleged inferiority of African blood—no matter how little of it one possessed—was used to rationalize the continued social and political subordination of Blacks. Wisely, Blacks made a political virtue out of a necessity, asserting that we would not allow our heterogeneous ancestry to divide and render us politically dysfunctional—as many argue has been the case with Brazil's "Black" population.

I looked at Anna and listened to her ahistorical and apolitical diatribe. Her comments were a more extreme form of the kind of Black bashing I've often heard from multiethnics of African descent—usually ones who have had little contact with, or understanding of, the Black side of their heritage. I fear that the increasingly acrimonious nature of the debate among multiethnic Americans and African Americans is turning into a dialogue of the deaf. Pain and rage are the barriers. And though Anna often sees me as the enemy, I have always viewed her as a wounded sister. I understand the source of her rage.

Born in Japan and brought to the U.S. while in grade school, she knew little about her father's African American and Native American family. He died when she was young. Her mother, a Japanese war bride, raised Anna as only she could: to be a good Japanese daughter.

On the days Anna brought sushi to lunch, African American children teased her. But their mild teasing escalated to schoolyard terrorism: a group of Black girls pushing her down . . . cutting off her long, dark hair 'cause she swung it like a White girl. . . .

. . . a Black cop in L.A. ignoring her pleas for help after a fender bender injured her light-skinned son, then calling her a "half-breed bitch." . . .

From her perspective, the dark-brown, long-haired Polynesian-looking and Japanese-speaking woman has had the foot of an African American on her neck all her life.

"Communities of color are the most severe in doling out this kind of oppression," she says grimly. "The oppressed seem to oppress more."

In 1903, when Du Bois wrote that the "problem of the twentieth century is the problem of the color-line—the relation of the darker to the lighter races of men in Asia and Africa, in America and the islands of the sea," he referred to the domination of Whites over darker peoples. This remains true. But that domination has bred an insidious offspring: internalized oppression, that is, the installing of the oppressor's values within the psyche of oppressed people, so that—in a system of structured inequality such as ours—the psychological dynamics that help to keep the system in place function on automatic pilot. In effect, the mind becomes the last plantation.

One wonders if the assertion of a unique, multiethnic identity—particularly for a person of African heritage in the United States—is the ultimate expression of (or, through a synthesis of competing identities, an escape from) the divided consciousness that Du Bois said defined American Blacks. For where, save the United States—the New World—could an Anna be forged? Not just in the particulars of her ethnicity, but in the clear anguish, for many like her, such an amalgamation in an African-tinged package causes? Where else but in the United States does a slave master's economically motivated definition of identity reign so completely? Multiple souls, multiple thoughts, multiple "unreconciled strivings" warring "in one dark body, whose dogged strength alone," Du Bois wrote, "keeps it from being torn asunder."

Such contradictory feelings were not unknown to Du Bois. In *The Art & Imagination of W. E. B. Du Bois*, Arnold Rampersad notes that the twentieth century's greatest African American scholar was "not immune to the psychological subversions of white racism," often seeming ambivalent about his own "racial" identity. Aiming at this vulnerable psychic spot, the color-conscious Garvey sought to "discredit Du Bois before the bar of black public opinion" in 1921, writes Rampersad. Garvey insisted that the "mulatto" Du Bois was trying to be everything but a Negro. Sometimes, Garvey dug in, Du Bois claims he's a Frenchman, on another day Dutch, and only "when it is convenient is he a Negro."

In a 1929 issue of *The Crisis*, a less hostile commentator, writes Rampersad, noted ironically Du Bois's resemblance to "a sunburnt Jew, a Turk, an Italian, a Cuban or a German," anything but what he was *supposed* to look like: a Negro.

What is a Negro supposed to look like, then and now? How is one supposed to talk, walk, laugh, love, live—be?

Du Bois confronted these issues personally and politically throughout his life, providing a blueprint, at the jump of this century, for the "race" in *The Souls of Black Folks*.

But as a new century nears, ushering in the next millennium and unprecedented ethnic and "racial" diversity in the U.S., millions like Anna sound a disturbing and potentially potent riff on Du Bois's classic statement of color division. Further, given the tense, competitive relations between Blacks and other people of color vying for the dubious status of America's most significant minority, acute observers of the social landscape have correctly predicted that intraminority group conflicts will be a key factor leading to the fire next time. As Richard Rubenstein, former director of the Center for Conflict Analysis and Resolution at George Mason University, said in a July 12, 1990, *Los Angeles Times* article that anticipated the 1992 Los Angeles "riots" (specifically citing tensions between Blacks and Korean immigrant merchants and police brutality as causes), the nation is on the brink of "civil war."

Hedging so powerful an assertion in customary journalistic fashion, the article continued: "That grim prediction doesn't necessarily mean riots in the streets but a combination of [individual] sociopathic behavior" and "intensified intergroup conflict."

In California, which provides a microcosm of existing and, perhaps, future intraminority group relations, neighborhoods once predominantly Black, such as Watts, are shifting to Latino majorities. Typical of conflicts in these changing neighborhoods is the Latino charge that they are underrepresented on the staffs of hospitals in changing neighborhoods that have large numbers of Latino patients but too few Spanish-speaking nurses. In 1990, for example, the U.S. Equal Employment Opportunity Commission found "significant disparities" in the promotion of Latinos at the Los Angeles County–University of Southern California medical center. There, Latinos accounted for 14 percent of registered nurses but occupied only 4 percent of nursing-supervisor positions. In contrast, Blacks represented 20 percent of the nurses but 29 percent of the supervisors. Whites, however, still outnumbered everybody, accounting for 40 percent of the nurses and 46 percent of the supervisors.

Blacks argue that they should not have to give up jobs they fought for and won in the afterglow of the civil rights struggle and in the wake of the Watts rebellion. As one Black activist complained, "You don't see us going into East L.A. trying to take jobs from Latinos."

And then there is the much-publicized, sometimes deadly, conflict between Korean immigrant merchants and Blacks in many impoverished urban neighborhoods. Many of these merchants view Blacks as violent, ignorant, and unwilling to work, while Blacks see them as among the most arrogant and rude in a succession of exploitative middlemen entrepreneurs.

These variations on intraminority group conflict are related phenomena, in great part a consequence of what that brilliant analyst of the colonized mind, psychiatrist Frantz Fanon, called internalized oppression.

". . . so tell us who you are," said Love. ". . . was the darkest one in my family . . . heard my grandparents, my cousins, my everyone—whispering 'nigger-nigger-nigger. . . .' "

But Re-Evaluation Counseling theory has gone beyond the purely psychological consequences of oppression that Fanon explored. The theory weds the concept of internalized oppression to class analysis, creating what I think of as liberation psychology.

"I define internalized oppression as that process whereby a set of beliefs, attitudes, and misinformation about members of a target or oppressed group are put out by the dominant group to justify their subordination," says Love, both a professor of education at the University of Massachusetts at Amherst and a leader in the Re-Evaluation Counseling community. That misinformation becomes embedded in the psyche—the emotional domain of that target group, she explains.

"There is extensive internalized oppression within the Black community," Loves states unequivocally. "It was a deliberate part of the system of dehumanizing Africans who were brought to the United States and making them fit to be slaves. We were not fit to be slaves when we came here, so we had to be made to be fit—that is to go along with and participate in an oppressive system. And that process continues to this day."

Among the consequences of internalized oppression are "the ways in which we put each other down. The ways in which we play out the dehumanization that got inflicted on *us*, at *each other*," Love continues. It's the flip side of the oppression itself.

Tall, possessing skin with the soft patina of polished mahogany and disposed to wearing flowing African gowns, Love relates that her own sister had long hair and light skin. "If she tossed her hair in a certain way, she"—like Anna—"was accused of trying to act like a White girl. And the other kids jumped her." Why? "Because we have internalized this set of notions about what it means to be beautiful," says Love. "And what it means to be beautiful in this society is to be like Whites.

"The oppression says that by definition Black people cannot be beautiful. But if someone—because of our genetically mixed heritage—comes along looking like the dominant group, we say, 'If you're Black you are not beautiful—that is, you can't have long hair and here you've got long hair. It's wrong. We'll fix it. We'll cut it off and we'll put you back in your place. Because your place is to be like us: nobody.' "

Looking to the broader community of color, what happens when two historically subjugated people, culturally dissimilar, collide? In one notorious case, a Black teenage girl in Los Angeles was killed by a Korean American merchant after a dispute over a $1.79 bottle of orange juice.

The merchant, a then fifty-year-old woman named Soon Ja Du, was the daughter of a doctor and a literature major in college before she came to the United States with her husband and three children. She never adjusted to her loss of status as an immigrant who, because of language barriers, was compelled to work in a knitting factory for many years before her family saved enough to buy two combination liquor-and-food markets.

A devout Christian, Du reportedly never felt comfortable selling liquor or having to keep a gun in the stores, one of which was in the midst of gang-plagued South-Central Los Angeles—the Empire Market and Liquor Store. And she later told a probation officer she was afraid of, and didn't understand, the poor Blacks who frequented her store. "They look healthy, young," she said through an interpreter. "Big question why they don't work. Didn't understand why got welfare money and buying alcoholic beverages and consume them . . . instead of feeding children. . . . Didn't understand at first," she said. Eventually, she explained, "paid less attention," and decided that it was "their way of living."

Days after Black gang members had terrorized her adult son, Du saw fifteen-year-old Latasha Harlins walk into the Empire Market, take a container of orange juice from a refrigerated case, and placed it in her open backpack. With the juice visible, the girl walked to the counter with two dollars in her hand. Du accused her of stealing the juice. Harlins turned halfway to show her the exposed juice container and said she was paying for it. Du did not believe her, yanked Harlins toward her, pulling the arm of the girl's sweater.

What happened then?

Years before and months after the incident, commentators insist on calling the tensions between Blacks and Koreans an essentially cultural conflict.

At root, I think the conflict stems from economic and political inequality *exacerbated* by cultural differences. And the nation's White elite are not just *tsk-tsk-tsking* spectators. It has much to do with the way capitalism works. As Edna Bonacich, professor at the University of California in Irvine and an expert on the role of middleman minorities around the world, points out, "Korean Americans, to a certain extent, are fronting for the larger White power structure. They are both beneficiaries of the arrangement and the victims of it." The sale of liquor in the Black community is but one example of how Korean immigrant merchants, like Jews before them and Arab immigrants in others parts of the country, fulfill their middleman role.

Corporate-owned liquor companies sell their products through Korean-owned liquor stores in the Black community, Bonacich says. Koreans, who then distribute liquor in a community plagued by substance abuse, "bear the brunt of the anger the African-American community rightfully has against the larger system of oppression. Koreans become sort of foot soldiers of internal colonialism," asserts Bonacich.

Cultural and ethnic difference "are no doubt a small factor in these types of conflict," Bonacich contends, "but unless you deal with the structural problems, you do not solve the conflict."

But I would argue that we have to move on all these fronts—cultural (which includes psychological issues) and structural—simultaneously. Actions rooted in bigotry usually turn these simmering hostilities into social conflagrations. Even when people of apparent goodwill try to cooperate, an aide to Los Angeles Mayor Tom Bradley admitted, there is this "impenetrable veil" of hostility, based on ethnic stereotyping, that undermines joint economic and cultural ventures.

Traditional mediation and bridge-building efforts are too superficial to penetrate that veil. They don't get at the psychological terror, fed by bigotry, that lead the Soon Ja Dus of the world to shoot the Latasha Harlinses who inhabit the planet's inner cities.

A significant part of the problem lies in a failure to address the exaggerated psychological dimensions of intraminority group tensions. Most interethnic conflicts have a psychological aspect—rigidity of thinking, low self-esteem, compensatory behavior. But I think these are especially significant in disputes between historically subordinate groups.

In the case of Korean immigrants, they carry not only the historical memory of subjugation under the Japanese but the day-to-day reality of anti-Asian prejudice in the United States and the isolation caused by language and cultural differences. African Americans carry not only the historical memory of slavery but their status as American's most stigmatized minority.

In many respects, I believe Korean Americans and African Americans to be very similar. Accustomed to being targets of abuse, members of both groups are quick to defend themselves if anyone seems ready to violate their humanity. I see it especially in the often swaggering, chip-on-the-shoulder posture of African American and Korean immigrant men. I saw it in the quick defense of Latasha Harlins when she slugged Soon Ja Du three times in the face after Du grabbed her. I saw it when the battered Du threw a stool at Harlins . . . then took a gun . . . braced herself on the counter, and as Harlins turned to leave . . . shot the girl in the back of the head. Over and over, I watched the now infamous videotape of the incident in Du's store and saw the consequences of "internalized oppression."

In other words, when a battered wife stabs her husband in the chest after he's complained that the eggs are overdone again, it's a safe bet that the murder was over more than breakfast.

There are few safe places where oppressed groups can express their distress. The nation's power elite are not going to let poor people of any color riot on Rodeo Drive. Instead, much of that rage is turned inward—alcoholism, drug abuse, suicide—or directed toward those equally or more marginalized—Black-on-Black crime, child abuse, spouse abuse, violence against Korean merchants, ethnic-bashing between Blacks and Latinos.

The model I've seen that best addresses this phenomenon of internalized oppression is RC.

RC communities exist worldwide, with headquarters in Seattle. What Love and other RC counselors do, first one on one at the level of peer counseling, then in larger support groups, is help the "client" "discharge" the distress, born of the hurt, that keeps them numb or enraged and often irrational. Each person takes turns being a client and being a counselor. The goal is self-healing and clear thinking. When used by organizations, that clear thinking can be wedded to a pragmatic program of social change.

Says Love: When people are able to identify, talk about, and discharge their pain with the help of an aware, supportive human being, they "can take the information, minus the painful emotions" and reevaluate behavior. It's when the information is covered over with all that painful emotion that we get stuck and end up hurting one another rather than responding to one another from a rational place of thinking."

The healing work that RC communities and RC-influenced prejudice-reduction programs utilize (and there are many of the latter around the country, often presented by independent diversity consultants contracted by governmental agencies, schools, and corporations) is essential work; but it is not enough. I've yet to come across a conflict-resolution model that clearly connects the dots.

I believe we need a holistic conflict analysis and resolution model, one that comprehends the psychological issues that RC identifies but that more clearly articulates the need for institutional change and gives people the skills to do it.

Further, the model should show that it is only through building coalitions within communities and across all types of communities that structural change can occur—and this can only happen if the profound hurts all of us have suffered and the dehumanizing myths we have internalized about each other are "discharged."

Perhaps programs utilizing what people find valuable in RC should be established in every neighborhood, as accessible as twelve-step programs are. But unlike RC, which is not a political organization, the clear thinking that peer counseling facilitates should be applied to an agenda that participants develop themselves for social change—whether it be transforming the policing of neighborhoods, the nation's system of public education, or the United States government.

Certainly, people already engage in the work of social change everywhere—personal epiphanies happen and sometimes the people who have them join forces—but it's always too few doing too much. People get burned out, exhausted from the physical effort, drained by the negativity of others who attack those who do choose to lead.

People are not going to heal overnight, or, perhaps, even in a lifetime. But it's a process, once initiated and carried out systematically, as RC members do, that can give people enough "slack"—emotional and intellectual space—to act in their own best interest, which, politically, is to find common ground with other groups. In the post–L.A. rebellion era—in that city and elsewhere—few people have the slack to think in their best interest. They have circled the wagons, staked out tribal positions, and their hurt and rage are frozen. What that leads to is the societal equivalent of the criminal beating of White truck driver Reginald Denny by several Black men the first few hours of the L.A. "riot"—political revenge.

Even free, as is RC, relatively few people will make the effort to seek counseling of any sort. So what can we do? I write, and I hope that, just as I was influenced and inspired by Alice Walker to investigate the significance of colorism, what I say rouses people, beyond the halls of academe, to discuss in beauty parlors and barbershops, on radio and TV shows and in church, color conflict among our own people and relations with other ethnic groups of color—remember, we are likely to be the majority one day. We should, as well, reconnect with allies in the White community. The latter are often marginalized by their own community when they take progressive and honorable stands against racism. And as many young African Americans work through the morass of our own oppression, we push them away with the orthodoxy of a vulgar, compensatory nationalism—this era's version called Afrocentrism—that often denies their humanity.

These tensions have no easy remedies. But we have to work toward an atmosphere of cooperation rather than antagonism. If we don't, the bottom line for African Americans is this: our numbers are shrinking relative to the growth of other minorities. Like the poor, troublesome Black people are always with us, lament many Whites. But as one elderly Black xenophobe acknowledged, White people have some "new niggers" now ("I'm just a high-tech coolie," said one politically conscious Chinese American engineer)—ones that look more like them, act more like them, and don't haunt their days and nights with cries of "No justice, no peace." Know something else, in some parts of the country they vote more like conservative Whites. And when they marry into White families, some grandpas and grandmas (happy that at least their new child-in-law is not Black) are more than willing to lobby for a new mixed-race census category that might take some of the taint off their grandchild's color and may, eventually, make them honorary White people. (That's already the case with large numbers of Latinos, East Indians, and Arabs.)

Not long ago, I heard about a bumper sticker spotted on a car cruising down a Los Angeles freeway: *If I had known then what I know now, I would have picked my own cotton.*

Tired of reaping what they've sown, many White Americans will happily embrace the proliferating Asian American and Latino population in an effort to exploit intraminority conflicts and permanently marginalize Blacks, if we can't reach honorable political, social, and cultural compromises with other groups, particularly people of color.

As we approach this mine-laden social-psychological terrain, among the questions we should be asking is, What does it mean to be an African American at the end of the twentieth century? In the same breath we should ask, What does it mean to be an American? These questions are at the heart of the unresolved tension in discussions about cultural pluralism: balancing what is perceived to be universal with ethnic particularism.

Examine the lived American culture—as opposed to what usually gets funded by public television. It has been shaped by many groups and at its base is European, African, and Native American. It is not the exclusively Eurocentric artifact that Patrick Buchanan, for example, extolled during campaign speeches for the Republican presidential nomination in 1992.

Buchanan even sounded un-American to many other conservative Whites who cherish the notion of the melting pot. But most Americans don't really know what the "pot" represents: a process of assimilation that results in a homogenized end product. You know, the same Big Mac you get here you get in Oshkosh. If this were an accurate representation of America, as newspaper headlines commonly suggest— MIAMI MELTING POT BOILS OVER—the country would not be the contentious place that it is.

Jazz, the only uniquely American music, represents the cultural synergy that is the best part of the melting-pot process but the one least celebrated. What we embrace as "high" culture is European. The all-American social identity that we celebrate is the ethnic smelter's alleged "everyman": Jimmy Stewart in 1940, Kevin Costner today.

The New World synergy that produced jazz, tap, as well as the essentially creolized African American population and the mestizo-California culture seldom seems understood by the creators of tourist propaganda in prerebellion Los Angeles. They presented the "multi-cultural" city as either a paradise of separate but harmonious ethnic groups or, in an updated version of Anglo-dominated assimilation, a zesty tossed salad served on the American flag.

But, as a nation, we are more bound to each other than the metaphor of a mosaic, for instance, suggests. We seem more a tapestry with a series of patterns, some more dominant than others.

African American music, literature, dance, and our struggle to extend democracy have been central to that tapestry.

While the official culture pretends otherwise, we all know what Elvis was about, Fred Astaire, too. And in White suburbia, people still watch *Moonlighting* in reruns and smile approvingly at a favored American male image: Bruce Willis's hip White/Black man.

On this score, I am reminded as well of the recent evidence strengthening the claim that the voice of Mark Twain's *Huckleberry Finn*—the book from which "all modern American literature comes," claimed Hemingway—was inspired by a ten-year-old African American boy named Jimmy.

"This shows a real black root in a white consciousness," one literary scholar claimed. The actor Hal Holbrook, who for thirty-eight years has played Twain, told one interviewer he had sensed a Black strain in Huck's voice but never knew for sure.

"It's almost like the truth about something is so clear," he said, "that you look right through it."

It would seem, at this point in our history, African Americans can calm the warring identities in our consciousness. Assimilation is not a one-way street. It's a boulevard with multiple lanes of traffic, flowing two ways, intercut by persistent jaywalkers. But our trucks are so big we've been jamming the boulevard for decades. If we understand that, especially our young people, then we have the consciousness to engage, with confidence, in the political struggle (which multiculturalism represents) to assert the authority of our claim: We are central to the notion of an American identity.

If, then, America is largely us, who are we?

Clearly, African Americans are not just the descendants of enslaved Africans in the United States. My cousin Jeffrey looked like one of Ozzie and Harriet's kids. But what's unusual about that? African Americans are the product of a New World culture. It's been estimated that 80 percent of us have polygenetic backgrounds. And while U.S. custom and law have denied that multiethnic reality to perpetuate its own system of apartheid, calling America on it wouldn't be the first time Black people got hip to a trick bag—and out of it.

While many Blacks argue that they know they have mixed ancestry, they (1) don't acknowledge it because it would appear that they are trying to distance themselves from a socially stigmatized Black identity, of which they are not ashamed; (2) their non-Black ancestry is so distant they could not identify it precisely; (3) if they did know their non-Black ancestors, their descendants wouldn't accept them as kin; (4) most of their non-Black ancestors were White men who raped enslaved Black women and they want nothing to do with a kinship forged by brutality.

For these reasons, as well as the dictates of U.S. social customs and sometimes law, we have not *embraced* the fact that we are generically a creolized population. And the rise of Afrocentrism has encouraged the science fiction that we are an unadulterated ethnic group. No ethnic group is pure, as Du Bois pointed out long ago. For centuries, Africans mixed with myriad ethnic groups before any were enslaved and shipped to the New World.

While rape of Black women by White men was pervasive once we got here, not every sexual encounter between individuals of the two groups was coerced—to think so displays a fundamental misunderstanding of human nature.

But when rape did occur, we must remember that it is the perpetrator of the crime, not the victim, who bears the shame. And to constantly cast this criminal aspect of New World history as the cruel burden the descendants of slaves must bear is like stigmatizing a contemporary victim of sexual assault.

As far as I am concerned, every Black person with White ancestry should, no matter how they came by it, own it. That is not a rejection of African American identity, but an affirmation of the complex ancestry that defines us as an ethnic group. It will normalize what is erroneously treated as an exotic and, consequently, divisive characteristic among African Americans. Further, the acknowledgment of our ties by blood and culture puts the lie to the official silence on America's historically miscegenated identity.

But again, carnal knowledge of each other "across the color line" not only goes beyond rape but includes other non-Whites. Zora Neale Hurston once wrote: "I am colored but offer nothing in the way of extenuating circumstances except the fact that I am the only Negro in the United States whose grandfather on the mother's side was *not* an Indian chief." So where we once tried to find every drop of non-Black blood as a buffer against our caste status, we now tend to proclaim that all of us are exclusively the descendants of African princes, princesses, kings and queens. (You notice how no one ever claims descent from the village thief.) In reality, many social scientists estimate that most of our non-African ancestry is Native American.

As demographers point to the growth of the non-White population and the consequent "browning" of America, the already heterogeneous African American gene pool will become more so: Black, Korean American, Hispanic; Japanese, African American, and East Indian; Ethiopian, African American, Chinese, and Euro-American. In Los Angeles, I meet people with these and similar backgrounds frequently.

Is the African American community capable of embracing such diversity? Is it too much of a stretch for the traditionally defined African American population, which is essentially monocultural, to include people of African descent whose consciousness has been shaped by a multicultural family?

What should we expect if the Annas of the world meet African Americans who continually vent their own pain through the physical and psychological abuse of multiethnic people who have African ancestry but do not identify solely with the African American community? Is there any alternative but for people like Anna to reject us and work for a separate census designation and the social and political recognition that will result?

Certainly getting the personal pain that arises from these conflicts healed is essential. When that process is begun perhaps people can think more clearly about the question of a "multiracial" census category, and the notion of "race," period.

Says Love: "The question of whether there should be a new racial category has to be considered aside from personal pain and personal history."

Love believes, as I do, that "personal wishes have to be viewed in the context of what it means to live in an oppressive society where inequality is based on social identity groups. And where *race* is the fundamental criterion on which those groupings, and thus divisions, are made.

"If you go at it from a sociological rather than a personal standpoint, it is disastrous to create a new category, because the oppression itself is based on exactly that kind of division," Love argues. "We should be putting our energies into using the historic juncture of the year 2000 as a time when we will abolish all racial categories."

I know many multiethnic activists would argue that this is a progressive-sounding argument to deny them recognition and representation. But if their interest is the elimination of oppression—and not social vengeance against Blacks—then the elimination of classifications based on "race" is the only solution that makes sense. We should be challenging the nomenclature of oppression and attacking the philosophical underpinnings of racism—all a necessary part of dismantling institutionalized discrimination.

Finally, the exorcising of the psychological consequences of oppression that divide communities of color is a painful matter that many of us would rather deny or argue should be done out of sight and earshot of the enemy. But Black folks are among the most studied people on the planet. Who *doesn't* know our business?

As long as colorism and conflicts with other minority groups distract us from the larger issues of social and economic justice, the nation's system of structured inequality prevails. Which is why so many among the country's White power elite smile indulgently at the notion of a "browner," "newly multicultural" America. They know what the last plantation is, too.

The Last Great Battle of the West: W. E. B. Du Bois and the Struggle for African America's Soul

Alton B. Pollard III

It is but human experience to find that the complete suppression of a race is impossible. . . . This the American Black man knows: his fight here is a fight to the finish. Either he dies or he wins. . . . He will enter modern civilization here in America as a Black man on terms of perfect and unlimited equality with any white man, or he will not enter at all. Either extermination root and branch, or absolute equality. There can be no compromise. This is the last great battle of the West.

W. E. B. Du Bois[1]

William Edward Burghardt Du Bois (1868–1963) is a towering figure in the annals of African American intellectual life, one of the greatest social theorists and activists this nation has ever produced. A graduate of Fisk University and a Harvard Ph.D., Du Bois sought in his long

Alton B. Pollard is Associate Professor of Religion at Wake Forest University. He has served as professional consultant and national research advisor to several universities and been pastor at Baptist churches in Massachusetts and North Carolina. He is the author of *Mysticism and Social Change: The Social Witness of Howard Thurman* and has published widely in professional journals and newspapers. He continues to lecture on African American religion and music and multiculturalism in colleges around the country.

career as social scientist, educator, author, cultural pluralist, moral philosopher, and Pan-Africanist to challenge the nation's heavy legacy of slavery, segregation, and racial xenophobia. In 1900 he declared prophetically that "the problem of the twentieth century is . . . the color-line"—or, to be more precise, "the relation of the darker to the lighter races of men in Asia and Africa, in America and the islands of the sea."[2] Throughout his life, Du Bois would extol African America's rich cultural possibilities and champion democratic freedoms for every sector of American society.

The intent of this essay is not so much to focus on Du Bois's diverse activities, as these are brilliantly documented in his three autobiographies and other extensive writings.[3] Nor shall undue attention be given to the myriad personal complexities of his life—there was never Du Bois without paradox—as these have been well articulated by a number of scholars.[4] What is sought rather is some understanding of the significance of Du Bois's social vision, particularly that of the latter-day Du Bois, for America and its denizens of African descent in these final years of the twentieth century. More than anything else, his social thought represents both a moral and intellectual call to arms and also an admonition about the importance of cultural pluralism. A lifelong opponent of all forms of social injustice, especially where imperialism, anti-Semitism and women's oppression was concerned, Du Bois affirmed his basic faith in the democratic ethos, even when his own country would not. But simultaneously, he was a leading proponent of African diasporic cultural pride. Many events of late—most conspicuously the questionable addition of Associate Justice Clarence Thomas to the Supreme Court—suggest that we, as a nation, can benefit immeasurably from studying the thought of this American prophet.

The last quarter of the nineteenth century was a period of profound struggle and despair for African Americans. The mounting anticipation of "freedom and justice for all," which had accompanied the earlier periods of legal emancipation and Reconstruction, soon gave way before the crushing avatar of racial proscription.

As the twentieth century approached, whatever constitutional rights African Americans thought they had secured were in fact eroded. Racism was rife across the land. In the South and border states anti-Negro hate groups maimed, lynched, raped, rioted, and unleashed a furious barrage of bigotry. Social and political deconstruction, North and South, came equally as swiftly: the denial of the franchise, non-existent or at best deficient educational opportunities, injustice in the courts, discrimination in housing and on public conveyances, and subhuman working conditions.

The cruelty of media stereotyping encouraged further attack. African Americans were regularly depicted as miscreants—lazy, criminal, ig-norant, irresponsible and, in the final analysis, irredeemable. The social sciences generally concurred, declaring in good Social Darwinist fashion that the decadent condition of the Negro was innate, a part of "the natural order of things." Governmental bodies and agencies refused to argue with these conclusions; legal jurisprudence, after all, had no quarrel with such race-specific characterizations.

The attention of African Americans thus turned once more to pro-nounced struggle and resistance against a myriad of searing white pathologies, against the relentless conundrum of institutionalized ter-rorism. For African Americans, the dawn of the twentieth century opened as a time of great racial conflict, social disequilibrium, and economic disparity. Theirs was a world where the lines of equity had been carefully and conspicuously limited according to race. By mid-century, the future for most of the African American estate remained under an ominous pall of doubt.

Du Bois would not live to see the emergence of a broad stream of prophetic consciousness among African Americans. (By "prophetic con-sciousness," I am referring to the critical and organic linkage of per-sonal, communal, societal, and global dimensions of liberation.) On August 27, 1963, in Accra, Ghana, at the age of ninety-five, W. E. B.

Du Bois died. The news of his death reached the United States early the next morning on August 28, the day of the historic March on Washington. Roy Wilkins, executive secretary of the NAACP, addressed the vast assemblage on the Lincoln Memorial lawn, urging them to "remember that this has been a long fight. We were reminded of it by the news of the death yesterday in Africa of Dr. W. E. B. Du Bois. . . . [I]t is incontrovertible that at the dawn of the twentieth century his was the voice that was calling to you to gather here today in this cause."[5]

A worthwhile and appropriate point of view to be sure, to connect the deceased Du Bois with the burgeoning civil rights movement, and establish his as a singular "voice" in the "long fight" against racial injustice. Indeed, as early as 1903, in his epochal work *The Souls of Black Folk*, Du Bois had described the essential problem of African American life:

> One ever feels his twoness,—an American, a Negro; two souls, two thoughts, two unreconciled strivings; two warring ideals in one dark body, whose dogged strength alone keeps it from being torn asunder. The history of the American Negro is the history of this strife,—this longing to attain self-conscious manhood, to merge his double self into a better and truer self. In this merging he wishes neither of the older selves to be lost. . . . He simply wishes to make it possible for a man to be both a Negro and an American, without being cursed and spit upon by his fellows, without having the doors of Opportunity closed roughly in his face.[6]

The African American has been a distinctive presence in the Western Hemisphere, a profound conveyer and purveyor of that cultural precipitate known as soul. Regrettably, Du Bois's observations to this effect are now largely forgotten, neglected at a time when much of the legacy of the civil rights–black consciousness movement is itself enshrouded in doubt. As we approach the end of this century the racial lessons of the past have begun to fade from memory, it appears, a reflection of the powerful and prolonged processes which now and again have stalled the African American—and larger American—movement toward liberation. Early in his career, Du Bois expressed the fear—a fear that remained with him all his life—that African Americans might somehow be tempted to relinquish their birthright, to renounce their unique (but by no means superior) history of strident social protest and rich cultural gifts. In his essay "Of the Wings of Atalanta," he posed these disturbing questions:

> What if the Negro people be wooed from a strife for righteousness, from a love of knowing, to regard dollars as the be-all and end-all of life? . . . Whither, then, is the new-world quest for Goodness and Beauty and Truth gone glimmering? Must this, and that fair flower of Freedom which . . . [sprang] from our fathers' blood, must that too degenerate into a dusty quest of gold?[7]

Decades were to pass and Du Bois could still be found asking the same questions, struggling valiantly with the cultural and political implications of social division (and the deepening tension of his own convictions) spreading slowly through his community of origins. For Du Bois, the issues of culture were likewise inseparable from moral imperatives. His identification with race and his opposition to racism (as well as colonialism, capitalism, and sexism) both derived from that historical and spiritual encounter in which African Americans had wrested selfhood from an ignominious past. What would it mean, finally, to be both a person of African descent *and* a seeker of the kingdom beyond caste?

In a 1933 essay entitled "On Being Ashamed of Oneself," Du Bois reflects on the growing reality of class division among African Americans, a tragic caste-within-a-caste. In particular, he recoiled from the conventional view that racial equality could be realized within the existing hegemonic structures of Western industrial society. Du Bois challenged African Americans to be guided by a new ideal in relationship to the diaspora and to the world, delivering this plaintive warning:

> What are we really aiming at? The building of a new nation or the integration of a new group into an old nation? The latter has long been our ideal. Must it be changed? Should it be changed? If we seek new group loyalty, new pride of race, new racial integrity—how, where, and by what method shall these things be attained? A new plan must be built up.[8]

Du Bois proffered the "new plan" that he had in mind for the black middle class with characteristic candor—and not a little controversy. For him, the struggle of African peoples everywhere to maintain racial dignity and integrity was "the last great battle of the West." This struggle required considerable "group action," involving "the organization of intelligent and earnest people of Negro descent for their preservation and advancement in America, in the West Indies and in Africa; *and no sentimental distaste for racial . . . unity can be allowed to hold them back from a step which sheer necessity demands*"[9] (emphasis added).

No one in the United States could have possibly foreseen the full implications of Du Bois's prophetic stance prior to the *Brown* vs. *Board of Education* decision of 1954. But in the century between emancipation and the modern movement for civil rights, the felt desire among some Negroes "to escape from ourselves" and "the trammels of race" continued to be evidenced as a significant if muted social theme.[10] It is no wonder, then, that once a break began to appear in the wall of desegregation those who were able to take full advantage of the opportunities presented did so. Unfortunately, the social advancement of a relatively few individuals gradually, almost imperceptibly, began to take precedence over the welfare and concerns of the wider African American community.

The belief in "color-blindness" is largely a post–Du Bois condition among African Americans, a quality or approach to establishing a sense of self or identity that implies certain rites (and rights) of social entry without regard to race. For many if not all adherents to this position, rainbow declarations of a "color-full" society (the postmodern recognition of otherness, social heterogeneity, cultural difference, distinctive gender views, and so on) are highly suspect, an odious and irrational deception. Similarly, "race-conscious solutions," whether in the form of social initiatives (affirmative action and Head Start) or community efforts (independent African American institutions) are deemed outmoded and repressive, an albatross and snare to upward mobility. Equality of opportunity (access to the barbarism of naked capitalism?) is trumpeted with little regard to equality of conditions for the poor, the exploited, and the dispossessed (political non sequiturs all!). The new breed of "color-blind" African American sings a refrain that is distressingly as simple as it is symptomatic: "Rather than cast our lot with the race, we race to leave the caste."

As earlier noted, today much of the legacy of "the movement" years (from the early 1950s to early 1970s) is in doubt. During this period, the very processes which for the better part of three centuries had been designed to quarantine African Americans were themselves powerfully and widely implicated. The spirit of African American protest is historic, of course, but the scope and magnitude of these surging new protests were of a scale previously unknown.

There were thus set in motion necessary and prolonged processes whereby African Americans sought in the main to dismantle the institutional apparatus of racism. Desegregation rulings soon forced restaurants, hotels, and transit authorities to suspend *de jure* (but not *de facto*) discriminatory practices. Public-school systems from Little Rock, Arkansas, to Charlotte, North Carolina, had to extend a measure of educational equality to African American youth, and even the private sector was compelled to take the new job applicants seriously. By almost any criteria, conditions in the African American community improved as a result of movement efforts.

There was, however, one dissenting reality; a contentious caveat of major moral and social consequence. It is crucial to recognize that, for the American of African descent, along with incremental social gains also came the contradicting impact of larger societal values. Largely unanticipated as a consequence of legal desegregation, especially beginning with President Lyndon Johnson's "Great Society," was the torturous wrenching of the African American collective soul. However, in a 1947 essay titled, appropriately enough, "Can the Negro Expect Freedom by 1965?" Du Bois had already predicted as much:

> It [freedom] will bring, however, certain curious problems. How far will . . . young Negroes consider that their primary duty is toward the cultural group which they represent and which created them? If they had been born in Russia or England, in France or Japan, in white America, such a question would not arise.
>
> On the other hand, Negroes in the United States, being on the one hand American, and on the other hand members, more or less integrated, of the Negro group, will not have so clear a duty before their eyes. They may think of their preferment chiefly as their personal accomplishment and therefore as a chance to escape unpleasant environment and hateful conditions. They may look upon their careers as American, not Negro; withdrawing themselves from the Negro group as far as possible.[11]

In time, the rewards of civil rights integrationism proved less than the goals appeared to promise. Modest social and economic gains accorded some African Americans gradually led to an unquestioning acceptance of general societal values, complete with their often adverse effects. One of the underlying and rightful assumptions of civil rights orthodoxy during the 1960s was that African Americans were entitled to full participation in the nation's socioeconomic life. But seldom was there sustained discussion or recognition, Martin Luther King, Jr., and Malcolm X being notable exceptions, as to what kind of people, in moral and social terms, such "progress" might produce—namely, middle-class, white-collar African Americans who were disdainful of community and culturally amnesic. Du Bois recognized that the challenge of authentic social equality would be the preservation of African American "cultural patterns," as well as the nurture of institutions distinctive to the group. He offered these words as a caution, even a warning, against complete racial assimilation: "American Negroes must remember that voluntary organization for great ends is far different from compulsory segregation for evil purposes."[12]

It is hardly accidental that there is a tendency among some African Americans today to absolve themselves, as much as possible, of communal or racial (as opposed to merely national) responsibility. For the first time in the history of the United States, sufficient numbers of African Americans have been deemed socially and intellectually qualified as to make the phenomenon of *crossing over* (in opposition to the less savory historical activity of *passing*) the prize of great worth. However, the price of admission to the "mainstream" has often been high, including a tacit acceptance of extant social attitudes and arrangements, arrangements which from the beginning of this nation have effectively relegated the vast majority of African Americans, women, Native Americans, Latinos, and others to involuntary serfdom, government-dependent status, or worse.

If nothing else is clear with respect to the work of Du Bois, it should be that his life concern—which was a profoundly moral and spiritual concern—was for African peoples to endure with integrity, and never become mere clones or wards of any Western nation. Unfortunately, as historian Vincent Harding notes, by the time of the civil rights movement, Du Bois was already convinced that African Americans had been successfully "bribed to trade equal status in the

United States for the slavery of the majority of men."[13] The pursuit of socioeconomic success so preoccupied African Americans "that they are no longer a single body. They are different sets of people with different sets of interests."[14]

In the late 1940s, as the freedom struggle accelerated across the South, Du Bois, speaking before an audience at Wilberforce University, displayed his deep identification with prophetic African American Christianity (as well as his aversion to the institutional church) to startling effect: "Our religion, with all its dogma, demagoguery, and showmanship, can be a center to teach character, right conduct and sacrifice." And then he added, as if anticipating the Montgomery bus boycott and the emergence of Martin Luther King, Jr., "There lies here a career for a Negro Gandhi and a host of earnest followers."[15] A scant decade later, however, he solemnly concluded that "it is possible any day" that King, the "American Gandhi" could be assassinated. The African American and larger American moral center, it seemed, was falling apart.[16]

The logical conclusion to Du Bois's greatest fears—racial fragmentation and assimilation—find disturbing fulfillment in some of the more prominent African American voices of our day. There is little need to elaborate on the activities of those who figure so prominently (or at least publicly) in the struggle of which I speak. A dichotomous mass of voices is building which tend to espouse, on the one hand, the individual qualities of "self-help," and the common good of "the race," on the other.[17] Increasingly, affirmative action and other measures are being attacked by African American "savants" as a debilitating and deleterious retreat from nonracial reality.

It is rather curious to note that those ensconced in the "self-help" camp seldom find fault with a society whose war chest dwarfs its community chest and where, by all indications, human suffering continues to increase at an alarming rate (one noteworthy example: the current conjoining of "trickle-down" theory to affirmative action policies, which ensures that benefits fail to reach those most in need of them, the black poor). Historian John Hope Franklin perhaps said it best: "Self-help is admirable so long as it encourages initiative and achievement in a society that gives all its members an opportunity to develop in the manner best suited to their talents."[18] Current indications are that, as the (ofttimes) self-help minions of the Reagan and Bush administrations make their private climb up the ladder of success, the general condition of America's African progeny continues to deteriorate sharply.

Clarence Thomas, a product of the rural South and acknowledged beneficiary of the civil rights movement, has reached the pinnacle of success in American legal jurisprudence—supreme court associate justice. To be sure, we commend him for his achievements and for his determination. But how was Justice Thomas, a self-avowed political conservative (in the disbelieving words of one non-American observer, "but what do African Americans have to conserve?"), able to become so oblivious of the painful memories of the race? How is it that he was so easily able to separate himself from the events of recent history? Is this why Judge Thomas was caught off guard during the Senate Judiciary Committee hearings, seemingly unaware that he, too, could get his racial comeuppance? Indeed, the hearings were, to paraphrase Justice Thomas, a "high-tech lynching," but they were equally if not more so a case of "high-tech rape." Again, the words of Du Bois should give us reason to pause before the acrimonious debate accompanying the testimony of Anita Hill: "The present mincing horror at free womanhood must pass if we are ever to be rid of the bestiality of free manhood. . . . The world . . . forgets its darker sisters. They seem in a sense to typify that veiled melancholy."[19]

Numerous commentators have attempted to put the best face on the Thomas-Hill debacle, referring to the superlative credentials and composure that each displayed. The pertinent question, of course, is so what? Essentially, all of African America was placed on trial and, once again, justice was found wanting. Such a verdict, Du Bois would declare, is the modern paradox and inevitable consequence of this nation's racial Sin. "A group, a nation, or a race, commits murder and rape, steals and destroys, yet no individual is guilty, no one is to blame, no one can be punished. The black world squirms beneath the feet of the white in impotent fury or sullen hate."[20] The hearings served to remind us that even in the great "color-blind" society, admittance is no guarantee of acceptance.

We have looked at various aspects of the Du Bois legacy in some detail. As America and its communities of African descent prepare for the new century, numerous questions remain to be answered. Will the hopes and aspirations of African Americans continue to be founded largely on the strategies and understandings associated with the civil rights–black consciousness movement? Have we become, as many self-help proponents would charge, unquestioningly mimetic in our current practices, incapable of expanding on the liberating perspectives of an earlier period? Are there any prospects for new modes of activism, forms capable of simultaneously nourishing the African American soul while moving the nation beyond divisive social realities? Is it possible that a prophetic African American consciousness is emerging that is prepared to emancipate, elevate, and liberate—collectively? Herein lies the challenge.

Much of the evidence to date—the emergence of the urban griots of rap music; the social message of Afrocentricity and a proliferation of African American cultural groups; the resurgence of the historically black college and university; political identification with black South Africa, Mauritania, Grenada, Haiti, and others of the Two-Thirds World—do reflect changes of major moment. Yet one need but point to the fracturing of African America into two extremes—the prosperous and the desperate, the haves and have-nots, the already-haves and the never-will-haves—to realize that not even these commitments will suffice in the African American soul quest for dignity, well-being, freedom, and justice.

It is difficult to determine the depth and extent of this new prophetic consciousness, or even the current condition of the African American soul, but the evidence of its stamina is irrefutable. There is abroad in the land a contagious pride, a dogged determination, an exciting confirmation of the Du Boisian dictum: "We must accept equality or die."[21] No apologies are being offered, no invectives hurled, no denial of our best selves, but progress—the renewed sense of our own humanity—born of struggle. Yes, I hear the dedication of America's African communities as it reverberates in the spiritual's soaring refrain:

> Done made my vow to the Lord,
> And I never will turn back.
> I will go. I shall go.
> To see what the end will be.

Notes

1. Cited in Manning Marable, *Black American Politics: From the Washington Marches to Jesse Jackson* (London: Verson, 1985), p. 74.

2. W. E. B. Du Bois, *The Souls of Black Folk* (Greenwich, CT: Fawcett Publications, 1961), p. 23.

3. Outstanding among Du Bois's numerous works are *Suppression of the African Slave Trade* (1896); *The Philadelphia Negro* (1899); *The Souls of Black Folk* (1903); *Darkwater* (1920); *Dark Princess* (1928); *Black Reconstruction* (1935); *Color and Democracy* (1945); and *The World and Africa* (1947).

4. See, for example, the excellent perspectives provided by Arnold Rampersad, *The Art and Imagination of W. E. B. Du Bois* (Cambridge, MA: Harvard University Press, 1976); Manning Marable, *W. E. B. Du Bois: Black Radical Democrat* (Boston: Twayne Publishers, 1986); Gerald Horne, *Black & Red: W. E. B. Du Bois and the Afro-American Response to the Cold War, 1944–1963* (New York: State University of New York Press, 1986); and Robert Franklin, *Liberating Visions: Human Fulfillment and Social Justice in African-American Thought* (Minneapolis: Fortress Press, 1990).

5. Recounted in Marable, *Du Bois: Black Radical Democrat*, p. 214.

6. Du Bois, *Souls of Black Folk*, p. 17.

7. Ibid, p. 69.

8. Meyer Weinberg, ed., *W. E. B. Du Bois: A Reader* (New York: Harper & Row, 1970), p. 13.

9. Ibid., p. 15.

10. Ibid., pp. 11–12.

11. Ibid., pp. 332–33.

12. Cited in Marable, *Black American Politics*, p. 101.

13. Vincent Harding, "W. E. B. Du Bois and the Black Messianic Vision," in *Black Titan: W. E. B. Du Bois* (Boston: Beacon Press, 1970), p. 67.

14. W. E. B. Du Bois, "Whither Now and Why," in *The Education of Black People* (April 2, 1960), pp. 149–58.

15. Herbert Aptheker, "W. E. B. Du Bois and Religion: A Brief Reassessment," *Journal of Religious Thought*: 11.

16. W. E. B. DuBois, "Will the Great Gandhi Live Again?" *National Guardian*, 9 (February 11, 1957): 6–7.

17. The political classifications are wide-ranging, from Americanists, bourgeoisie, neo-conservatives, and reactionaries on the one hand to Africanists, subversives, leftist radicals, separatists, etc., on the other.

18. John Hope Franklin, "Booker T. Washington, Revisited," *The New York Times* (August 1, 1991).

19. W. E. B. Du Bois, *Darkwater: Voices from within the Veil* (New York: Schocken, 1969), p. 165.

20. Cited in Truman Nelson, "W. E. B. Du Bois as a Prophet," in *Black Titan: W. E. B. Du Bois* (Boston: Beacon Press, 1970), p. 141.

21. Du Bois, "Whither Now and Why," pp. 149–58.

The Black Table,
the Empty Seat,
and the Tie

Stephen L. Carter

Once or twice, when I was in law school, the "black table" (as we
called our solidaritied corner of the dining hall) was torn by a debate,
passionate but friendly, over the question of how we should think of
ourselves: as black people who happened to be Yale students? or as
Yale students who happened to be black?

The black table itself was a statement of need, and of difference.
We were law students, but we were not like everyone else, or at least
we didn't think we were. We were as grimly enthusiastic and as secretly
ambitious and as ready to work hard as anyone else; we all felt the
tug of professional attainment. But there were other pulls. The gray
corridors and cavernous classrooms of the Yale Law School were familiar
but never home. To be a law student, black or white or any other
color, is to be on edge, and also on display. All law students need

Stephen L. Carter is William Nelson Cromwell Professor of Law at Yale, where he has
taught since 1982. His fields of expertise include constitutional law, intellectual property,
and contracts. Professor Carter has published dozens of articles on subjects as diverse as
the protection of rights in computer software, racial disparities in administration of the
death penalty, the confirmation process for Supreme Court nominees, the war powers of
the President and the Congress, the regulation of genetic engineering, and the new
trademark act. He is the author of *Reflections of an Affirmative Action Baby* and the forthcoming *God as Hobby: The Trivialization of Religious Belief in American Public Life*.

outlets for frustrations, irritations, fears—and joys too. As black law students, we had other needs, as well, needs that seemed to us, at least, not exactly the same as the needs of other students. The need to escape, for example. The need to seek support from each other. The need to be together. And the need to figure out exactly what we were doing there, what our *purpose* was, led us into the fierce but friendly debate over just who we were.

Our argument, never authoritatively resolved, served to remind us of two important truths. The first was that we liked to argue. The second—the more important—was that something was happening to us, something like a coming change in status, as though we were caught in transit, balancing somehow between our origins and our destinations, not fully secure in either. We were all of us children of the civil rights movement: the nation had changed its laws and, in some respects, its ways during our childhoods and adolescences. We were living the opportunities for which generations of black folk had fought and died. Walking paths wet with the blood of our martyrs, we felt an uneasy fear that taking advantage of those opportunities was changing us.

As a law professor at Yale, I look back on those days with a gentle affection, perhaps a wistfulness for the ease with which we bantered. Our heartfelt discussions were themselves happiness of a sort; our enthusiasm was an expression of solidarity, a kind of truth. We were in it together, united by the awarenesses that our shared skin color made possible and the eagerness to know what was right, and no matter how vehement our political differences, the black table remained an axis around which our small worlds revolved. The ease of it all—I miss the ease.

The passage of time has left me in some ways happier, in others much more pensive. Our community seems more divided now, but that perception might represent the fresh perspective that comes when, at last, one must leave the table behind. The *need*, however, is as deep and nagging as ever. Racism was real to me then, in my early twenties, a brooding enemy one could almost touch; nowadays, something over a decade later, its presence is somehow more sinister, as though it has hidden itself but not really gone away. We are lawyers now, my classmates and I, with professional success behind us and ahead, too. Affirmative action? Who cares? Look at us now! Look at what we have done with the opportunities—

And yet there is this unsettling sense, this mistrust of the world out there. Time has passed, we have moved on, but we cannot honestly say—I can't, anyway—that racism has moved into the past. It is harder to point to it now, people are more careful in what they say and maybe in what they think, too. And yet one senses it there, in the shadows, lurking perhaps around the next brightly lighted corner as one walks the corridor of one's office. We are where we are, we obviously belong, that was settled long ago, and yet—and yet—

The racism. Not so much something to blame for our setbacks as something about which we might often wonder when we think of what we will do next. And yet, the truth is that there is no time to worry, no time and no space, not for the professional. We are too busy being busy to let racism slow us down. We are lawyers now, as I said, nearly all of us, and we have moved on in our profession, a profession defined and dominated by generations of white folk, mostly men, mostly dead, many of whose sour portraits line the corridors and classrooms of Yale and of other leading law schools. (The portraits: Once, when I was in law school, a group of students organized a conference around the theme of sexism in the legal system. Those of us who attended were divided into groups, and one of the assignments was to work out what the law school would be like were the force of sexism less apparent. One of the groups brought a hush, then loud applause, when it reported its solution: *More portraits of dead women on the walls*. Chilling, but precisely right. History is itself a message.) The profession has rules and standards and expectations, and to move upward is to swim in a sea of white people's making. The profession is more integrated than it once was, but the rewards, and most of the punishments, are still distributed by people who are white. Black lawyers in the United States of America number something above twenty-five thousand, a very impressive number indeed, until one realizes that the total number of lawyers is well over seven hundred thousand. There are people of color who deny the right of white folk to shape the profession and insist that other voices be heard—exemplified, in the legal academe, by the Critical Race Theory Movement—and one can but wish them well, even if one wonders which they suppose to be the voices that matter. Law itself remains a conservative force, even though lawyers themselves are more progressive than they once were and, in opinion surveys, are more liberal than the nation as a whole on almost every issue. In the meantime, the profession remains what it is, and the same question we argued over the table, yet unanswered, sits more heavily as one grows older. Who exactly are we, dark-skinned lawyers in a white-skinned profession? What have we gained by our choices? And what have we cast aside? Yes, we are black . . . but *how* are we black?

Differentiating

Let me begin with an uneasy truth: I scare people. I write these words as I sit on an Amtrak train hurrying south along the Northeast Corridor, a six-foot-three-inch male in a sober navy suit, blue oxford shirt, and conservative tie, bent over a laptop computer, the very image, one might suppose, of the seamless dull gray professional. But a professional, of course, with a difference, one that is brought home to me as I watch with mixed feelings the stream of fellow business travelers, the white ones, anyway, treating the seat next to me as though it is already occupied. Of white women this is particularly true: to sit next to a black man, even a well-attired one, is a choice to be made only when no other seat is available, and even then to be avoided if possible, occasionally by standing.

Few of us who are black and professional are unfamiliar with this circumstance. And in our irritation (although it is nice, in the abstract, to have the elbow room of two seats for the price of one), many of us readily describe the attitude of the white people so reluctant to sit next to us as racism. This description makes for an awkward and threatening world: since most white people pass the empty seat and leave it as they found it, most white people must be racist. As I sit here, waiting for the seat to be filled (and now, at last, it has been, by a person neither white nor male—the other seats, I note in passing, are all taken), I wonder whether my friends who so readily call the reluctance racism can possibly be right.

To be a professional is to be spared the worst ravages of racism, but the many small daily slights that are the price of living here add up to a miasma of racial exclusion. It is almost a cliché that if you are black you can't get a taxi in a major city, and it isn't quite true—but it isn't quite false, either. Even in a business suit, it can be difficult; if one is dressed more casually, it can prove impossible. When in New York, for example, if I am traveling with a white person, I frequently swallow my pride and allow my companion to summon the taxi as I hang back—for to stand up for my rights and raise the arm myself would buy only a tired arm and no ride. For a black male, blue jeans in New York are a guarantee of ill-treatment. There are the jewelry-store buzzers that will not ring, the counter clerks who will not say "Sir," the men's departments with no staff to be found. I shop mostly at Brooks Brothers, but I always dress for it, recalling, from my childhood, a complicated tale involving my paternal grandmother, a rude shopkeeper, an expensive fur, and a change of tune.

Ah, I sometimes think, to be able to hit them over the head with my résumé! In my mind's silly eye, I can see the paper slamming down, as I await the grimace, the shout of pain, then the recognition and apology. Oddly, that might even do some good. Social psychologists who study racial stereotyping report that even white people who indulge in a great deal of stereotyping will alter their opinions of black people who possess a variety of identifiable status attainments, such as advanced degrees. This will not alter by a single iota, however, their judgments on other black people, about whom they know less, which means that even in the act of dressing to shop I am putting a distance between myself and my people. So there, already, is a division among us, a tax that racism imposes on success: Yes, we will treat you differently from the way we treat your brethren and sistren, but only if you first mark yourself as different. If I am willing to divide myself from the whole, even symbolically, I earn a reward for it. How terrifying!

Still, I do not insist that the taxi drivers who will not stop unless I am dressed as they prefer—unless I send the right signal of my difference from those they fear—are racists in the same sense that members of the Ku Klux Klan are racists. People are more complicated than that, and I have little doubt that some of the same people who will not open the doors of their jewelry stores when I am in my blue jeans will send large contributions to the Southern Poverty Law Center to do the good work of keeping the Klan at bay. For doing so, I charge them with neither insincerity nor hypocrisy—simply with normal human complexity. Similarly, I do not insist that my colleagues are racist when their evaluations of the work of a person of color differ from mine; or that law firms are racist when their record on hiring people of color is less impressive than I might like. To choose "racism" as a category to capture all of that complexity is much like suggesting that those who opposed the Persian Gulf War were not supporting America or that those who think the First Amendment protects exploitative pornography support the oppression of women. Each is a clever rhetorical point that drains the principal horror—racism, treason, sexism—of most of its normative content. Yes, of course, there is racism in the legal profession, but we must not be so blinded by our search for the covert kind that we miss the overt kind. There are people out there, people with power—fewer, I think, than some fear, but clearly too many—people with power who hate us. A white collar is no insulation against either side of *that* relationship. And dressing to shop, or to work, will change the relationship marginally, but one must not make the mistake of thinking (or desiring) that this cosmetic change also works a change in morphology sufficiently dramatic that there is a sudden and sharp discontinuity in one's life situation. There is a better job and more pay (and more white friends if that is what one desires); but there is also the lingering question, from the days of the black table, about what else one puts on when one puts on a tie.

Which brings us back to the train. Where I do wear a tie, always as careful in dressing for travel as in dressing to shop. I am not a different person with a tie than without one, even though some people's perceptions of me will change with my clothes. Even my fellow passengers, reluctant as they are to take the seat next to mine, probably look at me *a little bit* differently than they would were I in my jeans. They do not want to sit next to me, but they are not rushing to the conductor to demand that I be tossed off the train. And besides—not to put too fine a point on it—in the end, who cares about them anyway? Beyond a certain point, reached very early in my dialogue with myself, I lose interest in their opinions of me, or even in whether they are racists or not.

Not long ago, I published a book entitled *Reflections of an Affirmative Action Baby*, in which I urged those of us who are in the professions to quit worrying about what our white colleagues feel, to meet the "qualification question"—*Did you get here because of affirmative action?* —with a studied *Yes, so what?* I also argued that the best way to frustrate our detractors is to overachieve, to shape ourselves into a generation of black professionals too good to ignore.

Some black professionals were angered by what I wrote. I was told that I was naïve, that there was more racism in the professions than I evidently supposed, so that hard work alone would not be enough to get ahead. Others took me to task for worrying too much about what white people think. And some suggested that the call for over-achievement was unfair and ill conceived, suggesting that I was the shade of Booker Washington come back to life, urging us to cast down our buckets where we are, to work hard to please the white man.

I had thought that I answered all of these points in the book, but perhaps I did not write as clearly as I should have. The objection that I was worried too much about what white people think particularly rankled, however; it was my intention to argue the other way around, that we who are black worry too much about what white people think, and that our obsession with their good opinions—the same obsession, incidentally, that in the minds of some black people transforms affirmative action into a stigma—has got to stop.

Still, back on Amtrak, still heading south,* I cannot quite succeed in the pretense that the white people who will not sit next to me do not actually exist. I know they are there and I know they are avoiding me—how could I not? And while their behavior does not make me think less of myself, it does seem to me to demand a bit of analysis as one works through the matter of one's professional identity, and of why one wears a tie. As I have noted, the usual explanation for their refusal to sit next to black people is racism. I see little point, however, in being so harsh on my fellow passengers, or indeed, for marking them as particularly culpable. All they are doing, really, is thinking in racial terms. They are using race as shorthand for other characteristics that they find unpleasant: a tendency toward criminality, perhaps. Before one rushes to say that this is precisely what is meant by the word *racism*, let me caution that using race as a shorthand for other characteristics is precisely what affirmative action (to take the most obvious example) necessarily does. People of color who are swept, willingly or not, into the swirling maelstrom of racial preferences are presumed to share a common history or a common perspective or a

* This part of the description of the train ride was *not* written while on board.

common disadvantage or a common need or whatever the most persuasive justification might be. And although their motivations and results obviously differ, there is no *logical* distinction between the assumptions about race underlying affirmative action programs and the assumptions about race underlying the empty seat. Using race as a "bad" shorthand is, of course, far worse than using race as a "good" shorthand, and sometimes doing the second is important. Still, in both cases, the person of color who is the subject of the assumptions is treated as a representative of the people—it is simply that the white people who refuse to sit down, like the black people who pronounce upon the attitudes that one must hold to be truly black, are arrogating to themselves the right to decide what aspects of the people the one that they are looking at represents.

So the problem of the empty seat is not quite like the problem of being the last kid picked when choosing up sides for softball or football back in grade school, for the judgment has nothing to do with skill. Indeed, the fact that it has nothing to do with skill—that none of those who pass the seat know or care whether I am good at my job—makes it much like the forms of exclusion that often cut at the professional soul. One of the reasons that it often makes sense to use affirmative action to lever open the doors is that they are closed for reasons other than a racist desire to oppress; they are closed, rather, because of the prevailing racialist stereotypes that render black people beneath the notice of white people. Affirmative action can force white people to take notice, and, if they are not truly or deeply racist, once they take notice, quality will out. For it is their ignorance as much as their hatred that keeps the barriers up—the same reason that I sit alone on the train. There are times when, sitting thus, I long for some instrument of coercive authority, a means to force one or more of the passersby not only to sit but to talk, and to listen. But only brief times. The honest truth is that the good opinion of the people passing by matters to me less and less, both on the train and professionally; what I find I like is the elbow room.

Claiming

So let me begin to explore the question of professional identity at a slightly different place: not with the vision of blackness imposed from without, whether by people who are white or by people who are black, but with the vision of blackness selected from within. For prior to one's professional identity can be, should be, a *personal* identity. One selects it: that's easy, delightfully so, for I'm black and would not be anything else if I could. Yes, I work in a mostly white profession, and, yes, I work at a mostly white law school. But that is not all there is of me and need not even be most of me. My ties with the black community, with black people, are richer and stronger than my bonds to the white. I have no generalized view that white people are racist or insensitive; still, I must confess, the good opinions of black people, to put it simply, matter to me more. That is my choice, and I cannot imagine ever making another.

The choice is partly cultural, partly social, and partly political, but it is mostly affectional. One selects a milieu. It is a choice not about where one lives or how one votes but whom one loves. And the issue is less romantic love (although my wife is black, I recognize that there is such a thing as genuine affection across racial lines) than a sufficient love of one's own identity so that it extends in a special way to the group. I have white friends too, and care for some of them deeply, but that is beside the point. Just as in the days of the black table, simply being around black people—among black people—having that respite, that trust, that common need fulfilled, that *being together*—is something I cherish and something my wife and I are determined to preserve for our children. Which is why, as a black couple living as we do in a mostly white neighborhood, we are not content to trust our social lives to chance, but are constantly on the lookout for new black acquaintances, associates, friends—with children if possible.

Identifying as black is in this sense a decision. Biology plays a role, but not a complete one, and the pressure of our racialist society to treat skin color as destiny is one that some prefer to resist. The pressure *is* oppressive, but resisting it does not require pushing in the other direction; rather, one can, in the manner of the martial artist, use the opponent's strength to go where one wants to go anyway. I realize that there are black people, especially among the professionally successful, for whom connections with people who are white become more important than connections with people who are black, and I feel sorry for them, for what they have lost. Still, that is their choice, and I wish them well of it; mine, however, goes in another direction.

But as for the rest, one's *professional* identity, all that one can do is try on the words, and see which fit. . . .

A law professor.

A black law professor.

A black person who is a law professor.

A law professor who is black.

The transpositions of words, like the ones we batted back and forth in the dining hall, are subtle, but important. A few years ago, I watched a television interview in which a black man who is prominent in the conservative movement was asked whether he preferred to be called "black" or "African American." Without a moment's hesitation, he replied, "I'm an American. That's what I want to be called."

Fair enough: I'm happy to call him what he wants to be called. But I am not happy to think of myself that way. I need the adjective that he seemed content, almost determined, to drop. Oh, yes, I am an American, and I certainly want to be that. I take as much pride in that, I am sure, as anyone. But I am not, in my mind or in my soul, I cannot be, *just* an American, anymore than I am, in my mind or in my soul, or can be, *just* a law professor.

To be a black professional is to lead a dual existence, but that existence need not be uncomfortable. There are some intellectuals—Shelby Steele and Richard Rodriguez perhaps foremost among them —who have suggested that the fact of moving ahead in a predominantly white profession creates a necessary distance between oneself and one's ethnic community. They have argued, in effect, that the new environment slowly destroys the old, that it is inevitable and perhaps even desirable to be thought of as (or to think of oneself as), say, a professor who happens to be black, rather than a black person who happens to be a professor. And while I have always appreciated the logical force of the argument, it seems to me to be dangerously wrong. My wife, for example, was the first in her family to attend college. By the Steele-Rodriguez argument, I should feel, automatically, a distance from her relatives. But the reverse is true. Slipping warmly and comfortably into the embrace of her family is the most natural feeling in the world.

There are sour moments—I admit it!—when I stride the halls of Yale Law School bitterly, angry at a world that insists on seeing me as a black person who is also a law professor instead of a law professor who is also black. But the moments are few, for most of the time the first of these is my image of myself as well. In that sense, I have resolved that after-dinner argument of so many years ago, and I am what I want to be: a black law professor? Okay. A law professor who is black? Yes, that too. But, better, a law professor who loves black people.

Racial solidarity, in the sense of self-love, is the key to our survival in a frustratingly segregated integrated professional world, just as it is the key to our survival in a frustratingly oppressive nation. Oh, the professions are all integrated now. There are black people in them, fewer than we would like, but more than our detractors would like. Affirmative action, whatever its flaws, has forever changed the face of professional America, and that is all to the good. But so have hard work and perseverance, the willingness to be less concerned with the fairness of the obstacles in one's path than with finding the best way over, around, or through them. Affirmative action can open doors; but running (never walking) through them is our job.

But as we run and run and run, rushing toward professional success before the tiny trapdoor in the glass ceiling slams shut, there remains the uneasy question from the black table, the question of whether in running toward one thing we are also running from another. I might explain my decision to wear a tie on the train, and elsewhere too, on the ground that the tie is demanded by the profession I have chosen to follow. The question is whether my willingness to wear the tie, or perhaps my insistence upon it, is itself an acceptance of the distinction that my longing for solidarity wants most to deny. If I will vary my plumage to please creatures more powerful than myself, what does that say about my relationship with the flock?

Perhaps it says nothing. Consider the words of Mario Baeza, a black man who is a member of New York's legal elite: "I'm integrated, but I've never tried to be white. That's not what I aspire to in life." Very well, one accepts rules of dress as one accepts rules of grammar, in order to get ahead. That requires a certain ambition, but ambition is not inconsistent with a love of one's people. Solidarity can be the bridge between our roots and our destinations. Claiming one's people gives one an identity. Selecting a destination gives one a profession. The question, then, is whether there is any reason one cannot have both.

Professionalism

In every profession, sometimes even near the top, there are black people, and none can afford to stand still. One moves in one's profession, preferably upward. But as one gains altitude, the ranks of one's people, like the molecules of the air . . . *thin out!*

The faster one advances in the white-dominated world of the professions, the greater the suspicions often generated that one has somehow left one's truest and best self behind. Probably this is truer in the law than in any other profession because law, unlike medicine or banking, say, has the public persona of an engine of policy. Perhaps it was ever thus, or perhaps this is something new, a way that lawyers (and courts) are viewed in a world in which the correctness of *Roe* vs. *Wade* is considered a matter of public opinion and the significance of *Brown* vs. *Board of Education* is a matter of folklore. Oh, those lawyers, those judges, those courts—always off changing the world!

If one has the power to change the world—the power with which popular imagination vests our courts—it is best that one use that power for the good. It is not only black people who feel this, but black people have been losers often enough to feel it more keenly than most. And nowhere was this more apparent than when Thurgood Marshall, one of the towering monuments of twentieth-century jurisprudence, announced his retirement after nearly a quarter century on the Supreme Court of the United States and President Bush nominated Clarence Thomas to take his place. Many black people supported Thomas in a show of racial solidarity, and, in some cases, because they agreed with him on the issues. But one must also recognize that millions of black people saw political cynicism rather than the turning of the wheel of history in the Bush Administration's decision to follow the greatest legal figure of the civil rights movement with a less distinguished legal figure from the conservative movement.

Thomas was damaged by a confirmation process in which millions of Americans believe he lied under oath in denying Professor Anita Hill's charges of sexual harassment. (I, too, believed Anita Hill.) Still, Thomas has a long tenure ahead, and he could eventually prove to be one of the great Supreme Court justices, although, as of this writing, the evidence is depressingly to the contrary. Of course, there remains the question of what being a great justice means. The answer returns to the image of the legal system as an engine of social change. Thus the real point for his most bitter ideological opponents (and here I exclude Anita Hill, who, despite some of the nonsense spread by her detractors, had no political ax to grind) was that Clarence Thomas was a *lawyer*, and that he would, as a Supreme Court justice, gain a considerable power that most would prefer to see exercised for the good, by which his opponents generally meant that he should vote as Thurgood Marshall did. But more was involved than the exchange of a liberal for a conservative. As a *black* lawyer, a *black* justice, a *black* policymaker, Clarence Thomas, according to the ideological story, carries a special responsibility to care for his community—and to show that caring by adopting particular political positions. Here is where the answer to the question we posed around the black table begins to cut more sharply than I had thought it ever could: It was not, I thought, our intention to promulgate standards for judging each other's commitment. I had thought we were simply after methods for evaluating ourselves.

To be sure, if some of Clarence Thomas's more vehement political opponents think he has left his community behind, one can understand their anger, for many of his positions are antithetical to the glorious tradition of the civil rights struggle. What must be borne in mind, however, is that all of us who are people of color and also professionals—especially those of us who are lawyers, and, within that group, particularly those who have moved to heights previously reserved for white folk, such as elite corporate practice, teaching at prestigious law schools, and, of course, the federal bench—are always one small step away from the same charge. The moment we put on our ties in order to gain acceptance, we make a choice. It need not carry us far from our origins, but if we are careless, it might.

Fortunately, should any black professionals grow so bold as to imagine that essential power relationships have changed because collars are white, there are sufficient episodes of racism to remind. For there remain many white people at the top who will never accommodate themselves to the presence of black people in the corridors of power, and many others who are not hostile but whose lack of familiarity with us makes our jobs harder. Certainly the glass ceiling still exists. But the glass is cracked and black faces are forcing their way through, even if it means taking some cuts and bruises on the way up. The face of professional America *has* changed, and changed forever. Who would have thought, back in the mid-sixties, when civil rights marchers faced brutal assaults and official murder, that within a quarter of a century leading figures in the national security establishment—not only the chairman of the Joint Chiefs of Staff but, less known, the principal Soviet expert in the White House—would be black? We are rising not because we are black but because we are good; we will be there forever because our skills are needed. We are being good to America almost before America remembers to be good to us.

As professionals, we can but do our best; that is the ethic. As black professionals, we *must* do our best. There are white people who can slide through life, leaving a trail of massive and unattributed incompetence, but black people, given our position in America, do not have that option. Our parents urged us all to work twice as hard as the white kids. We can do that and perhaps obtain a measure of professional success, but, of course, it comes with a measure of patronizing by white colleagues. The Best Black Syndrome, I have called it elsewhere: You're the best black lawyer or doctor or whatever that I have ever known, say many white people from their thin experience of black folk. Not the best, simply the best black. The enforced narrowness of perspective is infuriating. The legal scholar Patricia Williams has written that she longs to respond, "There are more and better of me"—people, in other words, who have never had a shot at proving what they can do. And the estimable William Coleman, lion of the corporate bar, when patronized by a politician who observed that he, Coleman, should be on a court somewhere, shot back that the man simply had never met the great black lawyers who had no chance, among them Charles Hamilton Houston, principal architect of the legal strategy culminating in *Brown* v. *Board of Education* and surely one of the canniest and most subtle legal minds of the century.

A reviewer, responding angrily to the book that I mentioned, was kind enough to say that she suspected that I was twice as good at what I did as my white colleagues. The empirical truth of the matter was not relevant to her rhetorical point. Her point, rather, and a sensible one, is that black people must be better than white people to get as far as white people can. That is an assumption that black people commonly make, and although it often makes white people uncomfortable, there is plenty of evidence to back it up. Some of the best evidence comes from professional baseball, where the addiction to statistics provides what are generally considered hard and clear measures of differences in talent.* Studies always show that the statistical averages of black players, who are the minority, are significantly above those of white players, who are the majority. How can this be? The answer cannot be that black people simply play baseball better than white people, because were this the case, the white players would have to be at least as good as the black players in order to get a shot, and the statistical differences therefore would not exist. The better answer is that there is discrimination against black players—that black players who are merely as good as white players will not get the same chances that white players do. The black players have higher statistical averages because they had to be better than the white players to get noticed.

Other professions—law and medicine, for example—lack the same hard data for comparison, but most black professionals take this bias as a given. To the extent that the bias exists, one would expect the performances of black people who are near the top of their fields to be better than the performances of white people who attain similar prominence. Maybe this is so; some studies suggest that black professors are paid more than white professors of similar background and achievements. Does this market data suggest a recognition that the black professors had to be better to get to the same place? It's hard to tell, because there have not been enough of us around long enough, not in the corridors of power.

For most of American history, the professions have been segregated.

* Except maybe even the hard statistics of baseball are less clear than one might hope. A Jewish acquaintance tells how, when he was growing up, it was an article of faith in his household that Hank Greenberg would have broken Babe Ruth's single-season home-run record in 1938 (the record was 60 and Greenberg finished with 58) but for the fact that he was a Jew and, therefore, the pitchers walked him or threw him bad pitches in his last few games rather than risk the chance that a Jewish player might become the all-time home-run champ.

Skilled black professionals were long forced—odd word!—to serve only their own people. Black lawyers and doctors and dentists and accountants and the rest served black clienteles because white customers would not hire them and, in any event, white professionals, ever mindful of the bottom line, would not allow the competition. (And here I think of Thurgood Marshall's twinkling eye, as he asked us, his law clerks, where we would rather be taken with a gunshot wound, to some nice, clean suburban place where the doctors have never seen one before, or to Harlem Hospital, where they come by the dozens every year?) There they were, generations of smart, hard-working black men and women, prevented from practicing their arts on the wider canvas. Who can measure their greatness now, when so many of them left so little impact on what some Afrocentrists call "white history" —that is, the received tradition of what counts?

Now there are many more of us out there in white-dominated professions, working, sometimes struggling, often achieving. It is said at times that affirmative action, broadly conceived, has skimmed the cream from the black community—that the people who would have been serving black folk in the days of rigid segregation are now, in the era of integration, serving white folk. That is precisely why many of the leading theorists of black nationalism thought affirmative action a terrible idea. Once upon a time, integration of the professions was justified, at least in part, by the role-model argument—the idea that I, as a black law professor, am charged with proving to black and white alike what black people can do. Not a bad argument, either, but one that is in an uneasy tension with the fear that many of the best and the brightest of black people are deserting their communities, in both the geographic and economic senses. Successful black professionals often move into mostly white neighborhoods and also are no longer dependent on black people for income.

The question, then, is whether integration of formerly white professions must inexorably lead to assimilation of "formerly" black professionals—the point of the conversation so many years ago around the black table at Yale. The question is far from absurd. To succeed in a profession, one adopts the profession's ethos, its aesthetic, its culture. One remakes significant aspects of oneself.

Consider the black lawyers who succeed at one of the most exclusive and least integrated areas of practice, corporate law in large law firms. On campuses and in inner cities, one continues to hear debates over whether what is often called "Black English" is a language with African roots, a dialect with regional American roots, or simply a set of common errors. No matter one's view on that proposition, it is perfectly plain that a legal brief written in Black English would not be an acceptable professional document. Back in the late sixties and through most of the seventies, when the large Afro was the hairstyle of choice among politically and culturally sincere black students, the hair would nonetheless be trimmed if one wanted to work on Wall Street. And today, when many activists in the inner cities favor what they describe as traditional African garb, a black lawyer who wants to work at a corporate law firm must dress in smartly tailored business clothes.* In short, the practice of corporate law demands an aesthetic that many in the black community would describe as imposed by others.

It should be possible to adapt to this professional aesthetic and yet retain one's cultural identity—what I have described above as a claim. True, if one wants to move on in a professional world run by people who are white, one must understand the relevant values and respond to them. If one wants to move upward in the professions, one must accept that most of the rewards one seeks will be distributed by white people, according to rules they have worked out. The rules might be fair, they might not be; they might be coherent, they might not be; but even though getting rid of the rules when they aren't fair is one respectable project, playing by them and winning, whether they are fair or not, is another. The second of these, playing by the rules and

---

* This should not be taken to condone the ridiculous abuse of power by the judge in Washington, D.C., who recently threatened to punish a black lawyer who appeared before him in a kente cloth.

playing as well as everyone else, is what most professionals doubtless desire, and it is what all the best professionals attain. Black professionals can do that, too, and usually we must, at least if we want to move toward the top. And this is an awkward task, because it often will, *pace* Shelby Steele, feel like a surrender to white power.

But all it really is, is wanting to be good at what one does. To want to be a good doctor has nothing to do with wanting to be a white doctor. The fact that professional standards have been laid down before significant numbers of black professionals came on the scene does not by itself prove racism; the need of multinational business firms for skilled legal negotiators is not a function of whether the founders of the firms are white. It is a function of the markets in which the firms must operate. The market in a sense defines the tasks for which it will compensate, and moving up the ladder requires doing one of those tasks better than others.

Being good is not, of course, enough—not always. Black professionals will often question the willingness of white colleagues to be fair, and there is frequently reason to wonder. Bias and favoritism are still rampant. Many of us learn this as a legacy from our parents: white people, we are told, will not be fair to us. This undeniable (if sometimes overbroad) fact of life can point children in two directions: some children might be paraylzed by despair, certain that achievement is impossible; others might be charged with a fiery desire to prove the critics wrong. Our destiny as a people turns on this choice; our hopes must lie with the children in the second group; and our efforts must be to get as many of our children into it as we can.

A principal point of the Black Power movement (and, I hope, a principal point even now of racial solidarity) is to keep us away from the downward slope, to help us find support not simply in the good opinion of white people but in the good opinion of black people, too.

Still, it is possible to take a good thing too far. When, as may happen, one is denied the good opinion of black people for *political* reasons, there might be a temptation to lurch into the arms of a welcoming white institution. Everyone, after all, wants a home. One of the reasons that I despair at the vehemence with which the political divisions in our community are nurtured is that there is so tremendous a risk of losing sharp minds to those some would call the enemy. Moreover, a growing ethic in many inner-city schools insists that achievement itself is somehow a sign of a lack of solidarity—that doing well in school is something that only white people, or black people who are trying to be white, would seriously want to do. Consistent, if depressing, social science data bear this out. Such ideas as Afrocentric curricula and special schools for black boys are touted as solutions to this problem, and, if they generate a degree of pride that in turn leads to achievement, they might solve some part of it, a possibility that itself might make them worth a try. But one must be cautious, for the Afrocentric curriculum runs a substantial risk of creating a dogma no less damaging than the assertedly Eurocentric curriculum that is deemed the enemy, while the special schools for black boys carry some risk of stereotyping and seem to overlook the fact that black girls are also at risk. Besides, millions of black kids in the past performed quite well in schools—even segregated schools—without the need for special curricula. What their parents and teachers inculcated instead was the importance of training the mind as a way of getting ahead. The world was different then, but one might reasonably conclude, even today, that what our kids need more than a redesigned curriculum is an end to the foolish and destructive notion that achievement is a betrayal. What is needed most is a rededication to excellence.

Of course, I say all of this from the standpoint of one who has, rather obviously, been seduced by the standards under which my white professional world judges achievement. I have always liked the idea that my résumé should be the equal of the résumés of the best of the white kids—or, nowadays, the best of the white adults. Maybe it is, maybe it isn't, but that is hardly the point. The point is that my goal in life, at least since eighth grade, has been to beat them—the white folks—at their own games, whatever those might be. I didn't need an Afrocentric curriculum to do that; I needed the burning drive to prove the racists wrong. It has been with me a very long time and it has carried me a very long way.

But the distance I have traveled is only a professional distance. The drive to succeed in the white man's world has not carried me far from my community, except in the geographic sense; on the contrary, it has, in many ways, brought me closer. In my junior high school and high school years, as the only black kid in a series of honors and advanced-placement courses, I suffered occasional estrangement from other black kids, who often seemed to me to share a secret world that I yearned to enter, could I but find the key. Adolescent silliness, of course—all I had to do was try—but a springboard, in later years, for my delirious dive into a form of nationalism and, later, into a stronger circle of friendships and common needs, culminating, at least for me, in the glory of the black table. I will never lose touch with this circle, or these needs, because without them I would drown in a sea of whiteness.

Assimilation

So one claims. In America, with all the constriction that its swirling racial consciousness implies, claiming is a kind of freedom. Every ethnic group suffers its crisis as members of a fresh generation reject the claim as the last generation understood it, although, to the new generation, the claim is not rejected but transformed. The word that describes the process is *assimilation*. Among those who cherish solidarity, the word *assimilation* often carries a mildly pejorative content, and no wonder, for its many guises include alienation, intermarriage, the possibility of a turning away. And as each face turns, a culture creeps nearer to absorption, a transformation that also means demise. What does not change, they say, cannot survive; unfortunately, what changes cannot survive either. Thus does the image of America as a melting pot become an image for many to fear.

The professional ethic can cause the same dislocation, the same sense of rootlessness. Despite the overheated rhetoric of many otherwise thoughtful critics, the professional ethic—hard work in accord with the disciplining rules that define the profession itself—is not white, male, and Eurocentric. It is not even, in any comprehensible sense, ideological. It reflects, rather, a relentless pragmatism, the American tradition of solving problems rather than envisioning the world. Theorists of the left once imagined that America's brash style of capitalism would fail precisely because it lacked a pure vision which a variety of more disciplined ideologies across the world possessed. Better ideas would beat out better products.

But they didn't. In the struggle for hearts and minds, to the general astonishment of even its most passionate defenders, capitalism has triumphed. The question that professionalism raises is whether solidarity can beat better products: more to the point, as one rises in one's profession, is there a real risk that one will be trapped in the problem-solving methodology of one's training, and therefore lose the purer vision of group love that solidarity at once entails and requires? Some fear that the answer is yes; but the answer, surely, is the claim.

Again, one claims. One claims one's people. The claim is not of a politics or a culture or an aesthetic, or not purely of any of these. The claim, rather, is a love.

But what is the form that it takes? Even if we proudly proclaim that we are black people who happen to be lawyers, not the other way around, what, concretely, is the difference that this proclamation makes? Does it imply a habit of mind? An aesthetic sensibility? A political program? Many people would argue that it means some or all of these things, that to vary or reject is to grow estranged from one's roots. This is when the ugly battles begin over which black perspective is the authentic one—and those battles, for the sake of our people, are best avoided.

Perhaps what the claim of one's people implies is something rather different, something personal, a choice within a choice. The decision to claim solidarity is something internal, a joining of neurons rather than of hands. To claim solidarity, to claim to love one's people, is to accept a responsibility of living and working and helping—that is, to love one's people is to crave a kind of familyhood with them. But one may live a very long way from one's family and love it no less. For some people, love of family demands constant contact; for others, a card every other Christmas is sufficient. The great majority of people must surely fall somewhere between these extremes. The choice within a choice that the claimant must make is what love demands.

This means, of course, that every one of us who is black and a professional becomes insulated from the cruel suggestions that we have left our people behind, because only *we* know that. Many will not feel comfortable unless they are actively involved in assisting the worst-off members of their communities. Others will make choices about where to live, whom to love, how to vacation. Some will reach down the ladder to pull others along. Some will spend their days redesigning the ladder itself. But even one who spends her career simply being the best she can be at what she does can, if fired by love, insist that she, too, has made a claim—and so I would say she has. Moreover, she has even carried her burden of working and helping, for each of us who shatters the stereotypes advances the cause.

Why must solidarity ever demand more than this? To love and to choose—to choose to love—isn't this enough? There, at the black table, the answer was so difficult to see. We wanted greater complexity, wanted obligations to impose on one another, as though choosing for others what constitutes love would prove our own commitments. We thought that we were proving something of value if only we could show that the duality of our selected futures, our blackness and our professionalness, should be irreconcilable, or at least should pose us a challenge. In a racist world especially, we were sure there must be something more. Putting on the tie—it *had* to make us less. We were not prepared for the possibility that it merely made us different.

And now, more than a decade after my classmates and I left the black table, now when I am well along in my professional career, solidarity continues to tug, deep inside me, gently, insistently, lovingly, and a little desperately, like something afraid of being left behind. But I cannot leave it behind, and would not if I could. I carry it. I cherish it. More important, I try to nurture it—for the light of solidarity, like the light of love, will go out if not carefully tended.

Race is a claim. A choice. A decision. Oh, it is imposed, too. The society tells us: "You are black because we say so." Skin color is selected as one of many possible characteristics of morphology used for sorting. Never mind the reasons. It is simply *so*. It is not, however, logically entailed. Many years ago—in high school, I think—I happened upon an interview with the leader of one of what used to be called the emergent Caribbean nations. The interviewer asked the president how it felt to be the leader of a newly independent black nation. The president (or prime minister or whatever his title was) replied that he was the leader of a newly independent *white* nation. When pressed by the incredulous interviewer, the president explained (with a twinkle in his eye, I like to think) that he had read somewhere that in the United States anybody with more than one thirty-second black blood was considered black. "Well, here in my country," he concluded, "we define white in exactly the same way."

The president was not, I think, rejecting the interviewer's imposition of blackness upon him and his people; he was lampooning it, and with some force. "You are black because we say so" is oppressive. The liberating answer to such cruel nonsense, the answer that solidarity suggests, is: "No, I am black because *I* say so."

That answers the tug and paints an identity for me, or the start of one. But to make race a claim, to say that I am black because I say so, proposes that it is also up to me to decide what that state of blackness entails. For me as a professional, as a scholar, as a person who is black and has made that claim from love, this is an autonomy that matters.

79

Who Are We?
Where Did We Come From?
Where Are We Going?

Stanley Crouch

Whatever I have to say essentially results from two things, my being an American and my being a writer. As an American I am heir to a heritage far more intricate and compelling than most of what is said about it, regardless of the sayer's skin tone or class. As a writer, I am often asked to serve in an army whose purposes I consider dubious and whose leadership I look upon with great reservation. Therefore, like most of us, I am always working to avoid being pinned down between the race game and the human game. If one embraces the race game, one submits to a certain set of limitations; if one champions the human game, the charge yowled through the bullhorn of frustration is one of naïveté. As we know, there are those who consider that charge too great a burden. I'm not one of them. No matter what I might have felt when younger and more gullible, it no longer pains me to be out here by myself when I have to be, since part of what I consider my duty is adherence to the intellectual

---

Stanley Crouch is an actor, playwright, poet, and essayist. He has written for *The Village Voice*, *The Soho Weekly News*, *Harper's*, *The New York Times*, *The Amsterdam News*, and many other publications. He is a contributing editor to *The New Republic* and has served as artistic consultant for jazz programming at Lincoln Center since 1987. In 1991, Crouch received the Whiting Writer's Award. His biography of Charlie Parker will be published by Doubleday in 1993; a collection of jazz essays and reviews will be published by Oxford University Press in 1993; and his epic novel, *First Snow in Kokomo*, should appear in 1993 as well.

claustrophobia any writer seeking an individual sense of life feels when invited—or commanded—into the martial cattle car of presuppositions and clichés.

So what I have to say in this essay is where I think we come from as Negro Americans, where I think we are right now, and where I think we're going. Experience and study have led me to a tragic optimism that allows no interest in idols beyond the reach of human feeling and human failing, neither building nor tearing them down. The assignment given every generation is far more complex—either sustaining or expanding civilization. That chore demands combat with sentimentality, the overwrought failure of feeling. In this eternal conflict, the writer intent on laying demons low raises weapons formed of intellect and passion against either chaos or the straitjackets tied closed by Gordian knots of received ideas. In the following piece, my intent is to look at some things my own way. But, as most writers secretly hope, perhaps my perspective can rhyme with yours.

I.

No isolated aspect of the national biography, the epic tale of the Negro's journey from property to full participation has been at the center of our perception of the United States for two hundred years, and the sweep from eloquence to balderdash it has inspired is as impressive as it is repulsive. The Negro's social evolution called for the expansion of American democracy and quite obviously set agendas for other groups suffering from only partial interplay with the ideals of the nation. But that struggle was also connected to elemental aspects of the culture's consciousness, for the moment that the idea of a country separate from the British Empire began to form most seriously, there was an understanding that this dream nation of unprecedented democracy had to strain itself against the measure of the European past and adapt to the conditions of a world part civilized and part wilderness. The debates and policies that arose in reference to the question of who and what the Negro was in basic and potential human terms helped let us know just how civilized we were at any time and just how much of the American wilderness existed in the very spirit of the country itself.

That ongoing conflict between civilized vitality and anarchic wildness maintains a special position in the arena of ethnic identity, at least partially because the question of being an American and a Negro has held a perplexing and enlightening position in the long procession of triumphs and tragedies that have given our national life its vigor as well as the gloom we so often shroud in hysteria. As an issue, the identity of the Negro remains king-sized because identity is such a dilemma to Americans at large and because the insecurity involved in figuring out what one actually is within the context of this country too often allows for manipulation and shallow thinking. So many theories and misapprehensions appear, particularly ideas that are as confused as they are lacking in any real sense of their sources, few of which are domestic and none of any significance from Africa. That may be hard for many to swallow but the cup remains before us. Our history, like the history of the world since the Enlightenment, is either one of adopting, expanding, and acting on the vision of universal humanity or rejecting it, since there can neither be thorough democracy nor a world morality based on the recognition of fundamental commonality without universal humanism.

The upshot is that, in the long process of thinking out our Negro American identity during these roller-coaster ethnic debates and in face of national policies, we have had to either accept or reject or at least feel somewhat bemused by the cosmopolitan character of our position in this beautiful, elusive, exasperating, and violent culture. That culture includes new features and hair textures, new shades of eyes and skin tones, providing us with physical metaphors for the kaleidoscopic nature of the miscegenated national heart. Said national heart has always been as mysterious as any in history. Yet, in our own time, we should be able to easily see things that might not have been so clear to those predecessors who lived in eras when segregation, racial discrimination, and our own provincialism held in check real and imagined aspects of Negro life. Then our protracted social and psychological war against xenophobic superstition shaped political issues and determined how so many of us carried ourselves when we considered every public image and act proof or repudiation of the ideas that scandalized and beleaguered our part of the population. We might have believed ourselves more innately humble than we actually were, might have struggled against the interior devastation of the propaganda about our inferiority, perhaps even seen ourselves as captured angels socially crucified by moral cretins whose position in the world was backed up by brute force and brute force only.

In the intellectual history of these dilemmas, the idea of a "double-consciousness" has been raised in an attempt to explain the nature of the Negro, and that idea has become almost an automatic reference among those who are given to less than hard thinking about what it presupposes and what it purports to explain. Examined seriously, the idea is no more than another aspect of anarchic wildness overgrowing intellectual clarity. Conceived and laid out by W. E. B. Du Bois in the first chapter of 1903's *The Souls of Black Folk*, the condition somehow disallows consciousness of self and creates an aching split—"this sense of always looking at one's self through the eyes of others, of measuring one's soul by the tape of a world that looks on in amused contempt and pity. One ever feels this twoness—an American, a Negro; two souls, two thoughts, two unreconciled strivings; two warring ideals in one dark body, whose dogged strength alone keeps it from being torn asunder." Further, Du Bois writes, "The history of the American Negro is the history of this strife,—this longing to attain self-conscious manhood, to merge his double self into a better and truer self. In this merging he wishes neither of the older selves to be lost. He would not Africanize America, for America has too much to teach the world and Africa. He would not bleach his Negro soul in a flood of white Americanism, for he knows that Negro blood has a message for the world."

Here we have a muddle of ideas that purport to explicate an alienation between national and racial identity, casting them as "warring ideals." That muddle leads us away from the facts of American life and even now puts us at odds with the tasks before the writer who would recognize experience in the rich, mysterious, and disappointing ways that it always arrives. And since all social structures must address the tragic facts inevitable in human activity—folly, corruption, and mediocrity—what is "ideal" about either being an American or being a Negro? We are never really told but are immediately drafted into a bemusing intellectual struggle if we take Du Bois at his word and attempt to explain exactly what the resolution of "double-consciousness" into a "better and truer self" would be, especially when he says of it all that the "longing" circulates around the fact that the Negro "simply wishes to make it possible for a man to be both a Negro and an American, without being cursed and spit upon by his fellows, without having the doors of Opportunity closed roughly in his face."

Even that last derailing of his own train would be fine and dandy if it weren't true that Du Bois invested more in race than a set of surfaces that innately said nothing of the individual. Du Bois, sounding yet another of the many versions of the German nationalism rooted in the thinking of Herder, apparently believed that there was some sort of innate Negro identity, an identity comprised of "Negro soul" and "Negro blood." This identity was in an ongoing struggle with American that made for "two unreconciled strivings." Such a vision includes an acceptance of the sort of dubiousness that Ralph Ellison took on in *Invisible Man* when he argued not with Du Bois but with James Joyce by saying that Stephen Dedalus had the job of creating the features *of his own face*, not the "uncreated conscience of his race"! Ellison knew that the problem of a race consciousness of whatever stripe negates the question of the individual and imposes some sort of "authenticity" that can trap the single human life inside a set of limited expectations. Ellison was more interested in the incredible variety possible if any nation or any group truly grasps the idea of democracy and frees itself from all ideas that negate the broad human heritage available to enriching interpretation by individuals, no matter what their ethnic origin.

This is not something Du Bois missed completely, for *The Souls of Black Folk*—as a whole—swings back and forth between ideas about racial consciousness and a sense of greater humanity based in talent and sensibility rather than skin tone. The very confusion of the work as an entity suggests that if anyone had such double vision on the issue that an ongoing set of contradictions resulted, the culprit was Du Bois himself. Du Bois was so inaccurate that he went on in that first chapter to make claims for the effect of his double consciousness that push aside the fact that Negroes, as Americans, are caught in the middle of the national struggle between high and low, refined and rough, industrious and lazy, articulate and ignorant, moral and criminal, sincere and hypocritical—struggles that the best writers at any point or place in history have always seen as the overriding human tale, no matter the vernacular particulars.

Du Bois, however, so strongly believed race to have the upper hand that he could explain poor workmanship in the determinist terms of his double-consciousness, asserting that "The double-aimed struggle of the black artisan—on the one hand to escape white contempt for a nation of mere hewers of wood and drawers of water, and on the other hand to plough and nail and dig for a poverty-stricken horde—could only result in making him a poor craftsman, for he had but half a heart in either cause." The long tradition of Negro excellence at everything from seamanship to rodeo skills refutes Du Bois and was the crux of Washington's argument against the free ride the skin game gave European immigrants in blue-collar arenas where Negro ability was so well documented that there could be no *fair* restrictions raised against it. Continuing, Du Bois asserts that because of "the poverty and the ignorance of his people, the Negro minister or doctor was tempted toward quackery and demagogy; and by the criticism of the other world, toward ideals that made him ashamed of his lowly tasks."

Neither *The Confidence Man* nor *Huckleberry Finn* would allow one to perceive those problems of opportunism and lack of gumption solely in racial terms. They are central elements of the American dilemma, and the arena of color only puts its variation on them.

By claiming that the Negro who would become a person of letters "was confronted by the paradox that the knowledge his people needed was a twice-told tale to his white neighbors, while the knowledge which would teach the white world was Greek to his own flesh and blood," Du Bois both ignores America's anti-intellectual tradition and prefigures the wrongheaded James Baldwin of "Stranger in the Village," who hands over the highest literary, aesthetic, and architectural achievements of Western civilization to some Swiss ignoramuses by assuming that "the most illiterate among them is related, in a way that I am not." While implying all God's brown chillun got rhythm, Du Bois even figured out a way to choke off the inspiration of the Negro artist: "The innate love of harmony and beauty that set the ruder souls of his people a-dancing and a-singing raised but confusion and doubt in the soul of the black artist; for the beauty revealed to him was the soul-beauty of a race which his larger audience despised, and he could not articulate the message of another people."

Though we should not expect Du Bois to be a musicologist, and though he concludes his book with high praise of Negro music—albeit finally bogged down by a belief in race memory—we cannot allow him to slip by when he presents such a closed argument. Where is there *any* proof of his idea? The developments in religious and secular music, in dance and in comedy, don't support him anymore than the work of Ira Aldridge or Black Patti validates his idea that the Negro artist "could not articulate the message of another people." It is also true that those such as Frank Johnson, the popular and internationally celebrated Philadelphia bandleader of the early nineteenth century, William Henry Lane, the great dancer known as "Juba," James Bland, Scott Joplin, Buddy Bolden, W. C. Handy, Eubie Blake, Ma Rainey, Bessie Smith, Jelly Roll Morton, Sidney Bechet, Will Marion Cook,

James Reese Europe, and James P. Johnson had no trouble at all transforming into often innovative aesthetic design what they saw and heard in the Negro community, nor would the legions soon to follow them in show business, where the greatest Negro art appeared. None seemed overwhelmed by the opinions of any outside their own communities. Few artists anywhere in the world ever are; they are too busy interpreting and rendering the obvious and mysterious facts of humanity as they appear before them. But then the impression that Du Bois gives us, finally, is that he had little understanding of art or of the artistic process.

Perhaps as great an error as any in the double-consciousness formulation, particularly as it applies to our contemporary experience, is its missing the possibilities for varied nuance that are intrinsic to national experience. In fact, consciousness is much more complex than double. For instance, if one is Negro and a member of a long-term Boston family, or even one of two generations, that Negro most probably perceives identity in terms of the Eastern Seaboard, the city of Boston itself, of his or her neighborhood, block, class, and religion. That regionalism, which so deeply influences the way one apprehends the world, is true for every part of the country, and it is not neutralized by race. If one knows jazz musicians, for instance, pride of city and of region is basic, and it determines quite often the way in which musicians play. It also determines which musicians they celebrate apart from the figures who shape the national evolution of the musical language. And when gender is factored in, things take on yet another set of attitudes and interpretations of experience. None of these examples denies race as an element but all give a much richer sense of how varied the human dimensions of American experience are, regardless of pigmentation.

Du Bois, who was obviously the result of miscegenation, even opened the way for what would develop into abstract African racialism of the Negro kind when he wrote, "The shadow of a mighty Negro past flits thorough the tale of Ethiopia the Shadowy and of Egypt the Sphinx."

Since American Negroes are from neither Ethiopia nor Egypt, what we find lurking in the haze of that statement is the eventual idea of Pan-Africanism. Central to Pan-Africanism is a politics of race that assumes some sort of inevitable fairness in a group possessed of a commonality of complaint founded in struggling against the mutual ruthlessness of colonialism in Africa and the racial injustice of the Western Hemisphere. It purports a victimized but essentially royal "we." The brutal totalitarian history of postcolonial Africa should make clear just how naïve that idea was, not to mention the way the corrupt and irresponsible Marion Barry so cynically called for racial unity and claimed racism in an attempt to manipulate the black majority of Washington, D.C. As one Washington wag put it, "I hate it when niggers fuck up the motherfucking public trust, then, when they get caught, pull out their civil rights credit card and charge racism!"

2.

Given the poorly thought-out and contradictory positions of *The Souls of Black Folk*, why are those ideas that Du Bois presents in such unconvincing fashion still so popular, even when he isn't known as a source? Is it because those ideas remove Negroes from the weights of modern life as they fall upon everyone? Is it because those turn-of-the-century ideas allow for the avoidance of individual responsibility and make it possible to see Negroes in something akin to a pure state, or at least a state in which all is very simply white and black, Western and Third World, oppressor and oppressed? Today, given figures like Marion Barry, Uganda's Obote, Ethiopia's Mengistu, and South Africa's Winnie Mandela, there might even be nostalgia for those times, or at least for the simpler ideas those times allowed.

At this point, ninety years since *The Souls of Black Folk*, it is too late in the world for nostalgia, particularly the nostalgia that is no more than a cover for the bitterness felt when the homespun idea of being some sort of a chosen people is smacked by the persistent complexities of our humanity as we actually live it—in the pitch before dawn, or in the morning, or in public light, or in the evening's privacy when the sun goes down and nobody else is around. We should by now be fully aware of the fact that no ethnic group—or class—is either more or less susceptible to the richest ideas explicit in our social contract or to the steel-quilled sentimentalities of decadence. There is nothing preventing our overt involvement in the forming of either the national identity or national policy, and we also observe ourselves functioning in almost every capacity and exhibiting every inclination from the grand to the gaudy, from the idealistic to the shallow ethnic con delivered in the familiar rhythms of the church or the street, from the brave to the cowardly, from the pure to the absolutely corrupt and disgusting. Like all modern people, we see our humanity stretched across the rack of the media, where the tabloid inclinations of electronic journalism examine people not only with a microscope but also, as Richard Nixon so knowingly observed, with a proctoscope.

That brings us to a challenge demanding intellectual and emotional liberation from the clichés and political recipes that amalgamate into strange combinations of determinism, frantic fawning before fantasies of ethnic origin, and visions of paradise lost. None of those visions are sufficiently fluid or insightful in a time when the quality of our criticism should make it possible to address the riddling manifestations of the human spirit in the truest terms of our own technological moment, in the very same ways that the most uncompromising minds have always had to when struck by the demands and the revelations of the mechanistic age. But in order to do that we need to move toward a freedom that steps beyond the lightweight vision of racial solidarity that discourages the insights expected of serious writers and intellectuals.

Only the deaf, dumb, and blind wouldn't know that we have more than a little candor stuck in our craw. Yet so many of us are afraid of being called self-hating or neo-conservative that we function too often like espionage operatives who cannot be expected to tell the truth publicly for fear of being castigated unto unemployment or ostracized as traitors. The serious shouldn't be daunted by any of that and should realize that were a writer like Balzac presently alive and Negro and penning material about, say, Washington, D.C., the charge of self-hatred would quiver with rage from the pages of reviewers. A Negro Balzac would look at the folly, the corruption, and the mediocrity with humor, psychological insight, an extraordinary sense of place, class, and the particulars of occupation. He or she wouldn't get lost in the problem of public relations because the tragedy and hilarious absurdity of human life form immutable facts no one with a grounding in the rich irony, criticism, and affirmation of the blues or of literature and true intellectual engagement could miss.

3.

If we are to rise above the mud of racial limitation and put our experience within the largest possible context, we have to go far beyond the overstated racial paranoia and insecurity that can ensure success. We have to assert our human heritage and understand where we truly come from in intellectual and moral terms, which means that we must be willing to let the dogs bark as our caravan moves by. We ought to know that no fundamental observations about the wonders or the horrors of human beings over the last two hundred years have originated with us because we came into the discussion of sophisticated modern life very late, with no great African texts—none. This does not mean that the Africans from whom we are at least *partially* descended were innately inferior, which was the argument used to justify the colonizing barbarism of those willing and able to set aside ethics when abroad. Yet much of the periodic hysteria about Africa's role in the beginning of civilization is a response to the fact that our level of intellectual engagement on the grand stage of the world was quite humble throughout our tragic arrival in the Western Hemisphere. No shadowy flitting around Egypt or Ethiopia. That humble level was the result of an environment benefiting neither from great ideas nor from significant technology, an environment as far removed from the bustle of intellectual cultivation as the world of the most distant rural peasantry in Europe.

Any honest examination shows that the indigenous arenas for West African genius were much narrower than the best Europe had developed, were neither in architecture nor the sciences, in literature nor philosophy. To stand up and accept those facts within the context of our American experience is also to celebrate the extraordinary flexibility of human beings, which is the essence of the democratic ideal. After all, so many can recall those classes in which Negroes superbly taught their students math, science, history, literature, art, and so on, preparing them for careers that swept the gamut made possible by the unsurpassed clearing house of information that, finally, makes Western Civilization the wonder that it is.

Interestingly, the Third World students who do so well at our universities rarely have any problem recognizing the wonder of Western Civilization. Unlike too many glib academics and substandard intellectuals, those foreign students aren't as often overwhelmed by the ethnic versions of being parlor pinks. They aren't especially impressed by those among us who lounge like lizards in the comforts of this civilization while pretending our society is inferior to systems in which the opposition is either jailed or murdered, exiled or "reeducated." Those students have had to face the limitations of their own societies and quite frequently aim to work at bringing the poetic values of their traditional cultures in line with the endless vistas of information amassed by the Western world, information that has come from *everywhere*, which is the essence of the victory against provincialism that allowed for scientific inquiry to supersede the brutalities that usually accompanied exploration or quickly followed it.

But initially because they were in conflict with the moral underpinnings of Christianity, those very brutalities within our American context didn't go down as smoothly as many so given to listing them like to claim. One need not be religious to see that Christianity's access to all was perhaps the earliest vision of universal humanity, a vision that would have indelible impact on the struggle against slavery and the eventual fall of racism written into the policy of law. And however many examples one can find of Christian leaders willing to align themselves with colonial savagery, there is the equally significant fact that from the very moment African slaves were brought into America there were those who debated the issue and saw the business of bondage as antithetical to the ethics of the religion.

Conversely, it is important to face the fact that *there was no great African debate over the moral meanings of slavery itself.* There is no record whatsoever of an African from a tribe that *wasn't* being enslaved arguing against the very practice of capturing and selling other Africans. Historians in or out of Africa have found no African William Lloyd Garrisons, no African abolition movement, no African underground railroad, no African civil war in which the central moral issue was slavery. As Nathan Huggins observed in his gloriously unsentimental *Black Odyssey*, "The racial irony was lost on African merchants, who saw themselves as selling people other than their own. The distinctions of tribe were more real to them than race, a concept that was yet to be refined by nineteenth- and twentieth-century Western rationalists."

Even so, the distinctions of race are less important to this argument than the fact that the conception of universal humanity never arrived to thunder against the conventions of those African cultures in the way that it did in Europe as a result of the Enlightenment, when the most extraordinary thinkers sought to identify with others beyond the limits of nationality, language, and the styles that characterized European societies, that made them French or German or British or whatever. The degree and the rate at which this nation's democratic ideals expanded into the furthest reaches of the society were determined by the victories in the conflict between the idea of universal humanity and the prejudicial attitudes that allowed for slavery and racial discrimination. Then, moving outward from Europe and America, the conception of universal humanity has come to take such a position that no contemporary leader of a nation—regardless of his or her real feelings—feels free to suggest that any other people from any place in the world are somehow *innately* inferior. Such political conventions have no precedents in world history and are the result of ideas that have developed since the American and French revolutions, our own Civil War, and the scientific research that has proven universal humanity much more than a good idea, resulting in remarkable achievements such as blood transfusion and organ transplants.

But whenever the question of universal humanity is raised in the context of Negro American history, we must know that figures such as Frederick Douglass, Harriet Tubman, Rosa Parks, and Martin Luther King have a significance far beyond the provincial. Two examples of that significance were observed in the singing of "We Shall Overcome" in Prague and the carrying of placards that read those same words in Tiananmen Square. Seriously examined, those Negro leaders and symbols of resistance to dehumanization have a moral ancestry rooted in the ongoing Western debate that has led to the redefinitions of society and of the rights of the people in it. That Euro-American ancestry, far more than anything from Africa itself, also fuels the combination of ethnic nationalism and evangelical liberation politics domestic Negroes bring to high-pitched rhetoric over the issue of Nelson Mandela and his struggle.

Making these observations, however true, puts one at odds with the patronizing idea that Negroes are somehow so incapable of existing as adults in the contemporary world that they should always be handled like extremely fragile children who must be fed the myths that "make them feel good about themselves." But the world will be what it is no matter how much anyone attempts to pretend otherwise. And what is needed in every sector of our society is a willingness to look at issues for what they are, to recognize the complex dimensions of our identity, to embrace the tradition of the serious writer and intellectual in Western civilization and reject ideas as flimsy as the ones Du Bois puts before us in that first chapter of *The Souls of Black Folk*.

Though some might argue that Du Bois was doing well for his time, I say that we can do much better for our time and for all time. We have behind us, about us, and before us a tale as inspiring and depressing as any in the history of the modern world. It is filled with politics, intrigue, war, romance, humor, victory, loss, illumination, treachery, adventure, despair, epiphanies, and all of the components that traditionally inspire everything from epigrams to epics. If we are to do better by this tale, we must follow the examples of writers as far removed as André Malraux and Ralph Ellison, Thomas Mann and Albert Murray, Lincoln Kirstein and David Levering Lewis, F. Scott Fitzgerald and Charles Johnson, H. L. Mencken and Gerald Early. In order to do so, we have to sharpen our intellectual swords and take to the field, intent on drawing blood as the demons of anarchic wildness bear down on us again, filling the air with dust and expecting to run us over. No matter the numbers of those demons and no matter the thunder of their mounts, as the incremental delivery of work resulting from midnight oil and accurate observation always guarantees, an upset is in the making, one that will result from the unsentimental but affirmative dictates of the miscegenated national heart that has made us all that we finally are and all we will ever be.

Confessions of a
Wannabe Negro

Reginald McKnight

I can't say when I first noticed my blackness. Such things fall upon
one like sleep, appear like gray hairs on the head. One moment we
are not aware of some aspect of our being, and the next we are saying
that we have never known ourselves any different. I do, however,
remember the very day I noticed that my blackness made me different.
There was this girl named Marsha on whom I had what you could call
a crush, young as I was. Her hair was white as sunlight on a web, her
eyes were as blue as plums. This was so long ago, thirty years or better,
that I can't remember the context within which all of this took place,
but I do remember that it happened in school, and I remember that
we were indoors, queued next to a row of windows that cast light only
on Marsha. I stood in line dead next to her, inhaling her Ivory soap
and whole-milk scent, watching the light set fire to that delicate hair.
Some kid behind me had been trying to engage me in a conversation
for more than five minutes, but I was having little of it. I only wanted
to consume Marsha's presence. But, through sheer persistence, the kid

Reginald McKnight currently teaches at Carnegie-Mellon University in Pittsburgh, Penn-
sylvania. He is a winner of the O. Henry Award and the Kenyon Review New Fiction
Prize, as well as the recipient of a 1991 National Endowment for the Arts Grant for
Literature.

broke through. I heard him say, ". . . born in California, just up the road. Where was you born?" "Germany," I answered, and drifted back to Marsha, her elbows, the backs of her knees, the heels of her saddle shoes. Then she turned around . . . to look at me . . . to speak to me . . . to cast her radiance my way. She said, "Coloreds can't be born in Germany." Of course I felt humiliated, embarrassed, angered. My stomach folded in on itself, my hands trembled, my face burned. I couldn't have explained it to you then, but I had never felt this way before, never felt singled out on account of my color, and at first I thought Marsha had misunderstood me, so I replied, "I didn't say I was German, I said I was *born* in Germany." But she stuck to her guns, empty as their chambers were, saying, "You're just a liar! Colored people do not come from Germany." And I told Marsha, as gently as I could, of course, that I most certainly had been born in Germany. Just ask my mother, etc., etc. But the more I asserted my claim, the more incredulous Marsha, and then a growing number of my school-mates, became. I remember one boy telling me that he was Catholic, and that, ". . . um, in the Catholic Church? um, if you lie? um, you'll, ah go to H.E.L.L." I had only one supporter that morning, a kid whose name I can no longer recall. She tried to defend me by announcing that though she was Chinese she'd been born in Tennessee. Marsha, for some reason, saw no logic in this, and said, "Well, maybe so, but that doesn't mean a colored can be born in Germany."

I was six, I think.

A few years later I remember walking home from school with my neighbors, my friends, the Weatherford kids, Ginny, Kathelynn, and Junior. The Weatherford kids were white, but at the time I didn't think of them as white. If I thought of them in terms of a class, or a type, or a category at all, I thought of them as Southerners, children, friends, and so forth. The afternoon was windless, cool. The bone-dry, yellow, tan, and evergreen of a typical Colorado autumn. We strode down the sidewalk, mindful of little outside the foursquare of ourselves. Junior, as he usually did, boasted about some impressive thing he had done or had thought that day in school. Kathelynn and Ginny bickered about which of them had made the bigger mess that morning in the room they shared. I bounced my Car 54 lunch box off my thigh, pretending to listen to Junior, while giving my full attention to his sisters, and somehow being aware of the magpie-fashion hollering of the flock of boys who walked behind us half a block or so back. Though they themselves drew no nearer to us, their words incrementally became more distinct to me. Dummy in the blue shirt. Dummy in the blue shirt. Dummy in the blue shirt, they were saying, and I knew they were talking about me, even though I was wearing not a blue shirt but a blue sweater. It made no difference that I was the only one of the four of us wearing blue. I would have known even if all four of us had been swathed from collar to ankle in blue. Dummy in the blue shirt. Dummy in the blue shirt. "Hey, Dummy, turn around." "Yeah, look at us, Dummy!" "Hey, look at us!" "Were you too dumb to take a bath this morning, Dummy?" "Yeah, you sure are dirty." "Phew! I can smell you from here."

Of course the Weatherford kids heard this too, and one or two of them told me I ought not turn around. I thought that was a good idea. Junior, my man Junior, turned around, though, and hollered back, "You're the dummies. . . . Shut up!" Then he turned to me and said, "They're the dumb ones, not you." Just then a chunk of feldspar, the size of an eight-year-old's fist, zinged a couple of feet over my head and skittered down the sidewalk several feet ahead of us, and came to rest in the grass. "Hey, Dummy, turn around."

"Just ignore them, Junior," Ginny said.

This nonsense went on for several blocks, ending only when we turned right, heading down our own street. Just before we turned, however, I finally did glance back at the kids. They appeared to be a couple of grades ahead. I didn't recognize any of them. Neither did I expect to.

I said nothing to my family about this, that day, but the following morning I told my mother about the incident while she was knocking a few naps out of my hair with a very small-toothed comb. It wasn't till I was about three quarters of the way through the story that I realized I'd made a mistake. In the first place, my mother has never been a "morning person," and she went about all her morning tasks with great flame and fury even when things were running smoothly. But as my story unfolded I noted she began combing my hair with increasing vehemence. It felt as though some great bird were swooping down on me, clutching my head with its blade-sharp talons, and by degrees, plucking the bone away to get to the meat. Quite honestly, I had expected her to lay the comb aside, set me on her lap, and coo rather than caw. But Mama said, "What were you doing? Were you acting like a dummy?" And I said, "No, ma'am, I was just walking." "Well," she said, combing with still greater heat, "you must've been doing something, boy." I was pretty sure my scalp had begun bleeding. "Hold still, boy," she said. Then, "I tell you *what*—if I *ever* catch you acting the fool at school or anywhere else, I'll skin you alive— you hear me?" And I said, "Yes, ma'am, I did, but I didn't do a thing except walk home from school." "I said hold still, boy! You better not be lying to me, Reginald." I was in tears by this time and all I could manage to say was what I'd already said before, that I'd just been walking, and so forth. Then, in a last-ditch effort for sympathy, I mentioned the rock they'd chucked, and that it had just barely missed hitting me smack on the head. "Well, why didn't you throw one back?" Mama said, and then she said she'd be damned if she was going to raise anybody's sissy. But I heard something catch in her throat, and she laid the comb on the rim of the basin, then rested her hands on my shoulders. I was too ashamed of my tears to look up into the mirror and at her reflection. She turned me about, drew me into her warm bosom, held me, talked about how ignorant some people were, that I shouldn't let a bunch of stupid boys upset me, that the world could sometimes be a tough, mean, petty place and I was just going to have to toughen up right along with it. She said a few more things, which I can no longer remember, but I do remember that her warmth and the sounds that issued from her throat, dozy, lugubrious, made my belly heat up and glow, made my legs tremble, made me want to sleep. But Mama said, "Come on now, son, you got to be strong." She took me by the shoulders again, turned me back around, and resumed working on my hair.

I think I was about eight then.

And by this time I thought I was getting it, thought I had discovered the difference, and what it meant, but in that same year I made a second discovery, something that made it clear to me that I was different, but not different in the way I thought I was. That year my grandfather took ill and the air force granted my father a special two-month leave so my mother and he could go to Waco and tend to family needs. At first I was delighted, for I thought my father's leave meant a leave from school for me and my siblings. I was wrong, of course. One of the very first things my parents did when we got to Waco was enroll my sisters and me in school, and for the first time in my life I attended a segregated school.

For the first two or three days it was quite nice. The teacher seemed to adore me, unlike previous teachers I had had, the majority of whom treated me with a benign indifference. But with this new teacher, Mrs. Wood, it appeared I could do no wrong. She enjoyed having me read aloud, often stopping me midsentence and asking my classmates to mark the way I'd pronounced a particular word. The schoolwork seemed easy to me, and Mrs. Wood would invariably make positive comments on my work as she handed our assignments back to us. To this day I don't know whether I did well in school because the school, as some of my friends have suggested, was substandard, or because, as others have said, for once I'd felt comfortable amid my peers and didn't feel like the usual dummy in the blue shirt. Perhaps it was both. Perhaps it was coincidence. I can't be sure because in those days I was a very quiet kid, very shy. I felt no comfort in the teacher's special attention. I felt no comfort amid my peers, whether black or white, and I don't recall the work being significantly different from what I'd had at previous schools. It was the first school I ever attended, however, that permitted the practice of corporal punishment. Perhaps that made all the difference.

In any case, one afternoon, as I was leaving the campus at the end of the school day, two boys jumped me from behind and tried to tackle me to the ground. Not only was I surprised by the attack, but I was surprised by the ineptitude of my attackers. Neither of them attempted to slug me even though several onlookers standing nearby were hollering, "Hit 'im. Hit that white paddy. Hit that boy." One of my attackers, as he gripped me in a headlock, kept saying, "You think you something good, huh? You think you the teacher's pet, huh?" The other one said, "Git his legs, git his legs, git his legs." And he finally decided to get my legs himself and they brought me down, though I had boy number one in the headlock, rather than he me. Boys as small as we were could hardly do one another any harm, but all the dust we kicked up, all the pounding we exchanged, all the yelping of our spectators, not to mention the surprise of the attack, had me extremely agitated. Extremely nonplused too, because I wasn't clear as to whether they were simply playing, Texas style, or really trying to do me harm. While I lay prone, still holding the one boy in the headlock, and as the other boy, rather than slugging me, tried to peel my arms from around his friend's head, my Uncle Bill, who was responsible for picking me up from school each day, approached us and very coolly asked me, "You okay?" I felt the grips of both boys slacken a notch, but as I would not let go, they would not let go.

"I'm okay."

"What y'all fighting about?"

"Don' know. Just jumped me. Just started fighting me."

"Why'd y'all jump him?"

"Teacher's pet," said one.

"He think he white," said the other.

"Yeah, he think he something."

Uncle Bill said, "Y'all know this is my sister's boy?"

"Naw," said the first boy as though he didn't care, but I felt him slacken his grip still further, and this allowed me to throw my leg over his belly and straddle him. The other boy then got *me* in a headlock. "Awright," said Uncle Bill, "that's enough. I got some errands to run." Then Bill hoisted me up by my belt, swung me over his shoulder, and carried me to my grandfather's old Willie.

As the Jeep vibrated away from the school, I noticed, after a while, that I had been staring at the backs of my hands, and alternately glancing at the hands of my uncle. After a while I said, "Uncle Bill, do you think I look white?" And without looking at me, he said, "Do you think you look white?"

"Don't look white to me," I said.

"Me neither," he said.

And I didn't. I don't. I'm the color of a well-worn penny, as dark as, or darker than, any of my classmates in that Texas school. What on earth could they have meant? As the old woody rolled down the street, rattling the windows of Piggly Wigglys, hardware stores, barbershops and five-and-dimes, streets in this part of Waco where whitefolk were seldom seen, rarely thought of, I recalled a conversation I'd had just a week or so before with a classmate, this bullet-headed boy who sat two seats in front of me in Mrs. Wood's class. We were at lunch, and I remember being fairly amazed at what his lunch consisted of, rice buried in sugar (sugar?) and milk (milk?), two boiled eggs, and an orange. We were just getting acquainted, and he began by asking me the usual sort of questions: Where you from? Where's that? Why you move here? and so on. Then rather suddenly he asked me —and it seemed so incongruous to the previous questions—"Is your mama white?" And I said no. "Your daddy white?" No, I told him. "Hm," the boy said, "then why you talk so funny?" and he waited for my reply. I really didn't know what to say, but ended up with "I don't know. I don't think I talk funny." Then he asked me, "Why you walk so funny? Walk like you afraid to move, like you Frankenstein. Walk like a whiteboy." He chugged his milk, then wiped his mouth with the heel of his hand. "You act funny, too."

I turned toward my uncle and said, "Uncle Bill, what's a white paddy?" Bill shrugged, shook his head. "Aw, it's a whole lot of things, Reggie. Someone who looks white or acts white. Someone who acts sidicty, you know, like he better than everybody else. Something like that. Those boys are just ignorant, Reggie. They don't know nothing about nothing. Somebody don't act the way they do or look or think the way they do, and they wanna call him white paddy. You take my advice: Don't even study people like that."

But I did study them, as I suppose they studied me. I studied people both black and white, both critical and congratulatory. I studied the buck-toothed, tube-headed, freckle-faced whiteboy named Mike who called me nigger when I struck out in a softball game in the fourth grade. That happened in Colorado. It was the first time anyone ever called me nigger. I studied the two little Waco black girls who tossed rocks at me and my cousin Valencia as they chanted, "White paddy, white paddy." I remember the relief I felt, though it was only momentary, when I thought the girls meant that both Valencia and I were white paddies. It turns out I was mistaken, though. They meant just me. What mystified me at the time was that they hadn't even heard me speak, hadn't seen me walk. What were they seeing? I asked myself. How could I hide it? What was I doing? I studied the Colorado brother who, in school one day, replied to my "What's happ'nin', man?" with "Tom." And he coolly rolled away like mercury on glass, leaving me utterly bamboozled. I didn't know the guy, had never seen the guy before. Another high school acquaintance, a guy named Keith, used to joke with me, from time to time, by calling me Uncle Tunk. I studied him, too, discovering that he sincerely liked me but just thought I acted white. I studied the white boys in Louisiana who called me Charlie Brown, Coony, Nigra, Hippy Nigger, Boy, Monkey, Spade, Jig, who sincerely disliked me, and thought of me as typically black. I studied the six kids who spat on me as I walked past their bus parked in front of the school one day. As I approached the bus, each of them poked his head out the window and chanted, "Fuck a duck. Screw a penny. Nigger's dick's as good as any!" And then they showered me with their poetic residue. I must admit that though I studied the poem I never quite understood the intent. The spittle, though, was as legible as big black lettering on a yellow school bus.

I studied those who said to me, intending kindness, I suppose, "You know, you're really not that colored at all." Or "Were your family ever slaves? I mean, you don't act like other colored folks at all." "You know," a black friend said to me once, "I can't tell whether you're ahead of your time or behind it . . . cause you're one funny black man. You know?" A white friend asked me on a number of occasions whether I would be interested in dating his sister. I asked him, "You've told her I'm black, haven't you, Mike?" "Black," he laughed. "Yeah, right." And I remember the lanky, Dead Head blonde woman, who sat in front of me in a college Linguistics class, asking me whether I could speak like "other blacks." Deciding to forgo the mighty-righteous question "Just what the hell do you mean by like *other* blacks?"—I knew, I knew—I told her I could. "Let's see," she said. I crossed my arms and said, "Whaddaya mean, 'Let's see'? You don't believe me? Anyway, it's a matter of context. I just can't leap into it on command." She smirked, shrugged, and said, "Really, Reg, don't have a cow. It's okay." I felt like sliding from my chair, dropping to one knee, and singing, "I'd walk a million miles/ for one o' ya smiles/ my M-a-a-a-a-mmy," or something by the Righteous Brothers, or Joe Cocker. Minstrels. But I didn't because she might not have caught the irony. In fact, she might have said either, Wow! That was good, or, Well, I didn't think you could do it—either of which would have left me more deeply flummoxed than I already was.

I think these people have been trying to suggest to me that though I exhibit blackness I perform it rather poorly. I believe they are trying to tell me that there are a limited number of valid ways to express blackness, and that my own expression of it is, at best, shaky. Trey Ellis talks about this sort of thing in his essay "The New Black Aesthetic." Ellis says, "It wasn't unusual for me to be called 'oreo' and 'nigger' on the same day. . . . I realized I was a cultural mulatto."[1]

But when I say that I am a cultural mulatto, I don't mean to suggest that the majority of blacks in this country (or anywhere else) have some unwitting propensity toward resisting cross-cultural influences in the same way that a duck's oily feathers resist water. In a certain sense all Americans are mulattoes of one shade or another. But when whites "do blackface," people don't so much as blink (though a few would call them nigger lovers; a few would accuse them of exploiting black art/culture for lucre and fame or power and diversion). I daresay they are looked upon by many with a kind of admiration. They are lauded as hip white cats, down whitegirls, soulful purveyors of the "suchness," if not the substance, of negritude. As for blacks who are influenced by expression that is not, as some would say "preponderantly black," the response is rather more ambiguous. Charlie Pride, for example, or Richie Havens, or Jimi Hendrix, or Tracy Chapman may be praised for their talents, their virtuosity in the "pure" sense, but I know of no one who lauds such artists for their mastery of art forms that could be referred to as decidedly "white," except a handful of rock bands who argue, and quite rightly, that rock is a product of black culture as much as it is of white culture, if not more so. There may or may not be such a thing as "blue-eyed soul," but there is certainly the language for the concept. I know of no such term, however, for blacks who perform, in one way or another, to whatever degree, the white "thing" except for the term "crossover" which applies not only to blacks but to everyone else as well. Why the difference? Are we to conclude that this difference lies in the notion that blackness-as-performance is more neatly extricable from blackness-as-being than whiteness-as-performance is from whiteness-as-being? Is blackness-as-performance somehow regarded as a free-floating entity, belonging to no one in particular, while whiteness-as-performance can, and *should*, only belong to whites? After all, it appears to me that black-influenced whites are very often thought to be deepened and ennobled by such processes, while white-influenced blacks are regarded as weakened, diluted, less black.

Of course, it should come as no surprise that some blacks resent certain other blacks who seem willing to accept Eurocentrism, either in part or wholesale, given our history of having it shoved down our gullets. But I have seen whites reveal the same sort of resentment toward white-influenced blacks, as if blackness-as-performance belongs to anyone who would grasp it, master it, even extend upon and recreate its various forms, while its opposite doesn't or shouldn't belong to anyone but its primary producers. Are we to suspect, as Timothy Maliqalim Simone does, that whites may be engaged in "a new form of parasitism"? Simone asks, "Is the assumption of black ideas and worldviews simply a virulent means of recuperating white identity, so that it may resuscitate a waning confidence in its legitimacy to dominate others?"[2] Both of these questions are exceedingly difficult to answer, largely because I'm not sure we know what we're talking about when we talk about "everybody." And also because, ". . . like it or not," says Henry Louis Gates, Jr., in a recent *New York Times Book Review* essay, "all writers" (and from here I extrapolate musicians, painters, sculptors, etc., as well as a number of individuals who are not artists—black, white, yellow, etc., etc.) "are 'cultural impersonators.' "[3] It almost goes without saying that the nature of being human has a great deal to do with mimesis, adaptability, absorption, shape-shifting, souleating.

Like Ellis I was reared in predominantly white environments for most of my life. Though there were schools I attended where I was the only black person in the class, or my grade, and on one occasion, the entire school, for the most part I went to schools where the ethnic representation reflected national ethnic proportions. The neighborhoods in which I grew up were also integrated, being, most of them, military bases established or demographically reconstituted after 1947, the year that the armed forces were integrated. As a result of my upbringing, I learned quite early that the meaning of being black is always, always, always a matter of context. On the sliding scale of my personal history I have been adjudged to be both an Uncle Tom and a Hippie Nigger Bigot. In a 1988 interview with Bob Edwards of National Public Radio's *Morning Edition*, I described myself as a victim/beneficiary of the Civil Rights movement. Since that time I have heard others use the term (though I'm not here implying that I coined it. Historians have suggested that there are times in certain societies when things reach a critical mass of sorts, and ideas, more or less, invent themselves) and I've no doubt that the term implies a grudging affirmation that the movement succeeded to a certain degree. It also implies its failure. The term "victim/beneficiary," just like the word "mulatto," connotes the tragic, leaves us with the image of the heart and mind shred in two by the exigencies of two parallel but inherently incompatible worlds. Success is the irresistible force, failure, the immovable object. The result is either a new creature, a fresh-born slippery babe, yet half veiled by its own steam, but leaving us breathless with hope and wonder; or it is a mutant bastard, a monster, without a place, without a voice, illegible, indecipherable, not worthy of our trust; or it is nothing, a heartless, brainless wonder worthy of neither hope nor scorn. Has the successful failure, the failed success of the Civil Rights movement, left blackfolk in the same slough, left us with the same "sense of always looking at one's self through the eyes of others, of measuring one's soul by the tape of a world that looks on in amused contempt and pity" that W. E. B. Du Bois speaks of in *The Souls of Black Folks?* Are we still left with that "double-consciousness . . . two souls, two thoughts, two unreconciled strivings; two warring ideals in one dark body"? I think it has, I think we are, but with one significant difference, a difference, however, that was not promulgated so much in the Civil Rights era, but in the era of Du Bois himself. As Julius Lester puts it:

> Dissent and disagreement have been the hallmark of black history. Though Booker T. Washington, the most politically powerful black American in history, sought to control the minds of black folk with that power, W. E. B. Dubois {sic}, the preeminent

intellectual and the founder of the NAACP, fought publicly with him over whether the minds and souls of black folks were better protected by protest and the vote or accommodationism and economic nationalism. Later, Dubois [sic] and Marcus Garvey, the ideological father of today's black separatists, would not even pretend that they liked or respected each other.[4]

The phenomenon Du Bois talks about ought not really be regarded as mere bifurcation, for it is not the nonblack world alone that is engaged in the act of being touchstone and measuring tape of the black world, but we ourselves. The "double-consciousness" of which Du Bois speaks isn't really so much a double-consciousness as it is a poly-consciousness. Someone who's black like me doesn't feel particularly torn between one thing and another, but rather among a multiplicity of things. For the better part of this century, many of our leaders, and a good many of us who have followed them, have insisted on toeing one ideological, aesthetic, political, spiritual, or intellectual line or another. Many of us have assiduously searched for the essence of blackness and again and again returned to the inner self empty-handed. What does one have to be or do or believe to be truly, wholly, mono-lithically black? Some have suggested to me that the wearing of European clothing is unblack, while others have preached the Black Gospel while dressed like Young Republicans. Others have said that the consumption of pork is unblack, while others have insisted that to eschew pork is to deny one's cultural roots. Some have insisted that marrying a nonblack spouse is unblack, while others have said, When you get down to it, we're all African. Some would judge one's level of blackness as being manifest in one's level of knowledge of the history and culture produced by blacks, while others say that very few products have been invented in a vacuum, that when one straddles the interstices of culture and history one begins to trace all the borrowings, the purchases, the thefts, the loans, the imitations that lead to the artifacts that one group or another claims as theirs, that when we are honest with ourselves, the best we can say is that this thing or that thing is a product of our species.

Many say that the term "black" itself is inadequate, and substitute for it African American, Afro-American, Afrikan, and so on and on. . . . Many say so much, so often, with such fervor and conviction that I can't tell rectitude from attitude: *"Hey, man, them shoes ain't black." "Look, here, brother, that ain't the way a brother's supposed to talk to a sister." "Dag, 'B,' brothers don't supposed to read that kinda shit." "Hey, don't talk to me about that Africa stuff, cause I've never been to Africa. I don't know the first thing about the place. I'm an American. Period." "Look here, baby, I don't know what that is you listening to, but it ain't music." "Understand something, little brother, I'm the last black man. That's right. You kids don't know a thing about dancing or walking or thinking or making love under the moon. Don't know about knocking whitey the fuck up the side of his head when he needs it. You kids don't know a thing. When I'm dead, that's it. No more black men."* For a long, long time I've let myself be pulled from joint to joint, pulled by the joint. I've stood up and praised her praise song, cursed his condemnation, then changed places with myself. Weren't they all authorities, all valid, all experts when held up to my pathetic little narrow-behind wavering blackness? My inability to put it all together, find the center, swim away clean, black, and sanctified was my fault, no? I thought so. But all the while in the back of my head I sensed something missing, felt some still and empty point that was always out of reach. I soon discovered, though, that what was missing was my own voice.

The thing that has accounted for at least half of the trouble that the performance of my blackness has brought me is the way I speak. *"Now, listen to the way Reginald* enunciates *when he reads that paragraph again, class. Go ahead, Reginald. Start from the top of the page."* I don't know if Mrs. Wood knew that since the "standard" form of any language is established on political rather than purely elocutionary imperatives, no dialect conveys meaning any better or sounds any better—depending on who's doing the listening—than any other dialect. It's just a matter of which dialect the ruling class chooses to make its own. I know for certain that I didn't know this, way back in second grade. I suppose that to some ears I speak the patois of the ruling class, though to my own ears it is more of an ideolect that has resulted from living in a household in which my father's Alabamese and my mother's rather un-Texaslike East Texas accent, and the various accents of all the places we lived have mixed rather curiously upon my tongue. Nevertheless, people have responded to my use of English as though I were an impostor, a usurper, as if I were puttin' on airs, stubbornly willing myself to speak in a way that wasn't natural to "my kind," and by doing so have marked myself as an adopted (at least adoptable) member of the ruling class.

Some have assumed that I come from a privileged background, upper-middle class, college-educated parents, and so on. And beneath this assumption lies the suspicion that I feel little more than contempt for black people and that I would wish nothing more than to assimilate more deeply into the dominant culture. Well, I would be more than a fiction writer if I say I have never felt anger toward certain black people, or have never admired certain whites, but since I have experienced few constants in terms of my innumerable encounters with members of both groups, there have been few times in my life when I felt any particular way about anyone until I became acquainted with her or him. I have never consciously desired to be white. I have never even imagined what it would be like to be white, outside the confines of what I do as a writer. But there were definitely times I was made to feel I wasn't black enough, and wished somehow that I could get a handle on being so, being properly black. I felt this way, even though, when I want to, I can use my father's dialect, as well as a number of others, that are considered to be more or less black. But I kept silent for a long, long while, not because I had nothing to say, but because I thought I had nothing with which to say it. When I spoke in my own ideolect, I lacked authority. When I borrowed my father's I felt like an impostor, and still lacked authority. Having traveled as much as I have I've acquired a fairly decent ear, but my natural speech is my natural speech, and if I don't fit in because of it, I think that's absurd. And I am beginning to suspect that I am as black as I can possibly be. I don't think it would make any difference, in this respect, if I spoke with an Irish brogue. When I lived in Senegal, a friend who had recently introduced me to his family said to me, "You know, they like you, but they just can't get over the fact that you come from a country where all the black people speak English. English!" I asked him if he had considered the notion that I came from a place where blacks might be just as mystified or surprised as his family that there are countries where nearly everyone speaks (at least some) French. "I see what you're getting at," he said. "But to me, it seems natural for a black person to speak French. But English. Man, that is so strange to them. To me, too, to tell you the truth."

From Marsha with the plum-colored eyes to my friend Mike who wanted me to date his sister, people are trying to tell me, as I say above, that there is something essential that I exhibit but poorly perform. At times this poor performance troubles some people, at times it brings others comfort. From southern "rednecks" to northern "rustnecks," from southern "geechees" to northern "Malcolmists," from the privileged to the dispossessed, I had grown up feeling hard-pressed to find a genuine place for myself, a general consciousness upon which to draw. I felt I had no group with whom I was completely at peace or for whom I held unbending antipathy, no permanent corre-spondences based on culture, color, class, race, sex, gender. Be this as it may, I never believed that I was wholly unique in terms of how I performed my blackness or perceived my position in the black world. But I am not saying that I had or have "risen above" the constraints or the licenses of culture, class, race, and so on. And I don't mean to suggest that the relative isolation I have experienced has given me any special insights into any of the apparent enclaves through which I have traveled and by which I have been shaped. All I know is that it is my responsibility to carve out a "space" for myself in the black world without giving up my individuality. In fact, the whole idea of there being a world in which the individual does not fit seems, to me, to be antithetical to the very idea of a "world." As Julius Lester puts it, "The intellectual and spiritual health of any group is secured only to the extent that its members are permitted to be themselves and still be accepted as part of the group."[5] It's really very simple, and wholly without climax when you get down to it.

For all I know, there may be some essential blackness, but I tend to think it won't be found within the architecture of any particular ideology. In fact, if it is to be found at all, it will likely be found to be a sort of palimpsest, upon which is written all names, ideas, philosophies, arguments, fears, projections, productions, hopes, extrapolations, histories, even silences. But it ought to be the sort of palimpsest upon which there can be no erasures. I have grown weary of my differentness being used against me, or being used as a lever to force me to the banks of our dark and dusky river of being, when, in actuality, my differentness, my relative uniqueness, expands the black world, makes it more complex, contributes to our wherewithal to survive sudden or gradual changes in the political environment. If we insist on a definition of blackness it will have to be predicated on something other than a set of codified and repeatable performances (though this is not to eschew our traditions), for blackness is a process, ever changing, ever growing. I think only lemmings should move in lockstep.

I am not merely asserting that "We are not all alike." Those who aren't aware of that would not likely read this essay or anything like it. What I am saying is that generalizations from within are every bit as fragmenting as scrutiny from without. From my boyhood I have read and heard all manner of statistical facts and figures about black people. Really, they've told me very little about who I am, let alone who we are. We're too big for that, and as individuals too complex. I'm not so sure we should ever find ourselves in the position of saying this general thing or that general thing about black people, expecting our words to discover the essence of our "true self-consciousness," for when we do, we will be doing no more than talking *about* black people, talking *around* them, never quite getting it right, never pinning us down, never quite turning sound into substance, and never—much like the way sharks course around caged divers—ever able to sink our teeth into flesh.

We are, from the bottom to the top, as polymorphous as the dance of Shiva. We are not a race, not a culture, not a society, not a subgroup, not a "breeding group," or a cline, not even simply an agglomeration of individuals. We are, in my mind, a civilization, a collection of cultures, societies, nations, individuals, "races." We are ancient and new, Christian, Muslim, Jew, American, Trinidadian, Zimbabwean, female and male, gay and straight, brilliant and stupid, wealthy and poor, mocha and almond and ripe olive. We are at times a "We" and a "Them," an "Us" and "The Other." Being a civilization does not mean we will always like one another, agree with one another, or even—though this is not wise—listen to one another. But I hope it means that my name will be written on this great palimpsest, my ideas, my contributions, my voice, right next to yours. Let all be included. Let none be cast aside.

Notes

1. Ellis, Trey. "The New Black Aesthetic," *Callaloo*, Spring, 1989.
2. Simone, Timothy Maliqalim. *About Face: Race in Postmodern America*. Auton-omedia Brooklyn, 1989.
3. Gates, Henry Louis, Jr. " 'Authenticity,' or the Lesson of Little Tree," *New York Times Book Review*, November 24, 1991.
4. Lester, Julius. "What Price Unity?," *The Village Voice*, September 17, 1991.
5. Ibid.

Black Is the Noun

Nikki Giovanni

*It is late. The poet has just opened her second pack of cigarettes.
The poet smokes like a chimney. She fears the day when the
possession of cigarettes, not just their use, will be illegal. The
light is on in her den though her window blinds are closed.
She did not wear her seat belt today. They know. She knows
they know. Contemplating her fingernails she notices, to her
horror, a speck of grease. She has, once again, eaten fried
chicken. It won't be long before they come for her. What should
she do? Finding no answer, she ambles to the refrigerator,
opens the freezer, and takes out peach sorbet. If she must go,
she will go her way.*

I've had my fun . . . if I don't get well any more.

— **J. McShann**

I knew I was old when, one evening last spring, I was driving from
Blacksburg to Princeton to attend a party. I had finished early but a
friend was driving with me and she couldn't get off from work. We

---

Nikki Giovanni is a poet, whose latest book, *Sacred Cows . . . and Other Edibles*, has extended
her reach into the personal essay. She is a professor of English at Virginia Polytechnic Institute
and State University.

left about five-thirty in the evening, driving my car, a candy-apple-red MR2. We had on the requisite jeans and T-shirts. I am always cold so I had on a sweatshirt. We were short-coiffured, medium-nailed, no-makeup, modern sort of women on a fun drive to a fun place. We stopped for coffee, smoked, munched the sandwiches we had made—were, in other words, going about our business. Ginney has two talents that I not only do not possess but do not aspire to: she can spell and she can read a map. My idea of getting around is to go to the furthest point and make the appropriate ninety-degree turn. For example, in order to reach Princeton from Blacksburg, I would go to Washington, D.C., and turn left. But Ginney can read a map so she angled us onto the Pennsylvania turnpike, around Philadelphia, and onto the New Jersey turnpike. I don't like to be picky about things because I lack certain skills myself, but I do think it is not asking too much for employees to know where things are located. You know, you go into Kroger's looking for, say, tomato purée. You would expect to find this in the canned-vegetable section, only it isn't. It's located with sauces. You ask someone wearing a Kroger shirt and you should get that answer. You expect the turnpike officials who take your money at the toll booths to know which exit to take for something as well known as Princeton.

I have an aunt, well, actually I have two aunts, but I only want to talk about one of them. My aunt, and I will not designate which, has trouble with her night vision. She is not quite as blind as a bat but she . . . well . . . has trouble. And there are, possibly, these genetic transfers. I don't think I've reached that stage yet but sometimes it is difficult to see what exactly the signs are saying. It had gotten quite dark, we had stopped for coffee several times, and I, as driver, was happy to be on a turnpike with large green signs. When we were handed off from the Pennsylvania to the New Jersey I asked the woman in the booth which exit I should take for Princeton. Had she just said, "Honey, I ain't got no idea where no Princeton is. It's been a long day and nothing has gone right. My left foot is hurting 'cause I cut that corn but it's not healing right and maybe I have diabetes. You know when a corn won't heal that's a sign of diabetes. My mother had sugar and she lost her whole leg right up to the knee . . ." or something like that, I would have been understanding. "Yes," I would have said, "I've heard that corns that won't heal are a sign of sugar. My mother's best friend, Ann Taylor, from over in Knoxville was just telling me about it when I was passing through last June." And she and I could have visited a bit while Ginney looked at the map and plotted our course. But no, she says, with authority, "Take Exit 19," and we set out with the confidence of the innocently assured.

We were lost immediately; there was nothing that made sense on that exit, it was three-thirty in the morning, and, worst of all, I began to despair. We turned the light on in the car so that Ginney could see the map but, golly, those lines are very, very small and the car was in motion and bingo! The blue lights were shining in back of me. I pulled over, popped the Dells tape out of the cassette, ground out my cigarette, grabbed my seat belt, and waited for the highway patrolman. "Your registration and license, please." I had the registration with my gas card in the front but my driver's license was in my purse in the trunk. I looked up to explain my problem when he turned his flashlight into the car. He saw two McDonald's coffees, an ashtray full of cigarettes, and us—two lost, tired old ladies. "Where are you coming from?" he asked. "Roanoke, Virginia." I always answer Roanoke because nobody knows where Blacksburg is. "How long have you been on the road?" "Since about five-thirty. We're lost. We're trying to get to Princeton." "Well," he explained, "you're way out of your way. You've got another fifty miles to go." He gave us directions and said, "Drive carefully." "I'll get my driver's license now," I offered. "Oh, no, ma'am. You-all just get where you're going. Have a safe evening."

Something in me clicked. A few years ago he would have given me a ticket. A few years ago whether I was lost or not I would have been written up. But we were just two little ole ladies in what he probably thought was my son's car in the middle of the night trying to get to Princeton. I turned to Ginney: "We are old. He saw old women. You drive."

Going to Chicago . . . sorry but I can't take you.
—W. Basie

In *Star Trek II: The Wrath of Khan*, Khan, a criminal Kirk was responsible for putting on some planet way the hell out of nowhere, finally makes his escape. He is living for only one reason: he wants to kill Kirk. Khan and Kirk fool around for a couple of hours while Khan tortures and kills people and . . . finally . . . gets *The Enterprise* in his grip. Spock, of course, sees the problem and goes to the rescue. The awful weapon is turned on Khan and he is killed. But wait! Khan will have the last word even after death. Khan has trapped *The Enterprise* and it will implode because the crystals it needs cannot feed the engine. They all will die and Khan, the evil Ricardo Montalban, whom I actually liked in *Fantasy Island*, will prove that evil triumphs over good even when evil can't be there to gloat about it. Spock knows the answer but Kirk cannot bear to see his friend give his life. Spock understands that either he gives his life or they all give their lives. He sneaks away from Kirk only to encounter McCoy. He uses the Spock maneuver to knock McCoy out but at the last minute whispers: "Remember." And does his mind meld. Spock steps into the chamber, feeds the engine, and awaits his death. By now Kirk is on the deck, upset, quite naturally, about losing Spock. "The needs of the many," Spock says, "outweigh the needs of the few . . . or in this case, the one. I will always be your friend." He gives Kirk the Spock sign with the split fingers and dies. The next thing we see is Spock's funeral service and *The Enterprise* pushing his casket out into space. By this time I am embarrassing my son by actually heaving in the theater. I cannot believe Spock is dead. I will not accept it. But Tom points out to me that Spock's casket is headed for the Genesis planet. *Star Trek*

III will bring him back. I cannot see it. If he's dead, how can he come back to life? In all our myths only one man was able to do that. But Spock did tell McCoy something: "Remember."

I love *Star Treks*. They are nothing more than Greek myths of heroic people doing extraordinary deeds with style and wit. No one on the good ship *Enterprise* will ever be short of courage. The television series, which was actually quite short-lived, marked a new era in television by obliging audiences to respect—and even to admire—differences among people. They talked to rocks in "The Huerta" and spirits in "The Companion"; they came back to defy death at the OK Corral by not recognizing the power of bullets; they stopped a war between two planets by making them confront the reality and pay the price of the killing; they gave us television's first interracial kiss. But Spock said: "Remember."

The Search for Spock opens with Kirk and McCoy meeting Spock's father with a flag. Spock's mom is Jane Wyatt, formerly married to Jim Anderson on *Father Knows Best*. No one ever mentions the divorce but when you see how the kids came out you could easily see why she might have wanted to make her way to another planet. Mrs. Spock, Jane, is not seen. Since she is human she's probably off crying her eyes out over losing her only child. Mr. Spock, the Vulcan, is not emotional so he stands to talk. "Where are his memories?" Mr. Spock asks. He knows his son is dead and he can accept that. But where are his memories? Kirk and McCoy have no idea what he is talking about. "My son was a great man," Mr. Spock all but bellows. "His memories are valuable to us. We can store them so that others will learn from what he knew. You must find his body and retract from his brain his memories."

Star Trek perfectly epitomizes the sixties vehicle. You had a cou-rageous white boy; a logical Vulcan; an Asian scientific transportation officer; an Irish, emotional doctor; and, the ultimate genius of *Star Trek*, Uhurua, a black woman who was the voice of the entire feder-ation. Toni Morrison once wrote: "The Black woman is both a ship and a safe harbor." Uhurua proved that. Of all the possible voices to send into space, the voice of the black woman was chosen. Why? Because no matter what the words, that voice gives comfort and welcome. The black woman's voice sings the best notes of which Earthlings are capable. Hers is the one voice that suggests the possibility of harmony on planet Earth. Scholars are now studying what made the slavers bring females on the slave ships. The slavers could not have been so stupid as to think they could get as much work from a woman as from a man. There is the theory that since the women ran the markets and worked the farms the white man understood that in order for his agriculture to prosper he would need the women. I think not. I think there was a cosmic plan; a higher reason. In order to have a *civilization*, the black woman was needed. In order for one day this whole mess to make sense, the black woman was needed. So that one day forgiveness would be possible, the black woman was needed. I need not, I'm sure, point out the fact that the first black child born in what would become the United States was a black female. The first poet. But more, I believe the first voice to be lifted in song was the voice of a black woman. It may have been the "faith of our fathers," but it was our mothers who taught it to us. And when that faith was transformed what do we have? A half Earthling, half other-world being, saying to the doctor: "Remember."

Like Alex Haley's ancestor, who preserved his past by passing along his name, the slaves told their story through song. Isn't that why we sing "Swing Low, Sweet Chariot"? Isn't that why we know "Pass Me Not, O Gentle Savior"? Isn't that the reason our legacy is "You Got to Walk This Lonesome Valley"? "Were You There When They Crucified My Lord?" To W. E. B. Du Bois, the spirituals were sorrow songs, perhaps because he saw himself as so different from the slaves who sang them. But the spirituals were not and are not today sorrow songs but records of our history. How else would a people tell its story if not through the means available? And as James Cone has said, the spirituals testified to the *somebodiness* of our people. We made a song to be a quilt to wrap us "in the bosom of Abraham." "Over my head, I see trouble in the air. . . . There must . . . be a God, somewhere." We knew "He didn't take us this far to leave us." We brought a faith to the barbarians among whom we found ourselves, and the very humbleness of our souls defeated the power of their whips, ropes, chains, and money. "Give yourself to Jesus." Not your money, not a new church that you will sit in with other white people like yourself, not a new organ, none of those things . . . yourself. And all we had was a song and a prayer. Who would have remembered us had we not raised our voices?

Had Spock been a black American, his father would have gone to church to ask the Lord for help. And his help would have come like the strength that came to Emmett Till's mother: "I know that's my boy," when the sheriff asked what she could contribute to the trial of Till's killers. "I know it's my boy," Mrs. Mobley, Till's mother, said when she opened the casket. "I want the world to see what they did to my boy." Didn't she roll the rock away? Two thousand years ago the angels said, *"He is not here."* Mrs. Mobley said: "Here is my boy. Look." And the world was ashamed. Spock told McCoy to remember. And McCoy didn't even know what he had.

They went in search of the body and, movies being movies, they found a young Vulcan boy on Genesis and brought him home. But McCoy had the memories all along. He just didn't know what he had.

> Money won't change you, but time is taking you on.
>
> —J. Brown

Much evidence to the contrary, I am a sixties person. It's true that I didn't do T-shirts or drugs and I never went to jail. I argued a lot in coffeehouses and tried at one point to be a social drinker. It didn't work. I can't hold liquor at all. But I was nonetheless a sixties person and continue to be today because I actually believe in the people. That was never just rhetoric to me, though it has often been my undoing.

Believing in the people is dangerous because the people will break your heart. Just when you know in your heart that white people are not worth a tinker's damn and the future depends on us, some black person will come along with some nihilistic crap that makes you rethink the whole thing.

I was never more than a foot soldier and not a very good one at that. I observed and I wrote. And the more I observed, the more amazed I was by our need to deny our own history—our need to forget, not to remember. The contradictions were especially evident to me, perhaps, because I attended Du Bois's school, Fisk University. How ironic that Fisk's Jubilee Singers kept the spirituals alive, yet the students at Fisk were anxious to deny that their ancestors were slaves; if people were to be believed, nobody but me ever had slaves in their family.

The fact of slavery is no more our fault than the fact of rape. People are raped. It is not their choice. How the victim becomes responsible for the behavior of the victimizer is well beyond my understanding. How the poor are responsible for their condition is equally baffling. No one chooses to live in the streets; no one chooses to go to sleep at night hungry; no one chooses to be cold, to watch their children have unmet needs. No one chooses misery, and our efforts to make this a choice will be the damnation of our souls. Yet such thinking is one of the several troubling legacies we have inherited from Du Bois.

Du Bois needed to believe that he was different. That if only the "better" white people would distinguish between the "better" black folk, "the talented tenth," they could make a "better" person. I think not. The normal ninety have to be respected for the trials and tribulations they have endured. They've been " 'buked and they've been scorned." They bore the lash while they cleared the fields, planted and created in this wilderness. Am I against books and learning? Hardly. But just because my tools are words, I do not have the right to make mine the only tools. It is disturbing that wordsmiths like Henry Louis Gates, Jr., can say to those of physical prowess, "the odds are against your" succeeding in professional athletics (in a recent article in *Sports Illustrated*). The odds are more against any young man or woman of color being tenured at Harvard. Gates was not deterred in his determination to succeed in his chosen field and he does not have the right to discourage others. Those young men on city playgrounds know that, indeed, basketball is the way out. Without that skill no school would be interested in them . . . no high school . . . no college. The academically excellent can use their words to sneer but the young men know that's the only open door. Is it right? I think not. I would like to see choice come into everybody's life. But there are no good choices on the streets these days. The conservatives don't care and the black intellectuals are trying to justify the gross neglect of the needs of black America. The Thomas Sowells, the Shelby Steeles no more or less than the Clarence Thomases and the Louis Sullivans are trying mighty hard to say, "I am not like them." We know that, we who are "them." We also know that they have no character. We know they are in opportunistic service. The very least they owe is the honesty that says, "I got here distinguishing myself from you." Clarence is against affirmative action? Shelby is against affirmative action? Since when? Since the people fought so that neither of these men would have to die for their choice of wives? So that Yale would admit a poor boy from Pin Point, Georgia? When did affirmative action become an insult? Shortly after you were granted tenure at your university? You don't like being made to feel you can honestly do your job because affirmative action made someone hire you? There is a solution. Quit. You think life is hard for you because you're viewed as a group? Try living in Newark or D.C. or Harlem and knowing that you will never be allowed by what Margaret Walker calls "those unseen creatures who tower over us omnisciently and laugh" to realize your dreams and potential.

Am I blaming Du Bois for his children? You bet. The black conservatives belong to Du Bois. Booker T. Washington, born in slavery, reared in the coal-mining districts of West Virginia, walked his way to Hampton, worked his way through the Institute, labored in the red clay of Alabama among some of the most vicious white folks outside of Mississippi to build Tuskegee; he tried to empower black folks. Is there a quarrel with the Atlanta Exposition speech? Somebody, other than the black conservatives, show me where this nation is not still "as separate as the fingers of a hand" and how we would not all be better off if we would "come together as a fist" for economic development. Du Bois wanted to vote? So do we all. Didn't Martin Luther King, Jr., have something to say about "Southern Negroes not being allowed to vote while Northern Negroes have nothing to vote for"? Didn't Frederick Douglass ask, "What does your fourth of July mean to me?" Washington and Garvey wanted black people to come to the table with some fruits from their labor. Both Washington and Garvey knew we needed and need, in Margaret Walker's words, "something all our own." Why did Du Bois fight them? What an ironic twist of fate that Du Bois was the beneficiary of Garvey's dreams. That Du Bois was the Renaissance Man who spent his last days in Ghana, a black independent nation, under a black president. How ironic that Louis Sullivan and Clarence Thomas are beneficiaries of the struggles of the sixties.

> You better think . . . think about what you're trying to
> do to me.
>
> —A. Franklin

I am a black American. Period. The rest is of no particular interest to me. Afro-American, African American, whatever. I believe that if I remain a black American I force all others to become and claim their other Americanisms. They are white Americans, Irish-Americans, Jewish-Americans, or whatever hyphens they would like to use. The noun is "black"; American is the adjective.

I do not fool myself often. I laugh about definitions because laughter is, well, so much more pleasant. I am not a particularly well person. I have lived too long with sick people to think I have escaped their malady. Every now and then, for one reason or another, someone will ask to interview me or talk with me or I will skim back through what has been said of my work just to, well, more or less see how I am progressing. I have always laughed at the critics' saying I am bitter and full of hate. Nothing could be further from the truth. I am not envious or jealous either. I am just me. And I do have strong feelings about that. I do not and did not and most likely will not ever feel that I have to justify that. I do not have to be a role model, a good person, a credit to the race. When I look at Phillis Wheatly, Harriet Tubman, Monroe Trotter, Frederick Douglass, Sojourner Truth, Booker T. Washington, George Washington Carver, for that matter W. E. B. Du Bois, James Weldon Johnson, Langston Hughes, Nella Larsen, James Baldwin, and I cannot possibly exhaust the list but, hey, Malcolm X, Elijah Muhammed, Martin Luther King, Sr. and Jr., just to name a few, the race has built up a big enough account for me to charge whatever I'd like. Doesn't Toni Morrison have a character named Stamped Paid? Perfect. Black America is well in advance of the Sunday-school tithing of the folks with whom we live.

I had the great pleasure of meeting Anna Hedgeman when she visited Fisk University during, I think, my junior year. She was talking to honors history about Frederick Douglass: "Every time I see that statue of Lincoln sitting below the Emancipation Proclamation I want to have a statue of Frederick Douglass standing behind him guiding his hand." I could see that. Lincoln was an interesting white man who did the right thing, finally, by freeing the slaves in the states where he had no power to enforce his decree. But hey, why be so picky? He did it. True. But not for me. Not for Cornelia Watson so that she could birth John Brown Watson in freedom and he could marry Louvenia Terrell and they could conceive Yolande Watson and she could marry Gus Giovanni and they could conceive me. No. Not for me. Lincoln didn't care about Cornelia Watson. Nor conceptionalize me. Near the end of *Song of Solomon* Morrison has Milkman finally review his life: it is the women who wanted him to live. Or as the father in *Sounder* says to his son, "I beat the DEATH they had planned for me; I want you to beat the LIFE." Am I saying I'm glad we have Presidents' Day instead of Lincoln's Birthday and Washington's Birthday? No. I like my holidays to have real names. But I also know I don't owe those people any great affection or loyalty. They do not love me or mine. That, by the way, means I live in a narrow world. Well, maybe not so narrow. Maybe a more accurate way of looking at it is that I will not have my world or my worth determined by people who mean me ill.

It's been a long time coming . . . but my change is gonna come.
—S. Cooke

Like most people approaching their fiftieth birthdays (I was born in 1943), I have contemplated the meaning of my people. I have wondered why we were chosen for this great, cosmic experience. We were not the first slaves in human history nor were we even the first chattel. We were, however, the first slaves who chose to live among the enslavers. That is about the only thing that gives me hope. If God could part the Red Sea for Moses, surely the Atlantic Ocean posed no insoluble problem. I have contemplated what life must have been like around 1865 or so when freedom became a possibility. Why didn't we seek boats to take us to Haiti, which was already a free, black republic? Why didn't we start great treks, not just a few wagon trains here and there, to the uncharted lands of this nation? What made us determined to fight it out essentially where we were? Some books tell us we loved enslavement—we didn't have to worry about our care or our duties. Some books say we didn't know where to go. Some books tell us we believed the promises of Emancipation that we would be given forty acres and a mule. Mostly I think it was cosmic. The spirituals show us a people willing to "wait on the Lord." Though "sometimes I feel like a motherless child . . . a long way from home," though we knew "the rock cried out No Hiding Place," though we had the "Good News" that "I got a crown up in the Heavens," we "were there when they crucified my Lord." We were chosen to be witnesses. Like Job in his patience, like Samson in his foolishness, "my soul is a witness . . . for my Lord." And without that faith there is no foundation for this nation. America may not be the best nation on earth, but it has conceived loftier ideals and dreamed higher dreams than any other nation. America is a heterogeneous nation of many different peoples of different races, religions, and creeds. Should this experiment go forth and prosper, we will have offered humans a new way to look at life; should it fail, we will simply go the way of all failed civilizations. The spirituals teach us that the problem of the twentieth century is not the problem of the color line. The problem of the twentieth century is the problem of civilizing white people.

When I was a little girl you could still buy things at the five-and-dime. You could buy those paddles with the ball attached that you would sit and whack for hours; you could buy jacks and pick up sticks. You could buy spin tops that you pulled a string around and the top would go spinning off. If your surface was rocky the top would falter and fall; if your tip had a nick it would jump and fall; if your release of the string was not smooth it would jerk and fall. If you wanted your top to spin the longest you did everything you could to get and keep things smooth.

You read my letter, baby . . . sure must have read my mind.
—B. Eckstine

The poet lights her fortieth cigarette. She will go over her limit as she opens a new pack. It is her favorite time of the day, when morning begins fusing itself into night, bringing that nether light to the sky. The poet recommends life. She likes the idea of the human experiment going forth. She knows her people are more than capable. The worst blows have been thrown and parried. This is only the cleanup. Perhaps, she thinks, she should treat herself to something wonderful. Fish.

Fried fish. The poet remembers her grandmother's joy at fried fish and extra salt. Yes. And maybe a cold beer to salute her mother. Good job, mommy. I'm here; not necessarily crazy; looking forward to tomorrow. No mother could do more. Maybe, the poet thinks, I'll buy a lottery ticket. The forty-first cigarette is lit. First thing in the morning. Fish and a lottery ticket. Hey . . . we're going to make it.

Racism,
Consciousness, and
Afrocentricity

Molefi Kete Asante

A Frame of Reference

I was born in Valdosta, Georgia, on August 14, 1942. My great-great-grandmother, Frances Chapman, had given birth to my great-grandfather, Plenty Smith, in 1866. My grandfather Moses Smith had moved his family from Dooly County, Georgia, to Valdosta, in Lowndes County. The Smith family had strong Asante and Mandinka ancestry despite the disruptions of slavery. My father, for whom I was first named, Arthur Lee Smith, married Lillie Wilkson, whose maternal grandmother was Muskogee. I was their first child, although my mother had three daughters, and my father, a son older than me. Eventually between them there were sixteen children in all. I lived in Georgia and Tennessee until May 1960, when I graduated from high school in Nashville, Tennessee.

Dr. Molefi Kete Asante is Professor and Chairperson, Department of African American Studies, at Temple University in Philadelphia. Professor Asante is the author of thirty-two books, of which the most recent one is *Thunder and Silence*. He is the creator of the first doctoral program in African American Studies; the author of more than one hundred scholarly articles; the founder of the Afrocentric philosophical movement and the National Afrocentric Institute; and the recipient of many honorary degrees for his educational and academic achievements. He is a poet, dramatist, painter, and gardener, and is now completing a book entitled *The Sources of the African Tradition*.

My early experiences certainly contributed to my racial consciousness by bringing me at once into the quicksand of the social environment that was the United States in the late 1940s and early 1950s. Subsequent events were to underscore the lessons of my ritual of passage into the world of southern racism, where whites often exhibited an anti-African phobia unfathomable to me as a young boy of Valdosta, Georgia, and Nashville, Tennessee. I went to a church boarding school in Nashville when I was eleven years old. Every summer and holiday I would return to Valdosta to crop tobacco and to pick cotton in order to have spending money for the next school year.

Realization

The whites I saw in this small Georgia town in the 1950s were neither more intelligent nor more industrious than the Africans I knew. The whites were wealthier and consequently more powerful by virtue of the false status bestowed by race in America. Living and growing up in Valdosta ruined the self-esteem of some Africans and brought our self-confidence into question. But in the end we were to have no problem of consciousness, the reality of being black in Georgia was too intimate, personal, defining. I did not reject my blackness; I embraced it.

To remind us of just how cruel the whites could be in the South, an African man was killed and his body dragged through the dirt roads of the two black sections of town, Southside and Westside. I was barely six when this happened, but the fumes rising from the anger in the black community colored the mental skies of a thousand children for several years. The damnable deed rained down hatred among us every time the story was told of how the poor victim had pleaded his innocence before they killed him. Whenever I heard the name Kill-Me-Quick, the area in Valdosta that the lynched man is said to have come from, I thought of it as some distant, foreboding community instead of the small satellite community of the Southside it really was. I never knew how it got its name, only that the name conjured up some strange sense of terror.

So lynching registered early and substantially on my mind; the effect of the monstrous crimes against innocent and often defenseless African Americans was permanent. Several years would pass before I understood the extent of the mental chains with which we had been shackled: African men and women harassed, mutilated, murdered in the stark piney-woods country or under the shade of the Spanish-mossed oaks.

The Element of Race

Shaped in the mold of segregation, I knew at a very early age that the world of America was black and white. The technicolor revolution of the Asians and Latinos had not penetrated the thick, gloomy fog of reality that hung over the question of race in Valdosta in those days. It would not be until I attended college in California that I would experience the multicolored reality that was becoming America. Here I was for all practical purposes a made-in-America person. Yet the making itself had not convinced me that I was truly a part of the process that governed the society. Black and white, two colors, two origins, two destinies, that is what intervened in the midst of reflections on place for a young African in the south of Georgia.

We were for all practical purposes the whole world. And when the young people of our church sang, "And he got the whole world in his hands," we knew that it meant both the Southside and the Westside and maybe the white people who occupied those big houses on Ashley and Patterson streets. I was sixteen before I ever knew anything about Chinese or Mexicans. In fact, the only Jew I had ever seen, besides the Nordic Jew Jesus whose picture hung on the wall of the church, was the man who ran Lazarus Brothers Pawn Shop on Ashley Street in Valdosta. This was the one store on the main street of the city that largely catered to a black clientele. Japanese we had heard of because of the war. They had been the comic characters in our books, the wild-eyed killers of the war comics. My impression of the Japanese was certainly warped by the information that went into my young mind. Puerto Ricans did not exist in Valdosta. Blacks and Protestant whites, that was it for the entire city, with the exception of the one Jew.

What I knew about race relations was just about all that the whites knew, too, I suspected. Their world was also black and white. We worked for the whites; they never worked for us. I observed this every time I was awakened at five-thirty in the morning by my mother so that I would not miss the truck that took us young children to the tobacco or cotton fields. A black man usually drove the truck to the farm. It would be an old truck, often a small pickup, loaded with about twenty or twenty-five people. Arriving at the fields before the sun came up, we would all pile out of the truck and put our cotton sacks on or hitch our mules to the sled, depending on whether it was cotton or tobacco. After a full day's work in the fields we were dead tired, dirty, hungry, and ready to be paid. A white man paid our driver, and would pay us when we had weighed the cotton of the day or accounted for the "cropped" tobacco.

Life had been like this since Emancipation. Sharecroppers and tenant farmers and hired laborers served the interests of the white farmers who made the economy of the region. Neither the whites nor we could have given a clear dissertation or disputation on the state of the world, so locked we were into the social cage of our existence.

Being About My Own Business

When I was twelve years old I thought I had to be about my own business. Work had never been far from our house. It sat outside our door at six o'clock every morning in the summer as a big truck with workers piled on it. Let us say that I had heard about twelve's being the age that a child becomes conscious of right and wrong, and let us say that this had a powerful impact upon my brain. In fact, at church they said Jesus had been about "his father's business" at that age. I had to be baptized and I had to get a job.

Nothing in the Bible my father and mother kept on the small table alongside the wall of the front room could have prepared me for the shape, the deep grooves, of the hatred whites held for us by virtue of our color. Although I was later to be told that it was also because of their fear of Africans, resulting from the five hundred years of war on African people. I am not so sure, however, that the Valdosta whites knew anything about five hundred years of domination. They knew about the whites' place and the blacks' place. It was all about location, and in their minds God had decreed these "places."

By twelve I had mastered the litany of possibilities for the African American: a schoolteacher, a preacher, a funeral-home director, and maybe a lawyer. My family had three or four root men and women and I was said to have been born with a veil over my face, meaning that I would probably be a root doctor or a preacher. Moses Smith, my grandfather, had practiced the roots openly and was known as a strong follower of the spirits. But his father, Plenty, my great-grandfather, carried even more authority in his combination of roots and Baptist tradition. He relied upon his own spiritual sights to heal and counsel people who made pilgrimages to his Dooly County home. Moses had made a convergence between dream books, Christianity in its Church of Christ fundamentalism, roots, hoodoo, and Yoruba. My father, Arthur, only dabbled in the spirits, often being told by his elders that he did not have enough faith in the healing or spiritual powers of the unseen.

With my father's lack of interest in the roots and stubborn rationalism I was not encouraged in the root line of work though it seemed to be a logical path for me. Eager to work and to show my own contribution to the family's economy, I started on the road to my profession with a shoebox that held shoe polish, a rag, and an old brush. I found a white barbershop down on Ashley Street willing to give me a chance to work on the shoes of the white customers. My very first customer, demonstrating for others in the shop his contempt for Africans, even a child, spat on my head as I leaned over his shoes. I knew what had happened. I did not say a word as I gathered up my shoeshine box, forgot about my payment, and walked out of the barbershop to the laughter of the man and a few other customers. My father, I remembered, was proud of me.

Unwelcomed as a child in the most elementary economic position one could have in the Deep South of the late 1950s, I came to expect nothing from whites. In fact, whites in the South were seen as the natural enemies of Africans. One spoke to them as if to strangers from another planet. They could wreak havoc in one's life with a word, a signal, a sign, or a whisper to the sheriff that you were "a bad nigger." I had come from a family of "bad niggers," whose Asante and Creek roots meant that there was a whole history of resistance to white hatred. Our family lived in poverty but never in shame; we were hard workers and prided ourselves on our ability to outwork anyone. If hard physical labor could make one rich, then all of my brothers and sisters would have been millionaires. Discrimination, prejudice, segregation, and the doctrine of white racial supremacy were neither innocuous nor benign in those days; they were real legacies rooted in the great enslavement of Africans. And often what we thought was benevolence on the part of whites, who would give our church their secondhand clothes, often turned out to be another statement of their alleged superiority.

Insight and Introspection

The tightly knit community of Africans who lived on the dirt roads of Valdosta never saw themselves as intellectually or physically inferior to whites. There existed no reference points outside of ourselves despite the economic and psychological poverty of our situation. Our social, political, and economic situations could be explained in terms of white racial preference. Whether this was true or not in every case, we believed it. For example, if only whites worked in the banks downtown as tellers and managers, we knew that it was because Africans were never given a chance. The proof came later when Africans were given jobs in the banks and department stores; the incredible thing is that whites were amazed that we could be successful in those positions, such was their ignorance. Whatever advantage whites had was directly tied to race. My grandfather Moses, a favorite name for males in my family, had often told us sitting around the fireplace eating boiled peanuts that if they gave a black person a chance to enter any sport —tennis, swimming, or golf—they would do just as well as the whites, if not better. It was a problem of access and money, he would say. Although we recognized our degradation, I do not ever recall wanting to be like whites; they were neither beautiful nor strong nor decent people.

I was a young adult when I really felt the rage against prejudice inside me. But I never allowed it to control me. My father had instructed me too well for that to happen. I controlled and directed the rage with committed vows made in the name of my great-great-grandmother, Frances Chapman, who lived and died in the piney woods of Dooly County, Georgia, about eighty miles north of Valdosta. Among the vows, I remember, was never to allow white racial supremacy to go unchallenged. As a student in elementary and high school in Tennessee, where I had gone from Georgia when I was eleven, my friends looked to me in any confrontation with whites because I

...nderstanding in my relationships with whites that
...al respect. During the school year I attended the Nash-
...nstitute and received religious education. My religious
...ned any desire I had for confrontation, although I was
always ...to defend myself.

Becoming a Christian at eleven, I tried preaching, since the ministry
was a natural extension of the roots tradition, in which I felt right at
home, until I became disenchanted with religion generally and the
way it was practiced in the Church of Christ specifically. After several
years I gave up the attempt and endeavored rather to demonstrate
propriety and good judgment in the face of ignorance. Relocating
myself from the Christian religion became a substantive pathway to
many future liberations. Whites did not only control the money in
the country, they also controlled the religion. I wanted no part of the
mind control that went along with a religion that had become the
deification of white culture, including white dislike, hatred, and fear
of Africa and Africans.

It seemed to me that whites demonstrated their fear of us in their
inability to allow us to share space in almost any enterprise. The whites
in Valdosta who rose above the petty, pedestrian attitudes toward
Africans were often ostracized by their neighbors. A few of them were
labeled "nigger lovers" by other whites. One year I saw the Ku Klux
Klan marching down the streets in their white robes shouting vile
remarks about "nigger lovers" and "niggers." I thought of them, I
remember, as a pathetic band of misfits; I was curious, however, about
who they were behind those hoods. The Klan was not just against
Africans, that little circle of frightened men was against whites who
thought Africans were intelligent, human, moral, and equal to whites.

The Terror of Reality

It has taken me considerable time to understand that the fundamental terror which resides in the white mind in terms of black-white relationships is rejection, that is, the fear that we will reject white values, standards, and ideas. But it is a deeper fear than, say, the fear that one might not be able to succeed in some venture; it is an existential fear, the fear that one might cease to exist without us to give them their sense of identity. To me, quite frankly, it mattered little how much whites feared the lack of existence because of their treatment of Africans. Almost every white I met felt some guilt about the condition of Africans but felt helpless to do anything about it. They recognized the historical nature of the racism that was daily poured into the African's cup. Every day brought other revelations, and whether it was social services or education, economics or housing, the situation was the same.

The attack on Africans in the academy, that is, the absolute difficulty some white professors have in granting excellence to African students or the immense problems whites have in giving tenure to African American scholars, is directly related to the fear of rejection. More amazingly, despite the Civil War, whites never allowed or wanted Africans to be truly "free" in America. Physical freedom did not mean psychological freedom, either for blacks or whites. Thus, confrontation is inevitable on almost every front because the white American is stuck with the heritage of the enslavement, unable to let the slave go free, and thereby refusing to see himself or herself alongside the African. They are forced by this position to oppose the African's leadership, creativity, innovation, and direction. Yet the African has vowed to be free. This is the source of conflict. I made that vow of freedom in the sandy piney-woods country when I was fourteen.

The feeling that you are in quicksand is inescapable in the quagmire of a racist society. You think that you can make progress in the interpretation of what's happening now only to discover that every step you take sinks the possibility of escaping. You are a victim despite your best efforts to educate those around you to the obvious intellectual mud stuck in their minds. For me, however, the course has always been rather clear, thanks to Arthur Smith and Lillie Smith's giving me the Francis Chapman and Plenty Smith stories when I grew up in Valdosta, Georgia.

The Illusion of Double-Consciousness

I was never affected by the Du Boisian double-consciousness. I never felt "two warring souls in one dark body" nor did I experience a conflict over my identity. Since I was a child I have always known that my heritage was not the same as that of whites. I never thought we came over here on the *Mayflower*. When I got up in the mornings to go to the cotton and tobacco fields, little white children got up to go fishing in the lakes or to camp. I knew that much from seeing them at the swimming pool, at the lakes, and at the parks as I rode those trucks back and forth to work. That was the experience it seemed of the white children I either saw or heard about; however, certainly somewhere in Georgia there must have been other whites with work experiences similar to mine. The point, though, is that most of the labor in the South during that period was performed by Africans. There were and remain in this country dual societies, one white and richer, one black and poorer. Perhaps in a great number of Africans these societies and the "two warring souls" converge to create a caldron of psychological problems; this was not the case with me or my family even when we were dysfunctional.

Valdosta, in all of its transparency, made my consciousness unitary and holistic. The starkness of the contrast was as evident as the paved streets in the white section of town and the muddy dirt roads on our side. My identity was solid, not fluid. My parents never gave any indication of suffering from low self-esteem or low self-confidence; they suffered from a severe income deficiency. Did I think that I shared something with these whites? Was I that crazy? Did I believe that I was an American in the same way whites were? Did I want to be like whites? No, we did not even go to the same Christian churches; our religion, although called Christian, was different. It might have been another matter if I had gone to school and to church with whites when I was younger. I might have suffered confusion, double-consciousness, but I did not.

The *orishas* captured us and sent us on a different way. The whites had no *orishas*. Our music was different. Our parties were different. Our clothes were different. Were there then two warring souls in my bosom? No, anger, resentment, and hatred for the people I thought had to be the most callous, inhuman, brutal beings on earth, that was in my heart. Was I conflicted about my identity? Not for one moment did I experience any sense of personal or cultural confusion about my origins, community, and struggle. There were no "two warring souls" in my personality. This is not to say that the hypocrisy of the United States in not living up to its guarantee of African freedom was not often present in my mind, but I was clear about the reality of America.

One discovers in this kind of situation that there is no beginning and no end, or so it seems. To think that a young person growing up in the South could decipher the situation in any realistic way is to attribute too much to experience and not enough to reading history and culture. This I was to come to much later in my life. But I had seen enough, heard enough, and felt enough to understand my predicament. Because I had such an insular upbringing in many respects, that is, the segregated schools kept me away from the longing to be white or to be accepted by whites that Du Bois must have felt in Great Barrington, Massachusetts. My whole world was black except on rare occasions when a lone white would enter our neighborhood to collect the insurance money, to hire an employee, to deliver some secondhand clothes, or to campaign politically.

Avoiding Psychological Trouble

I knew, however, that it would be necessary to avoid becoming either a misoriented African or a disoriented African in the maturing process. One could be misoriented by receiving and accepting false information. I had to cautiously weigh information that was presented to me. I had seen many young people, my own age at the time, totally disoriented about America. Disorientation occurred when a person got the wrong information, accepted it, and tried to act on the basis of it. My reading included everything from the King James version of the Bible to Marx and Fanon. We were into Fanon in the late sixties. His early death gave him a kind of martyr's status with me. Here was this clear mind, this brilliant analyst, who would help Africans to see how to liberate themselves. In a fundamental way, Fanon was one of the guides that I used to chart my own path out of the maze of disinformation and misinformation that surrounded me. Observing as a young man of the sixties, I could see an anti-Africanite in every opposition to our freedom and equality. I could discern the bogus use of equality as it was emerging in the counter use of the term to mean that affirmative action was reverse discrimination. The more sophisticated white reactionaries seemed to call it reverse racism. Of course, it was neither. Affirmative action was a down payment on the reparations that should have been granted to Africans who had worked in this country for 244 years for free. My youth had prepared me for the sixties.

The racist anti-Africanite was clearly in the ascendancy in the South of my youth. Almost every white person who occupied a political position was an anti-Africanite. Sometimes they campaigned for office on the grounds that they would be sure to "keep the niggers in their places." Could I possibly have been confused about where the sheriff of Lowndes County, Georgia, stood on issues of race? Only if I was crazy. This is not to say that "crazy" black people did not exist then. As now, we had individuals who felt that the "Lord gave the whites the power to rule" over us. If it were not so, they argued, then it would not be so. I saw the irrationality of our condition at an early age and was reminded that my great-grandfather, Plenty, did not like fools or ignorant people. His style was to maintain distance from the source of his irritation. I learned that lesson on one of my many visits as a child to my great-grandfather's farm in Dooly County, Georgia.

I am sure that there were misoriented Africans in Valdosta during that time. By *misoriented* I mean Africans who believed that it was better to identify with the "masters" rather than with the "slaves." I remember one black man who went around trying to convince other Africans that a certain white racist was better than another white racist because at least the white racist he was supporting for election "had never beat a Negro." Presumably, the other white racist had physically whipped some of his field hands.

The racist anti-Africanite finds the activities of the misoriented African comforting for his or her anti-Africanism. The misoriented African, much like Sartre's inauthentic Jew, runs away from his or her Africanity by attempting to deny it, conceal it, or attack it. Unlike the Jew, who seldom wishes to destroy his or her Jewishness, the misoriented African assumes that he or she is not African and therefore takes exception to those who remind him or her that he or she bears all of the major characteristics of resemblance to those who are African. Thus, the misoriented African, that is, the inauthentic African, allows the dominance of the single-consciousness of Europe to conquer him or her. At that moment, and not before, the misoriented African becomes for all practical purposes the spitting image of the racist anti-Africanite. Neither a victim of double-consciousness nor attuned to the consciousness of his or her own historical experiences, which would center the person, the misoriented African becomes disoriented and believes that he or she is actually a European.

Since one can only have one heritage despite the multiplicity of cultural backgrounds that go into that heritage, to assume that one possesses more than one heritage is to suggest contradictions in the person's heritage. Actually our heritage might be composed of many backgrounds but in the end we inherit a unified field of culture, that is, one whole fabric of the past rather than split sheets or bits and pieces. Otherwise what we inherit is not very useful.

Despite denial of Africanity, others see the misoriented African as African and box him or her into the existential reality which he or she denies. Denial may take many forms, including the idea that one is indeed different from those Africans who do not deny. A person who denies his historical reality means that he is not confident in his reality. He possesses a fluid identity. This is what I tried to avoid as a young adult in college, this fluid identity. I thank my *ori*, Obatala, for giving me a solid sense of identity. Therefore, I found every opportunity to learn from other Africans with solid identities.

There was always something in me that said you cannot flee from reality, you cannot escape the historical condition and remain sane. Denial assumes a larger and larger portion of the concentration time of those who have fluid identities. What I have seen in their lives is obsession, the obsession with denial-and-discovery. To deny the reality opens the possibility that one may be discovered to be authentically African despite all psychological efforts at denial. There is perhaps nothing worse than seeing an African who looks concretely African and who acts expressively African trying to deny Africanness but who is discovered to be African by the very people he or she is trying to fool.

Consciousness Transformed

In 1972 I visited Ghana during the first of what were to be eighteen trips to Africa over the next twenty years. UCLA had graciously consented to allow me to visit Africa in my capacity as the Director of the Center for Afro-American Studies. When I finally reached the library at the University of Ghana, Legon, I asked the librarian whether my book *The Rhetoric of Black Revolution* had reached his campus. He replied, "Yes, but I thought the author Arthur Smith was an Englishman." He could not understand how a person with an African phenotype could have an English name or so it seemed to me. Nevertheless, it was a profound encounter for an African American.

I vowed then and there that I would change my name. The name Arthur L. Smith, Jr., inherited from my father, had been betrayed by the dungeon of my American experience. Soon thereafter I took the Sotho name Molefi, which means "One who gives and keeps the traditions" and the Asante last name Asante from the Twi language. My father was elated. He said to me that had he been able to, that is, had he known an African name, he would have changed his name long ago. This made me very proud because I had always been supported by my father's sense of reason. I had no intention of ever masking or wanting to mask. I was straight up and down an African in my consciousness and that fact did not contradict my nationality as an American; it simply threw everything into the most ordered reality possible for me.

The Mask

I could never understand the aim of the Africans who sought to mask. Masking leads to masquerades. The first stage of masking is to cover up, whether sartorially or linguistically. Making certain that you wear the right fashions, have the right hairstyle, and affect the appropriate outward expressions of taste becomes the main preoccupation of masking. "Oh no, I couldn't be seen in those ethnic clothes," a misoriented African American once said to me while dressed in Italian shoes, an English paisley tie, and a French suit. Further masking is effected by using language to befuddle and mislead the potential discoverers. "You see, I'm only part Negro; my father's father was German" may be a correct statement of biological history but it is of no practical value in the American political and social context. There is neither a political nor a social definition within the American society for such masquerade. Neither biracial nor interracial has any political meaning in the contemporary setting of the United States. Thus, to employ the biological argument is to engage in a masquerade because the person seeks to escape the social and political definition for people whose biological history is essentially similar. Most African Americans have mixed gene pools, either one African ethnic group with another or African with some other ethnic and/or racial groups. Nevertheless, we say we are black and mean the word in all of the political and social dimensions it has in this situation. It is like calling the ancient Egyptians "black," which certainly they were in terms that we recognize today. That is, the ancient Egyptians looked no different from the present-day African Americans. In fact, the contemporary Egyptians in the south of Egypt can be mistaken for African Americans!

In the proving ground of America, some of us, and I am one, have been tested in every way. Yet as a lover of harmony I have thought that the most remarkable Maatic achievement of the human personality in this age would be the elimination of racism, prejudice, and discrimination. Perhaps I have wished for this because of the early rites of passage that I went through as a young man, but I would hope that my wish is a part of the celebration of the human possibility. Even from my young adult years I thought a precondition of my fullness, a necessary and natural part of my maturity, was the commitment to be who I am, to be Afrocentric.

One becomes Afrocentric by exploring connections, visiting the quiet places, and remaining connected. The furious pace of our dislocation, mislocation, displacement, off-centeredness, and marginalization, often brought on by the incredible conspiracy of the Eurocentric architecton, drives us further and further away from ourselves, reinforcing us in our dislocation and affirming us in our out-of-placeness. In such a situation, in the fringes of the European experience, pushed away from the center, we swirl around lost looking for place, for location. Afrocentricity is the active centering of the African in subject place in our historical landscape. This has always been my search; it has been a quest for sanity. Therefore, it was unthinkable for me to entertain ideas of living in the margins, being in the periphery of someone else's historical and cultural experiences. My aim was more fundamental, basic, the essential quality of being normal, uncomplicated. By being normal I do not reject the other; I embrace that which I truly know, i.e., jazz, blues, railroads, Obatala, roots, hoodoo, soul, rhythms, sweet mommas, Dunbar and Hughes, Sanchez, Mari Evans, and Charles Fuller, and so on, in ways that I do not know the products of the other, i.e., country music, mistletoe, Valhalla, Wotan, pale blonds, Frost, and Mailer. I recognize these products as a part of my experience in the large but they do not impact on me in the same way as those which seem to grow from the soil of my ancestors. With my own products I can walk confidently toward the future knowing full well that I can grasp whatever else is out there because my own center is secured.

True, I saw and see many who assume that for an African to strive to be European is the real normalcy. Such "Negroes" are often insane, suffering from a deep sense of self-hatred, which in the end prevents them from having a healthy relationship with the whites whom they admire merely because of their whiteness. Fortunately for me, I have managed to hold back the demons of double-consciousness by being who I am and trying, in Harriet Tubman's name, to be all that I ought to be.

The
Welcome
Table

Henry Louis Gates, Jr.

Let me set the stage. Take one young, eager black American journalist—that was me. One aging actress/singer/star—that was Josephine
Baker. And one luminary of black letters: James Baldwin. I was twenty-
two, a London-based correspondent for *Time* magazine, and I felt like
a mortal invited to dine at his personal Mount Olympus.

My story, for which the magazine had agreed to fund my trip to
France, was on "The Black Expatriate." One of my principal subjects
was Baldwin. Another was Josephine Baker, who, being a scenarist to
her very heart, put a condition on her meeting with me. I was to
arrange her reunion with Baldwin, whom she hadn't seen since she
left France many years ago to live in Monte Carlo.

Well into her sixties in 1973, Josephine Baker still had a lean

---

Henry Louis Gates, Jr., is W. E. B. Du Bois Professor of Humanities at Harvard University.
He has served on the committees and boards of directors of many professional organizations,
among them the Council on Foreign Relations, the African Roundtable, the Afro-American
Academy, and the Schomburg Commission for the Preservation of Black Culture. He has
received honorary degrees from several universities, including Dartmouth College and the
University of West Virginia. His numerous writings have appeared in leading scholarly
journals and he has been the editor of several volumes of works by other black writers.
His books include *Figures in Black: Words, Signs and the Racial Self*, and *The Signifying
Monkey: Towards a Theory of Afro-American Literary Criticism*, which won the American
Book Award in 1989.

dancer's body. One expected that. She was planning a return to the stage, after all. What was most surprising was her skin, smooth and soft as a child's. The French had called her *café-au-lait*, but that says nothing of the translucency or the delicate shading of her face. Her makeup was limited to those kohl-rimmed eyes, elaborately lined and lashed, as if for the stage. She flirted continually with those eyes, telling her stories with almost as many facial expressions as words.

I do not know what she made of me, with my gold-rimmed cool-blue shades and my bodacious Afro, but I was received like a dignitary of a foreign land who might just be a long-lost son. And so we set off, in my rented Ford, bearing precious cargo from Monte Carlo to Saint Paul de Vence, Provence, *chez* Baldwin. In case I was in any danger of forgetting that a living legend was my passenger, her fans mobbed our car at regular intervals. Invariably, she responded with elaborate grace, partly playing the star who expects to be adored, partly the aging performer who is simply grateful to be recognized.

Baldwin made his home just outside the tiny ancient walled town of Saint Paul de Vence, nestled in the alpine foothills that rise from the Mediterranean Sea. The air carries the smells of wild thyme, pine, and centuries-old olive trees. The light of the region, prized by painters and vacationers, at once intensifies and subdues colors, so that the terra-cotta tile roofs of the buildings are by turns rosy pink, rust brown, and deep red.

His house—situated among shoulder-high rosemary hedges, grape arbors, acres of peach and almond orchards, and fields of wild asparagus and strawberries—was built in the eighteenth century and retained its original frescoed walls and rough-hewn beams. And yet he had made of it, somehow, his own Greenwich Village café. Always there were guests, a changing entourage of friends and hangers-on. Always there were drinking and conviviality. "I am *not* in paradise," he assured readers of the *Black Scholar* that year, 1973. "It rains down here too." Maybe it did. But it seemed like paradise to me. And if the august company of Jo Baker and James Baldwin wasn't enough, Cecil Brown was a guest at Saint Paul, too: Cecil Brown, author of the campus cult classic *The Life and Loves of Mister Jiveass Nigger*, and widely esteemed as one of the great black hopes of contemporary fiction.

The grape arbors sheltered tables, and it was under one such grape arbor, at one of the long harvest tables, that we dined. Perhaps there was no ambrosia, but several bottles of Cantenac Braun provided quite an adequate substitute. The line from the old gospel song, a line Baldwin had quoted toward the end of his then latest novel, inevitably suggested itself: "I'm going to feast at the welcome table." And we did, we did.

I wondered why these famous expatriates had not communicated in so long, since Saint Paul was not far from Monte Carlo. I wondered what the evening would reveal about them, and I wondered what my role in this drama would be. It was the first time Jo and Jimmy had seen each other in years; it would prove the last.

At that long welcome table under the arbor, the wine flowed, food was served and taken away, and James Baldwin and Josephine Baker traded stories, gossiped about everyone they knew and many people they didn't, and remembered their lives. They had both been hurt and disillusioned by the United States and had chosen to live in France. They never forgot, or forgave. At the table that long, warm night, they recollected the events that led to their decisions to leave their country of birth, and the consequences of those decisions: the difficulty of living away from home and family, of always feeling apart in their chosen homes; the pleasure of choosing a new life, the possibilities of the untried. A sense of nostalgia pervaded the evening; for all their misgivings, they shared a sense, curiously, of being on the winning side of history.

And with nostalgia, anticipation. Both were preparing for a comeback. Baker would return to the stage in a month or so; and it was on stage that she would die. Baldwin, whose career had begun so brilliantly, was now struggling to regain his voice. The best was yet to come, we were given to understand.

People said Baldwin was ugly; he himself said so. But he was not ugly to me. There are, of course, faces that we cannot see simply as faces because they are so familiar that they have become icons to us, and Jimmy's visage was one such. And as I sat there, in a growing haze of awe and alcohol, studying his lined face, I realized that neither the Jimmy I had met—mischievous, alert, and impishly funny—nor even the Jimmy I might come to know could ever mean as much to me as James Baldwin, my own personal oracle, that gimlet-eyed figure who had stared at me out of a fuzzy dust-jacket photograph when I was fourteen. For that was when I met Baldwin first and discovered that black people, too, wrote books. You see, that was *my* Baldwin. And it was strictly Private Property. No trespassing allowed.

I was attending an Episcopal church camp in eastern West Virginia, high in the Allegheny Mountains overlooking the South Branch of the Potomac River. It was August 1965, a month shy of my fifteenth birthday. This, I should say at the outset, was no ordinary church camp. Our themes that year were "Is God dead?" and "Can you love two people at once?" (*Dr. Zhivago* was big that summer, and Episcopalians were never ones to let grass grow under their feet.) After a solid week of complete isolation, a delivery man, bringing milk and bread to the camp, told the head counselor that "all hell had broken loose in Los Angeles" and that the "colored people had gone crazy." Then he handed him a Sunday paper, screaming the news that Negroes were rioting in someplace called Watts.

I, for one, was bewildered. I didn't understand what a riot was. Were colored people being killed by white people, or were they killing white people? Watching myself being watched by all of the white campers—there were only three black kids among hundreds of campers—I experienced that strange combination of power and powerlessness that you feel when the actions of another black person affect your own life, simply because you both are black. For I knew that the actions of people I did not know had become my responsibility as surely as if the black folk in Watts had been my relatives in the village of Piedmont, just twenty or so miles away.

Sensing my mixture of pride and discomfiture, an Episcopal priest from New England handed me a book later that day. From the cover, the wide-spaced eyes of a black man transfixed me. *Notes of a Native Son* the book was called, by one James Baldwin. Was this man the *author*, I wondered to myself, this man with the close-cropped "natural," brown skin, splayed nostrils, and wide lips, so very Negro, so comfortable to be so?

It was the first time I had heard a voice capturing the terrible exhilaration and anxiety of being a person of African descent in this country. From the book's first few sentences, I was caught up thoroughly in the sensibility of another person—a black person. The book performed for me the Adamic function of naming the complex racial dynamic of the American cultural imagination. Coming from a tiny segregated black community in a white village, I knew both that "black culture" had a texture, a logic, of its own *and* that it was inextricable from "white" culture. That was the paradox that Baldwin identified and negotiated, and that is why I say his prose shaped my identity as an Afro-American, as much by the questions he raised as by the answers he provided. If blackness was a labyrinth, Baldwin would be my cicerone, my Virgil, my guide. I could not put the book down.

I raced through this book, then others, filling my commonplace book with his marvelously long sentences, bristling with commas and qualifications. Of course, the biblical cadences spoke to me with a special immediacy. For I was to be a minister, having been "saved" in a small black evangelical church at the age of twelve. (From this fate as well, the Episcopalians—and, yes, James Baldwin—diverted me.) I devoured his books: first *Notes*, then *Nobody Knows My Name*, *The Fire Next Time*, and then *Another Country*. I began to imitate his style of writing, using dependent clauses whenever and wherever I could—much to my English teacher's chagrin. Consider:

> And a really cohesive society, one of the attributes, perhaps, of what is taken to be a "healthy" culture, has, generally, and I suspect, necessarily, a much lower level of tolerance for the maverick, the dissenter, the man who steals the fire, than have societies in which, the common ground of belief having all but vanished, each man, in awful and brutal isolation, is for himself, to flower or to perish. (*Nobody Knows My Name*)

There are sixteen commas in that sentence; in my essays at school I was busy trying to cram as many commas into my sentences as I could—until Mrs. Iverson, my high school English teacher, forbade me to use them "unless absolutely necessary!"

Poring over his essays, I found that the oddest passages stirred my imagination. There were, for example, those moments of the most un-Negro knowingness, a cosmopolitanism that moved me to awe: such as his observation that, unlike Americans,

> Europeans have lived with the idea of status for a long time. A man can be as proud of being a good waiter as of being a good actor, and in neither case feel threatened. And this means that the actor and the waiter can have a freer and more genuinely friendly relationship in Europe than they are likely to have here. The waiter does not feel, with obscure resentment, that the actor has "made it," and the actor is not tormented by the fear that he may find himself, tomorrow, once again a waiter. (*Nobody Knows My Name*)

I remember the confident authority with which I explained this insight (uncredited, I suspect) about French and American waiters to a schoolmate. It hardly mattered that there were no waiters in Piedmont, West Virginia, unless you counted the Westvaco Club, which catered to the management of our one industry, a paper mill. It mattered less that there were no actors. How far was Paris, really? Baldwin wrote about an epiphany experienced before the cathedral in Chartres. In Piedmont, true enough, we had no such imposing monuments, but I struggled to collect his noble sentiments as I stood before our small wooden church, in need though it was of a fresh coat of white paint.

I, of course, was not alone in my enthrallment and, much as it vexed me, Baldwin was *not* my private property. When James Baldwin wrote *The Fire Next Time* in 1963, he was exalted as *the* voice of black America. The success of *Fire* led directly to a cover story in *Time* in May of 1963; soon he was spoken of as a contender for the Nobel Prize. ("Opportunity and duty are sometimes born together," Baldwin wrote later.) Perhaps not since Frederick Douglass a century earlier had one man been taken to embody the voice of "the Negro." By the early sixties, his authority seemed nearly unchallengeable. What did the Negro want? Ask James Baldwin.

The puzzle was—as anyone who read him should have recognized —that his arguments, richly nuanced and self-consciously ambivalent, were far too complex to serve straightforwardly political ends. Thus he would argue in *Notes from a Native Son* that

> the question of color, especially in this country, operates to hide the graver question of the self. That is precisely why what we like to call "the Negro problem" is so tenacious in American life, and so dangerous. But my own experience proves to me that the connection between American whites and blacks is far deeper and more passionate than any of us like to think. . . . The questions which one asks oneself begin, at last, to illuminate the world, and become one's key to the experience of others. One can only face in others what one can face in oneself. On this confrontation depends the measure of our wisdom and compassion. This energy is all that one finds in the rubble of vanished civilizations, and the only hope for ours.

One reads a passage like this one with a certain double take. By proclaiming that the color question conceals the graver questions of the self, Baldwin leads us to expect a transcendence of the contingencies of race, in the name of a deeper artistic or psychological truth. Instead, with an abrupt swerve, Baldwin returns us to them.

> In America, the color of my skin had stood between myself and me; in Europe, that barrier was down. Nothing is more desirable than to be released from an affliction, but nothing is more frightening than to be divested of a crutch. It turned out that the question of who I was was not solved because I had removed myself from the social forces which menaced me—anyway, these forces had become interior, and I had dragged them across the ocean with me. The question of who I was had at last become a personal question, and the answer was to be found in me.
>
> I think that there is always something frightening about this realization. I know it frightened me.

Again, these words are easily misread. The day had passed when a serious novelist could, as had Thomas Mann at thirty-seven, compose his *Betrachtungen eines Unpolitischen*. Baldwin proposes not that politics is merely a projection of private neuroses, but that our private neuroses are shaped by quite public ones. The retreat to subjectivity, the "graver questions of the self," would lead not to an escape from the "racial drama," but—and this was the alarming prospect Baldwin wanted to announce—a rediscovery of it. That traditional liberal dream of a nonracial self, unconstrained by epidermal contingencies, was hopefully entertained and, for him at least, reluctantly dismissed. "There are," he observed,

> few things on earth more attractive than the idea of the unspeakable liberty which is allowed the unredeemed. When, beneath the black mask, a human being begins to make himself felt one cannot escape a certain awful wonder as to what kind of human being it is. What one's imagination makes of other people is

dictated, of course, by the laws of one's own personality and it is one of the ironies of black-white relations that, by means of what the white man imagines the black man to be, the black man is enabled to know who the white man is.

This is not a call for "racial understanding": on the contrary, we understood each other all too well, for we have invented one another, derived our identities from the ghostly projections of our alter egos. If Baldwin had a central political argument, then, it was that the destinies of black America and white were profoundly and irreversibly intertwined. Each created the other, each defined itself in relation to the other, and each could destroy the other.

For Baldwin, then, America's "interracial drama" had "not only created a new black man, it ha[d] created a new white man, too." In that sense, he could argue, "the history of the America Negro problem is not merely shameful, it is also something of an achievement. For even when the worst has been said, it must also be added that the perpetual challenge posed by this problem was always, somehow, perpetually met."

These were not words to speed along a cause. They did not mesh with the rhetoric of self-affirmation that liberation movements require. Yet couldn't his sense of the vagaries of identity serve the ends of a still broader, braver politics?

As an intellectual, Baldwin was at his best when exploring his own equivocal sympathies and clashing allegiances. He was here to "bear witness," he insisted, not to be spokesman. And he was right to insist on the distinction. But who had time for such niceties? The spokesman role was assigned him willy-nilly.

The result was to complicate further his curious position as an Afro-American intellectual. On the populist left, the then favored model of the oppositional spokesman was what Gramsci called the "organic intellectual": someone who participated in and was part of the community he would uplift. And yet Baldwin's basic conception of himself was formed by the familiar, and still well-entrenched, idea of the alienated artist or intellectual, whose advanced sensibility entailed his estrangement from the very people he would represent. Baldwin could dramatize the tension between these two models—he would do so in his fiction—but he was never to resolve it.

A spokesman must have a firm grasp on his role, and an unambiguous message to articulate. Baldwin had neither, and when this was discovered a few short years later, he was relieved of his duties, shunted aside as an elder, and retired, statesman. The irony is that he may never have fully recovered from this demotion from a status he had always disavowed.

And if I had any doubts about that demotion, I was set straight by my editor at *Time* once I returned to London. They were not pleased by my choice of principal subjects. Josephine Baker, I was told, was a period piece, a quaint memory of the twenties and thirties. And as for Baldwin: well, wasn't he passé now? Hadn't he been for several years?

Baldwin *passé*? In fact, the editor, holding a wet finger to the wind, was absolutely correct, and on some level I knew it. If Baldwin had once served as a shadow delegate for black America in the congress of culture, his term had expired. Besides, soldiers, not delegates, were what was wanted these days. "Pulling rank," Eldridge Cleaver wrote in his essay on Baldwin, "is a very dangerous business, especially when the troops have mutinied and the basis of one's authority, or rank, is devoid of that interdictive power and has become suspect."

Baldwin, who once defined the cutting edge, was now a favorite target for the *new* cutting edge. Anyone who was aware of the ferment in black America was familiar with the attacks. And nothing ages a young Turk faster than still younger Turks.

Baldwin was "Joan of Arc of the cocktail party," according to the new star of the black arts movement, Amiri Baraka. His "spavined whine and plea" was "sickening beyond belief." He was—according to a youthful Ishmael Reed—"a hustler who comes on like Job."

Eldridge Cleaver, the Black Panther's Minister of Information, found in Baldwin's work "the most gruelling, agonizing, total hatred of the blacks, particularly of himself, and the most shameful, fanatical, fawning sycophantic love of the whites that one can find in any black American writer of note in our time." Above all, Baldwin's sexuality represented treason: "Many Negro homosexuals, acquiescing in this racial death-wish, are outraged because in their sickness they are unable to have a baby by a white man." Baldwin was thus engaged in "a despicable underground guerilla war, waged on paper, against black masculinity." Young militants referred to him, unsmilingly, as Martin Luther Queen.

Baldwin was, of course, hardly a stranger to the sexual battlefield. "On every street corner," Baldwin would later recall of his early days in Greenwich Village, "I was called a faggot." What was different this time was a newly sexualized black nationalism that could stigmatize homosexuality as a capitulation to alien white norms, and correspondingly accredit homophobia—a powerful means of policing the sexual arena—as a progressive political act.

A new generation, so it seemed, was determined to define itself by everything Baldwin was *not*. By the late sixties, Baldwin bashing was almost a rite of initiation. And yet Baldwin would not return fire, at least not in public. He responded with a pose of wounded passivity. If a new and newly militant generation sought to abandon him, Baldwin would not abandon them.

In the end, the shift of political climate forced Baldwin to simplify his rhetoric or else risk internal exile. As his old admirers saw it, Baldwin was now chasing, with unseemly alacrity, after a new vanguard, one that esteemed rage, not compassion, as our noblest emotion. "It is not necessary for a black man to hate a white man, or to have particular feelings about him at all, in order to realize that he must kill him," he wrote in *No Name in the Street*, a book he started writing in 1967 but did not publish until 1972. "Yes, we have come, or are coming, to this, and there is no point in flinching before the prospect of this exceedingly cool species of fratricide." That year he told *The New York Times* of his belated realization that "our destinies are in our hands, black hands, and no one else's." A stirring if commonplace sentiment, this, which an earlier Baldwin would have been the first to see through.

How far we had come from the author of *The Fire Next Time*, who had forecast the rise of black power and yet was certain that "we, the black and the white, deeply need each other here if we are really to become a nation—if we are really, that is, to achieve our identity, our maturity, as men and women. To create one nation has proved to be a hideously difficult task; there is certainly no need now to create two, one black, and one white." All such qualms were irrelevant now. In an offhand but calculated manner, Baldwin affected to dismiss his earlier positions: "I was, in some way, in those years, without entirely realizing it, the Great Black Hope of the Great White Father." Now he knew better.

In an impossible gambit, the author of *No Name in the Street* sought to reclaim his lost authority by signaling his willingness to be instructed by those who had inherited it: this was Baldwin and the new power generation. He borrowed the populist slogans of the day and returned them with a Baldwinian polish. "The powerless, by definition, can never be 'racists,' " he wrote, "for they can never make the world pay for what they feel or fear except by the suicidal endeavor that makes them fanatics or revolutionaries, or both; whereas those in power can be urbane and charming and invite you to those which they know you will never own." The sentiment in its unadorned rendering—that blacks cannot be racist—is now a familiar one, and often dismissed as an absurdity; but the key phrase here is "by definition." For this is not a new factual claim, but a rhetorical move. The term "racism" is redefined to refer to systemic power relations, a social order in which one race is subordinated to another. (A parallel move is common in much feminist theory, where "patriarchy"—naming a social order to which man and woman have a fixed and opposed relation—contrasts with "sexism," which characterizes the particular acts of particular people.) It cannot, therefore, be dismissed as a factual error. And it does formulate a widely accepted truth: the asymmetries of power mean that not all racial insult is equal. (Not even a Florida jury is much concerned when a black captive calls his arresting officer a "cracker.")

Nonetheless, it is a grave political error: for black America needs allies more than it needs absolution. And the slogan—a definition masquerading as an insight—would all too quickly serve as blanket amnesty for our dankest suspicions and bigotries. It is a slogan Baldwin once would have repudiated, not for the sake of white America—for them, he would have argued, the display of black prejudice could only provide a reassuring confirmation of their own—but for the sake of black America. The Baldwin who knew that the fates of black and white America were one knew that if racism was to be deplored it was to be deplored *tout court*, and without exemption clauses for the oppressed. Wasn't it this conviction, above all, that explained his repudiation of Malcolm X?

I should be clear. Baldwin's reverence for Malcolm was real, but posthumous. In a conversation with the psychologist Kenneth Clark, recorded a year and a half before the assassination, Baldwin ventured that, by preaching black supremacy, "what [Malcolm] does is destroy a truth and invent a myth." Compared to King's appeal, Malcolm's was "much more sinister because it is much more effective. It is much more effective, because it is, after all, comparatively easy to invest a population with false morale by giving them a false sense of superiority, and it will always break down in a crisis. That is the history of Europe simply—it's one of the reasons that we are in this terrible place." But, he cautioned, the country "shouldn't be worried about the Muslim movement, that's not the problem. The problem is to eliminate the conditions which breed the Muslim movement." (Five years later, under contract with Columbia Pictures, Baldwin began the task of adapting Malcolm to the silver screen.)

That ethnic scapegoating was an unaffordable luxury had been another of Baldwin's lessons to us. "Georgia has the Negro," he once pithily wrote, slicing through thickets of rationalization, "and Harlem has the Jew." We have seen where the failure of this vision has led: the well-nigh surreal spectacle of urban activists who would rather picket Korean grocery stores than crack houses, presumably on the assumption that sullen shopkeepers with their pricey tomatoes—not smiley drug dealers and their discount glass vials—are the true threat to black dignity.

The sad truth is that, as the sixties wore on, Baldwin, for all his efforts, would never be allowed to reclaim the cultural authority he once enjoyed. To give credit where credit is due, the media can usually tell the difference between a trend maker and a trend follower. What did the Negro *really* want? Ask Eldridge Cleaver.

I did. Several months after my visit to Saint Paul de Vence, I returned to France to interview the exiled revolutionary. We had moved with the times from cosmopolitan expatriates to international fugitives. ("How do I know you're not a CIA agent?" he demanded when we first talked.) This was not a villa on the Riviera. It was an apartment on the Left Bank, where Eldridge and Kathleen lived, and where he put me up in his study for a couple of weeks; here, ostensibly, was the radical edge that Baldwin now affected to covet.

Between Cleaver and Baldwin, naturally, no love was lost. Eldridge complained to me that Baldwin was circulating a story about him impugning his manhood. He wanted me to know it was untrue. He also wanted me to know that he would soon be returning and would take up where he had left off. The talk was heady, navigating the dialectical turns of Fanon and Marx and Mao and Ché. (Jesus would be added a few months later.) His shelves were lined with all the revolutionary classics, but also W. E. B. Du Bois, Richard Wright, and, yes, James Baldwin. Young Baldwin may have warned of "the fire next time," but Cleaver, determined to learn from the failures of his revolutionary forebears, was busily designing the incendiary devices.

What came as a gradual revelation to me was that Cleaver really wanted to be a writer, and that Baldwin was, perforce, his blueprint of what a black writer could be. He was at work, he told me, on a memoir, to be entitled *Over My Shoulder*; on a novel, to be called *Ahmad's Jacket*. But commitment, to be genuine, had to spill over the page. And in case I forgot our parlous position in the nether zone of the law, there was that hijacker—armed, dangerous, and definitely deranged—who insisted on staying with them, too. Eldridge, who had adopted me as a younger brother for the nonce, handed me a butcher knife to keep under my pillow and made sure I propped a filing cabinet in front of the door before I went to sleep at night.

Times had changed all right. That, I suppose, was our problem. But Jimmy wanted to change with them, and that was his.

We lost his skepticism, his critical independence. Baldwin's belated public response to Cleaver's charges was all too symptomatic. Now, with slightly disingenuous forbearance, he would turn the other cheek and insist, in *No Name in the Street*, that he actually admired Cleaver's book. Cleaver's attack on him was explained away as a regrettable if naïve misunderstanding: the revolutionary had simply been misled by Baldwin's public reputation. Beyond that, he wrote,

> I also felt that I was confused in his mind with the unutterable debasement of the male—with all those faggots, punks, and sissies, the sight and sound of whom, in prison, must have made him vomit more than once. Well, I certainly hope I know more about myself, and the intention of my work, than that, but I *am* an odd quantity. So is Eldridge, so are we all. It is a pity that we won't, probably, ever have the time to attempt to define once more the relationship of the odd and disreputable artist to the odd and disreputable revolutionary. . . . And I think we need each other, and have much to learn from each other, and, more than ever, now.

It was an exercise in perversely *willed* magnanimity, meant, no doubt, to assure us that he was with the program; and to suggest, by its serenity, unruffled strength. Instead, it read as weakness, the ill-disguised appeasement of a creature whose day had come and gone.

Did he know what was happening to him? His essays give no clue, but then they wouldn't. Increasingly, they came to represent his official voice, the carefully crafted expression of the public intellectual, James Baldwin. His fiction became the refuge of his growing self-doubts.

In 1968, he published *Tell Me How Long the Train's Been Gone.* Formally speaking, it was his least successful work. But in its protagonist, Leo Proudhammer, Baldwin created a perfectly Baldwinian alter-ego, a celebrated black artist who, in diction that matched that of Baldwin's essays, could express the quandaries that came increasingly to trouble his creator. "The day came," he reflects at one point, "when I wished to break my silence and found that I could not speak: the actor could no longer be distinguished from his role." Thus did Baldwin, our elder statesman, who knew better than anyone how a mask could deform the face beneath, chafe beneath his own.

Called to speak before a civil rights rally, Proudhammer ruminates upon the contradictions of his position. "I did not want others to endure my estrangement, that was why I was on the platform; yet was it not, at the least, paradoxical that it was only my estrangement which had placed me there? . . . [I]t was our privilege, to say nothing of our hope, to attempt to make the world a human dwellingplace for us all; and yet—yet—was it not possible that the mighty gentlemen, my honorable and invaluable confreres, by being unable to imagine such a journey as my own, were leaving something of the utmost importance out of their aspirations?"

These are not unpolitical reflections, but they are not the reflections of a politician. Contrast LeRoi Jones's unflappable conviction, in an essay published in 1963: "A writer must have a point of view, or he cannot be a good writer. He must be standing somewhere in the world, or else he is not one of *us*, and his commentary then is of little value." It was a carefully aimed arrow and it would pierce Baldwin's heart.

The threat of being deemed "not one of *us*" is a fearful thing. *Tell*

Me How Long depicts a black artist's growing sense that (in a recurrent
phrase) he no longer belongs to himself. That his public role may have
depleted the rest of him. There is a constituency he must honor, a
cause he must respect; and when others protect him, it is not for who
he is but for what he stands for.

To be sure, what Baldwin once termed "the burden of representation" is a common malady in Afro-American literature; but few have
measured its costs—the price of that ticket to ride—as trenchantly as
he. Baldwin risked the fate that Leo Proudhammer most feared: which
was to be "a Jeremiah without convictions." Desperate to be "one of
us," to be loved by us, Baldwin allowed himself to mouth a script
that was not his own. The connoisseur of complexity tried to become
an ideologue. And with the roaring void left by the murders of Malcolm
X and Martin Luther King, he must have felt the obligation ever more
strongly.

However erratic some of his later writing might have been, I believe
he could still do anything he wanted with the English essay. The
problem was he no longer knew what he wanted—or even what we
wanted from him. Meanwhile, a generation had arrived that didn't
want anything from him—except, perhaps, that he lie down and die.
And this, too, has been a consistent dynamic of race and representation
in Afro-America. If someone has anointed a black intellectual, rest
assured that others are busily constructing his tumbril.

In an essay he published in 1980, Baldwin reflected on his role as
an elder statesman: "It is of the utmost importance, for example, that
I, the elder, do not allow myself to be put on the defensive. The
young, no matter how loud they get, have no real desire to humiliate
their elders and, if and when they succeed in doing so, are lonely,
crushed, and miserable, as only the young can be." The passage is
eloquent, admirable—and utterly, utterly unpersuasive.

We stayed in touch, on and off, through the intervening years, often
dining at the Ginger Man when he was in New York. Sometimes he
would introduce me to his current lover, or speak of his upcoming

projects. But I did not return to Saint Paul de Vence until shortly after his death three years ago, when my wife and I went to meet Jimmy's brother, David.

Saint Paul had changed remarkably in the twenty or so years since he settled there. The demand for vacation homes and rental property has claimed much of the farmland that once supported the city and supplied its needs. Luxury homes dot the landscape on quarter-acre plots, and in the midst of this congestion stood Baldwin's ten-acre oasis, the only undivided farm acreage left in Saint Paul. Only now the grape arbors are strung with electric lights.

There we had a reunion with Bernard Hassell, Jimmy's loving friend of so many decades, and met Lucien Happersberger, the friend to whom *Giovanni's Room* is dedicated. After a week of drinking and reminiscing, David Baldwin asked me just when I had met Jimmy for the first time. As I recounted the events of our visit in 1973, David's wide eyes grew wider. He rose from the table, went downstairs into Jimmy's study—where a wall of works by and about Henry James faces you as you enter—and emerged with a manuscript in hand. "This is for you," he said.

He handed me a play, the last work Jimmy completed as he suffered through his final illness, entitled *The Welcome Table*. It was set in the Riviera, at a house much like his own, and among the principal characters were "Edith, an actress-singer/star: Creole, from New Orleans," "Daniel, ex-black Panther, fledgling play-wright" with more than a passing resemblance to Cecil Brown, and "Peter Davis, black American journalist." Peter Davis—who has come to interview a famous star, and whose prodding questions lead to the play's revelations—was, I should say, a far better and more aggressive interviewer than I was, but of course Baldwin, being Baldwin, had transmuted the occasion into a searching drama of revelation and crisis. Reading it made me think of all the questions I had left unasked. It was and is a vain regret. Jimmy loved to talk and he loved language, but his answers only left me with more questions.

Narratives of decline have the appeal of simplicity, but Baldwin's career will not fit that mold. "Unless a writer is extremely old when he dies, in which case he has probably become a neglected institution, his death must always seem untimely," Baldwin wrote in 1961, giving us fair warning. "This is because a real writer is always shifting and changing and searching." Reading his late essays, I see him embarking on a period of intellectual resurgence. I think he was finding his course, exploring the instability of all the categories that divide us. As he wrote in "Here Be Monsters," an essay published two years before his death, and with which he chose to conclude *The Price of the Ticket*, his collected nonfiction: "Each of us, helplessly and forever, contains the other—male in female, female in male, white in black, and black in white. We are a part of each other. Many of my countrymen appear to find this fact exceedingly inconvenient and even unfair, and so, very often, do I. But none of us can do anything about it." We needed to hear these words two decades ago. We need to hear them today.

Times change. Madonna, our very own zeitgeist goddess, has recently announced her interest in seeing a film made of *Giovanni's Room*, which was one of Baldwin's greatest hopes. (In the late seventies, Robert De Niro and Marlon Brando were said to be interested in the project, but nothing came of it.) An influential intellectual avant-garde in black Britain has resurrected him as a patron saint. And a new generation of readers has come to value just those qualities of ambivalence and equivocality, just that sense of the contingency of identity, that made him useless to the ideologues of liberation and anathema to so many black nationalists. But then, even his fiercest antagonists have now welcomed him back to the fold. Like everyone else, we like our heroes dead.

"I suspect, though I cannot prove it," Baldwin wrote a decade before his death, "that each life moves full circle—toward revelation." Once again, he leaves us with a question. For whose revelation did he have in mind: his, or ours?

Off-Timing:
Stepping to the
Different Drummer

Kristin Hunter Lattany

I would not "bleach [a] Negro soul in a flood of white Americanism" any more than Du Bois's American Negro would, for I have seen that happen, and I know that it causes spiritual death. Unlike Dr. Du Bois, I would, however, "Africanize America" if I could, because today we can disagree that "America has . . . much to teach the world and Africa." This takes nothing, I hope, away from Dr. Du Bois or his thought.

In Du Bois's day, "the awful shadow of the Veil," "the Veil that hung between us and Opportunity," and which strictly segregated Du Bois and his peers from whites, also distanced American society from blacks and made it seem to shimmer with an alluring veil of glamour. Draped in that illusion, America seemed, until recently, the brightest, the best, the most desirable creation the world had to offer. But now

---

Kristin Hunter Lattany is the author of eight volumes of young adult and adult fiction. One of her novels, *The Landlord*, was made into a film released by United Artists. Her first young adult novel, *The Soul Brothers and Sister Lou*, received many awards and was translated into several languages. Her other books are *The Survivors; Boss Cat* (for children); *Guests in the Promised Land* (short stories); *The Lakestown Rebellion*; and *Lou in the Limelight*, a sequel to *The Soul Brothers and Sister Lou*. She is a senior lecturer in English at the University of Pennsylvania, where she teaches fiction-writing workshops and courses in African American literature.

that veil, if not "the Veil," has been torn away, and we can see that America is not a glamour queen but a grisly skeleton, her only product death (death to the environment and death to human beings through war, Contras, sterilization of black women, weapons, and toxic products like Chemlawn, fluorocarbons, nuclear waste, tobacco, liquor, and drugs); her only lessons how to kill and how to die.

Signs of the grim death cult, which is the convulsive end of Euro-American world domination, are everywhere: skinheads, punkers, Jim Jones, channelers, satanists, thrash music and heavy metal, mass murderers, including Operation Desert Storm; the dark suits worn by European leaders as they attend ritualized conferences that are like their own funerals; S & M; films and TV shows that exalt death (*Highway to Heaven, Ghost, Ghost Dad, Field of Dreams, Flatliners, Dead Again*); organizations like the Hemlock Society, and a suicide manual, *Final Exit*, on *The New York Times* best-seller list.

African culture has many flaws—we should beware of romanticizing a place that cooperated with slavery, worships snakes, and devalues women—but it is, mainly, life-affirming, spiritually aware, and integrated with, rather than antagonistic to, nature. As long as, and to the degree that, white America was Africanized by African Americans—as long as whites were dancing to the rags of Scott Joplin in the Jazz Age or to the music of Little Richard and Chuck Berry in the 1960s; absorbing some of the sermons of Martin Luther King; talking the talk of street folk and musicians—there was hope for America's redemption.

But now I no longer see that hope. White adaptations of black music have succumbed to the great white death urge, going from bland rock to suicidal punk and homicidal heavy metal in less than twenty years. Skinheads, the Klan, and other forms of naked fascism are emerging on the American political scene. We must pull back from white America, because it is now a great rush of lemmings toward the sea. We have passed the point of deciding, in Malcolm's phrase, whether to integrate into a burning house; what faces us now is a decision to leap, or not to leap, into a mass grave. And if it were possible to construct a great grappling hook to snatch back our young, I would volunteer to help to build it. Sadly, too many of our youth have already joined the death march through drug addiction and armed drug wars.

The man's music is a triumphal military march to war and destruction, or a solemn dirge of death and despair. We can't afford to step to either one. We are about life. We must slip off his deadly beat to a rhythm of our own, and step right out of his gloomy cadence, sideways if necessary, into our joyous life-affirming dance.

Du Bois's generation and my parents', born respectively at the end of slavery and at the beginning of this century, did have a double- and perhaps even a triple-consciousness. They were proud of being black and of associating with black achievers; wary and watchful of whites, yet strictly disciplined so as to be acceptable to them, and scathing in their scorn for blacks who were not so minded and so disciplined. Products of the first Jazz Age, they taught us to off-time our private, subversive dances to the bewildering Afro-classical poly-rhythms of progressive jazz.

I use off-timing as a metaphor for subversion, for code, for ironic attitudes toward mainstream beliefs and behavior, for choosing a vantage point of distance from the majority, for coolness, for sly commentary on the master race, for riffing and improvising off the man's tune and making fun of it.

The cakewalk was off-timing, mocking the airs of Massa and Missy, and making the antics of Philadelphia's New Year's mummers doubly, deliciously funny to blacks in the know. Louis Armstrong's mockery of minstrelsy was definitely off-timing, shored up by his strong talent, as it had to be; one needs a strong sense of self to play off the master and his stereotypes. Those Hampton students who coolly ignored George Bush's commencement speech in 1991 were off-timing. Haitians who adapt Catholic saints to voodoo rites are off-timing. No matter what she says, when Marian Anderson appeared on the Lincoln

Memorial stage as a substitute for the DAR's—and opened her concert with "My Country 'Tis of Thee"—she was making dramatic and effective use of off-timing. The sister in Washington, D.C., who said, when asked her reaction to the Queen of England's visit, "Well, she's fascinating. But so am I," was definitely off-timing. Bill ("Bojangles") Robinson's tap routine to "Me and My Shadow" was a superbly elegant bit of off-timing, a mockery of the mocker that made a suave, ironic comment on racism.

Off-timing, I learned in my youth, was the subversive attitude we had to maintain if we were to survive in the man's society. It was Uncle Julius's sly devaluation of European values in *The Conjure Woman*, and Larnie Bell's knowing jazz renderings of Bach fugues in *God Bless the Child*, and was more a skewed, but single, ironic consciousness than a double one.

Later, when we reached our thirties, my generation, the Off-Timers, may also have been the first to develop a unified black consciousness, with the help of the fiery younger ones born in the 1940s who for a time became our teachers. Led by them, we moved from off-timing to rocking steady on straight doses of rhythm, blues, and Motown soul. I call the sixties radicals, with a nod to Amiri Baraka, the Soul People.

The ones who came after the Soul People, who were born in the 1950s and 1960s and came to maturity in the 1970s and 1980s, were the beneficiaries of the civil rights and integrationist struggles, which have been efficiently erased from their memories. They are as surely the products of the Reagan and Bush eras as any Yuppies. They are now between thirty and forty years old, with a five-year margin on either side of those boundaries. Some of them grew up in predominantly white suburbs and attended predominantly white schools; all of them were taught, primarily, by white teachers. They are the first African Americans—and, hopefully, the last—to have a purely white consciousness. With their pale contact lenses, permed hair, and bleached personalities, they are distressing to watch and even more distressing to listen to. They sound like tinny transistor radios. They aspire mainly to power positions in corporate America or in the drug economy, and to the possession of status objects. They think money, achievements, and possessions make their color invisible, and they think Bruce Springsteen can sing. They are, God help us, the Rock 'n' Roll Generation.

But take hope, and, maybe, take cover. The newest group, the Rap Generation, now under twenty-five, has come striding angrily on the scene in fade haircuts, kente, and beads. These youngsters are the first group of African Americans to have a purely black consciousness. They either do not know or do not care that if they are honest with the man he is likely to kill them, as is his historic habit. They do not believe, as I did in my youth, that subversion is necessary for survival, or perhaps they sense that their survival is at best tenuous, under the current conditions of race hatred, the failing economy, and the sick planet. Whatever the reasons, they are very open, and foolish, and vulnerable, and brave. Perhaps they sense that the millennium is at hand, and with it, the end of white power. But because I know that the powerful do not give up control easily, and because I love these young people, and want them to survive, I am afraid for them, even as I admire them.

I think that my parents and their contemporaries—Bojangles, Louis Armstrong, Marian Anderson—were the last to have the double-consciousness of which Du Bois writes. They respected themselves and other blacks, often laughed at the foibles of white folks, but believed that whites had advantages to offer which would be given if the supplicants of color were worthy and "ready." Hence their mockery was always subtle, never blatant or threatening, and only to be understood by folks in the know. For the generation before mine, which still believed in the possibility of acceptance by whites, the double-consciousness was real, I think, and life was lived on an edge of jagged glass and razor blades.

To me, Du Bois's double-consciousness implies duality, an unhealthy state for the individual and for the group. As Lincoln said, "A house divided against itself cannot stand." An individual in conflict with himself is only marginally functional, and if half his loyalty lies elsewhere, his community cannot trust him.

My father, an army man, admired Toussaint L'Ouverture more than anyone else. I am sure that my father's subversion, while he was serving in the man's army, was imagining that he was Toussaint or Dessalines, preparing to chase the French from Haiti. They were his heroes, just as Zora Neale Hurston, Langston Hughes, Sterling A. Brown, and Katherine Dunham are mine, and off-timing to the distant beat of the Haitian revolution helped him to be a great soldier.

I was raised to be a "race woman." This saved me from the confusions of assimilationism. I neither craved nor expected social acceptance by whites, though I attended integrated schools. I did not, for instance, feel deprived because my wardrobe was sparse and shabby compared to the clothes worn by rich white girls. I simply did not expect to compete with them on that level. This meant, ironically, that my family could not afford to send me to a black school, where I would have had to dress extravagantly, but could afford to send me to the best the white folks had to offer—an Ivy League university.

Being raised as a race woman also meant that my heroes and heroines were those noble and somehow depressing pioneers Sojourner Truth and Mary McLeod Bethune, Booker T. Washington, and the rest, including, of course, Dr. Du Bois himself. All these dreary prodigies of toil, determination, effort, and suffering were paraded before me by parents, by teachers (my first six grades of schooling were segregated, which makes an important difference) and by black newspapers, of which we had four locally in my youth. Their life stories, full of sacrifice, selflessness, and postponed satisfactions, seemed to me more depressing than inspiring. Somehow, biographers have failed black children. These historic role models bore, it seemed to me, both a double-consciousness and the double burden of convincing white folks that Negroes were worthy of whatever benefits white society might impart, and of uplifting the downtrodden masses who were less fortunate than they, even when their own good fortune was pitiably small—consisting, perhaps, of one good suit, a chicken on Sunday, and two rooms with a roof that did not leak. None of life's pleasures were enjoyed by these long-faced, unsmiling paragons, who were too seriously occupied with wrestling with The Problem to laugh or love or, heaven forbid, dance and sing. I did not want to be like them, though I was told, implicitly and explicitly, that I must.

Because of those early black achievers, I suppose, I associated utter dreariness with the term "Negro," though I never dreamed of identifying with any other group. I associated "Negro" with meek black Christians forever bowing in humility, and with unjust suffering on self-created crosses. The word and its gestalt depressed me and made me ashamed. I was glad when our designation was changed to "black," though I had never minded being called "colored," which suggested to me the infinite variety of black complexions and the vividness of our finery.

"African American" seems cumbersome to me, a tongue-twister and intrinsically double in its consciousness. Today, with the influx of "people of color," it seems likely that we will soon be called "colored" again, though if the term includes everyone who is not white it may be both a blurring of identity and another trick to cut the pie of opportunity into ever-smaller slices.

What do all these changing designations for our group really mean, anyway? The same thing, perhaps, as our exotic forays into the wearing of wigs, turbans, and, yes, gelées and dashikis, and to altered surnames (Roget for Rogers, Chambray for Chambers, Guillaume for Williams). The goals, I suspect, are dignity and respect; what we really long to be called is Mr., Mrs., and Miss. Rather than address us by those titles, as my husband has observed, American service workers adopted a policy of first-name familiarity as soon as we acquired civil rights.

Anyway, back down at the cross, I grew up learning about Negro leaders, and to me a "Negro leader" was a grim, Calvinist martyr who worked hard and never enjoyed life. I wanted to have fun and laugh. I wanted to avoid being like such people.

Luckily, I learned that I did not have to be like them. As my urge to write became apparent, my parents and mentors introduced me to heroes and heroines with whom I could wholeheartedly identify: Zora Neale Hurston, who had been my dad's classmate at Howard; Sterling A. Brown, whom he had also known in D.C.; and Langston Hughes, with whom I corresponded after he visited my parents' friends Bill and Lucille Walton Paul, in Magnolia, New Jersey. These folks were more like it: they were artists, they were "real"—i.e., comfortable and homey and unpretentious; and, most importantly, unlike the other models given me in childhood, they did not preach any doctrines of sacrifice. They produced art, they laughed at jokes, they listened to the blues, they worked hard, they helped others, but they believed in having a good time! They were black, maybe, or they were colored, but not "tragically colored" (Zora's phrase); they were not gloomy "Negroes." And they knew who they were; they did not suffer from a double-consciousness. Liking what they said and the way they said it helped me to like "colored me" (Zora's phrase again).

Zora, Sterling, and Langston helped me to become freer than my parents and to claim, like Simple, "my right to be a disgrace." We no longer have to be perfect to make white folks accept us: they are never going to accept us anyhow. In that bitter knowledge lies a wonderful liberation that lifts like wings and frees like the snapping of chains. A "disgraceful" black person now owns his or her disgrace—it does not reflect on me. In my parents' day, Joe Louis not only had to whip dozens of white hopes in the ring to claim his championship; outside it, he had to be "a credit to his race." In my day, Mike Tyson kicks butt in the ring, and his behavior outside the ring is a disgrace—but only to himself. I call this progress.

The writers who were my role models knew exactly who they were—they did not suffer from double-consciousness any more than they suffered from vicarious shame.

I think that a double-consciousness is a barrier to wholeness, to health, and to the development of integrity and authenticity of personality, which may be our main life's work as human beings. Although lacking a separate shell to protect the inner core leaves one vulnerable and open to pain, I prefer that vulnerability. To believe my consciousness double would be to label myself sick, schizoid, and I think I am well. Well because I have chosen to integrate my personality around a unified core of thoroughly accepted inner blackness. People who flee to other identities, to being "part Indian" or "part black" or who just "happen to be black" or who are, maybe, "people of color" (I'm not sure yet whether that phrase is the new millennium or just another evasive dodge) are risking the splitting of personality that leads to inauthenticity, spiritual death, and maybe, even, insanity. That's the real reason concerned elders don't want our young people to flee from their identities. We are not afraid of their rejecting us, but of the consequences of their rejecting themselves, and, mindful of the hazards of the struggle as well as of the preciousness of each family member, we don't want to lose a single valuable soul. The loss of the soul, as well as of "soul," which means contact with the core self, is an inevitable consequence of identity change.

For too many members of the generation that came to maturity and material success in the 1970s and 1980s, black consciousness was traded for a belief that race did not matter, and only "happened" to be part of one's identity. The hospitals will soon be filling with these poor lost children who are now approaching middle age, although, if we do not get national health insurance, the rest of us will have to become witch doctors and mambos in order to heal them.

Though our youngest adults, including those now in college, risk incurring the wrath of whites with their assertive black awareness, they are not in nearly as much danger as their parents and older siblings; they are not in danger of having the Devil take their souls, leaving them as blank as automatons. For the Devil is real in what is left of America. He is, in fact, in charge of this country; he is stalking its wreckage-strewn landscape in hip boots, and he is taking more than names.

The only healthy double-consciousness, in my opinion, is that which I have labeled "off-timing"—a mockery of white folks and their madness, which is grounded in a secure and solid sense of who we are—the salt and greens eaters, the lovers and life affirmers, the ones who are at ease in our bodies and in nature and who move to an inner rhythm as familiar as the beating of our hearts. Yes, natural rhythm, if you will. Existing in nature rather than trying to control it. Revering God and life, protecting and preserving children, and keeping in touch with the kinfolk are all black traits. The rest of American culture, from singles bars to the hydrogen bomb, can be summed up in the off-timed pronunciation of the phrase "white folks." Properly timed, accompanied by a shrug and maybe an eye-roll if you can do it, this says, "Well, what can you expect?"

Once, we danced off-time when the beat of jazz was too fast, employing cool, casual movements that seemed—but only seemed—indifferent to the music. We slipped in and out of the various verbal modes at our command with the same dexterity—most notably, using a white voice to talk their talk at work and slipping fluidly, instantaneously, into the race vernacular one minute after quitting time.

When black Americans ceased to be bilingual—perhaps because whites stole and transformed our language as fast as we could invent it—our survival was seriously in question. An entire generation—those who reached adulthood in the 1970s and 1980s—seems to have lost its biculturality and the dividing line between private and public selves, and, with it, the sense of race loyalty. I have learned the hard way that I cannot trust people whom I would once have regarded as my children. One dreadful year in Atlanta, for instance, the middle-aged black woman meat manager of a local Kroger's market helped us to survive by letting us know when prices were about to be reduced. This very real help ended one day when, not seeing our friend, I asked a younger black employee about her. This young woman immediately ran to the white store manager to inform him that some people were looking for Brenda, which aroused his suspicions and resulted in her swift transfer to another market, leaving us to pay the same high prices as everyone else. To insecure whites, two blacks conversing on white turf are a conspiracy, and three or four an incipient revolution.

As I have said, I always knew who *I* was and whose side I was on. And yet, for a while there, integration produced a most subtle and dangerous blending of my attitudes and concerns. I was reminded of this most forcefully in 1986, when the space shuttle *Challenger* self-destructed. I happened to be at the source when witnessing this event—at the source, that is, of our identities and attitudes and mindsets as Aframericans. I was in the deep South, in other words; to be specific, in Brunswick, Georgia, among my in-laws, gathered around the TV set. It was my husband's annual return to his roots, but in a sense, it was a return to my own roots, too—and one that, as it turned out, I desperately needed.

For I, like most Americans, had a special concern for the fate of one crew member—the appealing young white woman schoolteacher, Christa McAuliffe, who had won her chance to travel in space in a national competition for teachers. I said that I was sorry about her death. My remark was met only by blank stares—in fact, all of the commentary about the accident was received with total disinterest by my in-laws, except for one bit of information. When the name and photo of the lone black crew member, Ronald McNair, were flashed on the screen, they leaned forward with a single coiled movement, galvanized into intense attention. This one alone was ours, their posture reminded and rebuked me; this one was our concern, this man alone deserved our mourning.

As we watched *Challenger*'s destruction, some of us who had muttered, "God will not be mocked," at the hubris of its name were sad and respectful, simply to mourn Ron McNair. If he had not been aboard, perhaps a jubilant chord would have been struck that day; perhaps a ballad like "Titanic" (the one about Shine or that other one that used to be off-timed by blacks with the shout of "Hallelujah!" following "It was sad when that great ship went down") would have resulted. For then the accident would not have concerned us; it would have just been white folks reaping the consequences of their foolishness.

This attitude, the clear distinction between *theirs* and *ours*, which I lost briefly and regained that day, is a darkly hidden and necessary part of being black in America. Our lives are so hard and our history so wretched that if we identified with everybody's suffering we would never overcome our own for long enough to survive.

Experiencing *Challenger*'s suicide in that setting was enough to shock me clear back to the 1940s, when, as John Wideman says in *Sent for You Yesterday*, ". . . the white voice from the radio, the voice usually full of fancy words about England and France and parliaments and prime ministers and wars overseas, the voice which had nothing to do with colored people, this time [the time when Joe Louis lost to Max Schmeling] the voice was speaking to Homewood. And to all the homeboys and homegirls of America. For Joe Louis belonged to us, and we went to war, mainly, to avenge his defeat."

Uh-huh. And "Amen," and as the church ladies also say, "Yay-us." It's Saturday night. My favorite FM disk jockey, Bob Perkins (WHYY-FM, Philadelphia) just played Cannonball Adderley jamming on "Mercy, Mercy, Mercy," and, automatically, I got up and slipped into a comfortable off-time as easily as I would a pair of old slippers. It's a floating, gliding set of moves that can be done to all music and at all ages; you make it up as you go along, dipping into and slipping out of the mainstream beat, and it feels good. Homeboys, home-girls—wherever you are this Saturday night, I wish you the same feeling.

Junior and
John Doe

James McPherson

I

In 1961, Ralph Ellison made a prediction. "A period is going to
come," he wrote, "when Negroes are going to be wandering around
because we've had this thing [the assumption of black American in-
feriority] thrown at us so long that we haven't had a chance to discover
what in our own background is really worth preserving." Nine years
later, in an interview, I asked Ellison to elaborate on this prediction.
"I think that too many of our assertions continue to be in response to
whites," he said. "I think that we're polarized by the very fact that
we keep talking about 'black awareness' when we really should be
talking about black American awareness, an awareness of where we fit
into the total American scheme, where our influence is. I tell white
kids that instead of talking about black men in a white world or about
black men in white society, they should ask themselves how black *they*

James Alan McPherson is Professor of English at the Writers Workshop at the University
of Iowa and contributing editor for the *Atlantic Monthly*. His articles and short stories
have appeared in many publications, among them *The New York Times, Esquire, The Best
American Short Stories*, and *The Nation*. His works include *Hue and Cry, Railroad*, and
Elbow Room, which won the Pulitzer Prize for fiction in 1978.

are because black men have been influencing the values of the society and the art forms of the society. How many of their parents fell in love listening to Nat King Cole? We did not develop as a people in isolation. We developed within a context of white people."

At the same time that Ellison was responding to me, back in 1970, the polarization began shifting in the other direction as a deadly racial reaction gathered strength.

I remember San Francisco in 1974. This was the time of the Patty Hearst kidnapping, mass hysteria over an impending gasoline shortage, a time when someone named "the Zebra Killer" was shooting white people. At the height of this hysteria, all black males in the city were subjected to an all-night curfew, by order of the mayor, because the "Zebra Killer" was said to be a black male. I used to defy the curfew by sticking with my personal habit of walking when and where I pleased. One night, on a trolley car, a white male holding the strap next to mine leaned close to my ear and whispered, *"This had better stop! It had better stop* before we have to go to *war!"* Then, changing the tone of his voice, he said "Goodnight" to me in a friendly manner, and got off the trolley car.

I remember walking one morning to my favorite black-owned restaurant on Divisadero Street. I liked to go there for breakfast. As I approached the place, I saw seated at a table next to the window a black American friend, a writer, and a white male, an Irishman who lived in that mostly black neighborhood and who had a black girlfriend. I went in and sat down with them. While I had never trusted the Irishman because, officially, he was a policeman whom I considered "slick," I had accepted him as the constant companion of my black friend. My friend seemed especially nervous that morning. And the Irishman seemed especially sour and aggressive. I think he might have resented my intrusion. Whatever the source of his irritation, it soon drew my black friend into a ritual that frightened me. As we sat at the table, the white man would occasionally lift his finger, place it before the eyes of my black friend, and move his finger toward some scene or object on the other side of the café window. "Look at that," he would order. My black friend's eyes followed the directing white finger, almost as if the two organic objects were connected by an invisible string. "See that?" "Look at that!" "What's that?" The orders came again and again, and at each order my black friend's eyes moved with, or his independent will surrendered to, the authority in the single white finger. This single white finger seemed to be orchestrating my black friend's soul. Afterward, during this same stressful period, my black friend began speeding up his car, in anger, each time he saw groups of black boys taking their time while crossing street intersections.

It was during the early 1970s that I first began to get a new and curious message from black people. It was then that I first began to hear the word "they" being used in an unfamiliar, self-preempting way, a way that suggested that the pressure of the racial reaction had penetrated and was undermining the value sense, or the private idiom, of black Americans. An early warning came from a friend who had achieved early access to a private club habituated by the white upper class. He gave me some advice he had picked up during his rounds: "*They* say it ain't go'n be the way it *was*. *They* say all this bullshit is *over*!" I next heard this new integration of outside essence into personal idiom from a black colleague in response to my description of the homeless black people whom I had seen on the streets of New York. "Poor devils!" this professor of religious studies said. "Well, *they* won't get *me*!" And the next expression came from a personal friend, a poet who had postured militantly during the 1960s. In response to my account of some very vicious treatment to which I had been subjected by some whites, he said, "Maybe *they* don't like what you write. Don't you understand how much they *hate* you? Why don't you just stand pat and take your blows?" Then there was the black woman who stepped out of the crowd at a reading I gave at the Library of Congress.

"They've rewarded you," she whispered to me. "Now why don't you make yourself useful?"

Ellison's prediction did not really prepare me for the counter-polarization of black people during the 1970s and 1980s.

2.

Ellison's attempt to define a meaningful identity for black Americans came at a time when the attention of much of the nation, if not much of the world, was still focused on the self-assertions of black Americans. His assessments were made during a watershed period, when certain elites still remained poised to redefine the practical implications of the nation's ethical creed in new, other-inclusive ways. A great number of black Americans, those who were then called "integrationists," represented part of the force pressing for a redefinition of the ethical basis of the society. Traditionally, it has always been black Americans who call attention to the distance between asserted ideals and daily practices, because it is the black American population which best symbolizes the consequences of the nation's contradictions. This unenviable position, or fate, has always provided black Americans with a minefield of ironies, a "knowingness," based on a painful intimacy with the cruel joke at the center of the problematic American identity. At the core of this irony there used to reside the basic, if unspoken, understanding that identity in America is almost always a matter of improvisation, a matter of process; that most Americans are, because of this, confidence people; and that, given the provisional nature of American reality at almost any time, "black" could be in reality "white," and "white" could be in reality "black." Older Anglo-Saxons used to appreciate a few of the ironies in this minefield, or briarpatch. They had, in fact, created the circumstances which had given rise to it. When pressed, or when drunk, one of them might tell you in private, "We're all cousins. The only difficulty is that most people don't understand just how we're related."

The fundamental challenge of the 1960s and 1970s was to redefine this special quality of relatedness. The challenge was a simple but complex matter of articulating, or of dramatizing, how the black American idiom, the special flavor of black Americans, was then redefining in its own terms some aspects of the white American essence. This was the subtle, self-affirming dimension of black American and American experience that could not be comprehended by Du Bois's dualism through its either/or focus. What was needed during and after the 1960s was a creative synthesis, one that would lift the whole issue of black American and therefore American identity to a higher level of meaning based on commonly shared values defined by the experiences of *both* groups. What was needed was a revolutionary model of American identity, an imaginative aesthetic and moral foothold established in the future, with little attention paid to race, toward which all Americans might aspire.

It need not be emphasized that this did not happen.

Because it did not happen, just a few years after Ellison had affirmed his prediction, the minefield of ironies was very suddenly exhausted. Those years marked the true beginnings of the great racial reaction. Stated in terms of tragicomic ritual, or in terms of slapstick, those at the forefront of the charge into the sacred castle suddenly found the drawbridge being raised with most of the invading army still outside. Although no word as harsh as "prisoners" was used, prisoners were indeed taken. They were interrogated in terms of IQ scores, and in terms of the good cop/bad cop ploy of popular melodrama. The "bad cops" (racist social scientists) simply asserted, without any hope of scientific proof, that because of a genetic predisposition black Americans were inferior to white Americans. The "good cops" (sentimental liberals) answered with arguments that black Americans were inferior because of environmental factors. All ironic laughter ceased as this premise was carried forward in the mass media, and all debate about ways to improve the condition of the poor shifted to a discussion of whether or not they are human beings.

Those in the forefront of the movement were stunned, forced now to fight with weapons they had not forged on their own and instead with weapons held within the carefully guarded arsenals of others. The "good cops" won the day, without too many shots' being fired. The new black middle class was now isolated from the masses. The resurrected nature-nurture theory had done its work, and was retired to the keep of the sacred castle. Before the experiment in integration, the comic spirit grounded in the realities of the group idiom might have made light of this development with the usual irony. But after Moms Mabley, there was only Richard Pryor to provide the self-affirming communal gestures, grounded in ironic laughter, needed by the group as a safeguard against mechanical or aberrational behavior. Except for the early work of Richard Pryor, during the 1970s reality-based ironic laughter faded out of much black American expression. One result of this was that a large segment of the new black middle class became frightened, conformist, and strangely silent.

Toward the end of the 1970s, I began to hear, increasingly, other-directed allusions being consolidated in our private language. During this period the words "they" and "them" seemed to have become standardized ways of alluding to the relation of our inside world to the larger world outside our group. The old polarity between our idiom and the white American essence seemed to have been thrown into reverse, with the norms of white middle-class life becoming predominant. Beyond a continuing influence in the areas of sports and entertainment, our private idiom seemed to have lost its capacity to influence the values of the world outside our own. More than this, the passing fashions of the outside world—Du Bois's "tape" of an alien world—seemed to have invaded our very souls. The erosion of something fundamental and sacred began then, and has not stopped since. This great reversal of influences may not have destroyed the group idiom, but it did encourage many of us to allow our eyes to follow a directing white finger; and it did cause many of us to begin to express contempt for poor or unconscious black people who did not know enough to get out of the path of a speeding luxury car.

Sometime toward the beginning of the 1980s, all the "theys" seemed to me to have coalesced into a code of conduct, an acceptable guide to black behavior, the script of which existed outside of the group. This model of acceptable behavior began slowly to function as an internalized norm, causing some of us to begin policing the behavior of others in the group. This new norm was of very special interest to me. I had not realized just how powerful it had become until around Thanksgiving of 1980, when one of my earliest black teachers and his wife visited my home in Charlottesville, Virginia. My former teacher, an elderly man, had a nightmare during his first night in my home. All his life he had been sensitive to the nuances of naked white power. Only such a man could have drawn up into his dreams the unrefined images of white supremacy. On Thanksgiving morning, he reported to me the contents of his nightmare. He said he had dreamed of interviewing a black newspaper reporter who had just covered a top-level briefing of the military high command at the Pentagon. My former teacher reported to me what "they" said: "We should kill a million or so of them, just so the others will understand we mean business and won't start moaning about their 'civil rights.' "

My former teacher was, those many years later, still my teacher. He was prophetic in his expression of the deep fear that invaded the black American soul during the 1980s.

By the first years of the 1980s, I began to appreciate, in a deeply personal way, the consequences of the penetration of this new norm, this new sense of self, into the very core of the black American idiom. I saw the disintegration of whatever sense of self we still possessed. I saw the enthusiastic internalization of the assumed assumptions of "them," and I saw the beginnings of what has become an unending, self-negating, if not self-hating, conformity to the externally imposed model of an acceptable black self. Initially, I took an ironic stance toward this somewhat comic transformation. But when it began to condition the emotional and ethical responses of my family and my oldest black friends, when I saw that white hostility toward me was a signal for black hostility toward me, I abandoned some of my family, and many of my oldest black friends, and accepted a condition of internal exile in a small, isolated town in Iowa, as the only way I knew of maintaining myself whole. I accepted this burden of guilt as the price I had to pay for my own psychological freedom. But much deeper than this was my *fear* that the pointing white finger, the one I had observed in San Francisco and in other places, might direct a hostile and inwardly dead set of black eyes at me. For the first time in my life, I began to fear my own people.

Over the past twelve years, here in Iowa, I have often wondered whether I might have overreacted in putting great distance between some of my family and my oldest black friends and myself. There is always the temptation, if you are a writer, to be suspicious that your imagination might be overactive. But on the other hand, during these same years, I have had to deal with black men and women whom I sometimes considered alien. I have seen a colleague fly into a rage, using the appropriated language of his white peers, over my expression of independent thought. There were too many "theys" in his tirade for him to name. Another acquaintance, when I reported to him the way a black female student had used the bogus charge of racism to browbeat a "liberal" to give her a scholarship, laughed approvingly and said, "She's slick. She'll go far." Like my other colleague, he merely applauded *her* acceptance of the prevailing morality. But the very ease of *both* their acceptances was evidence that something was terribly wrong. Something humanly vital in them had been defeated, and they were involved in a constant process of self-improvisation, an improvisation relying on the "tape" provided by some external script.

3.

I do not believe that Du Bois, or even Ellison, could have anticipated the extent to which black people conformed to the white American model during the 1970s and 1980s. Both their analyses assume a limited absorption of white influences into the black American idiom. But traditionally, with black people, this reverse integration has been a highly selective process. Only those traits of the "other world" which could enhance the group's sense of self were selected by black people to be incorporated into the group's ongoing process of self-making. It was only under a new set of historical circumstances, during the past two decades, that a large segment of the newly created black middle class assumed that it had much more in common with that idealized other world than it had with the vernacular sources of its own vitality.

During these decades, a very large group of black people took a side trip, so to speak, by attempting to standardize an identity apart from the concrete conditions of the group ethos. Many stopped negotiating the complex balance between the moral and aesthetic feeling tones of our own ethos and the influences, or trends, abstracted from Du Bois's "other world." Many allowed an assumed corporate white consensus regarding the nature of reality to predominate over our own instinctive sense of reality. What was once viewed as a spectrum of choices, some of which were to be rejected and some of which were to be selected for incorporation because they "fit" (an enterprise undertaken by any group involved in the process of self-making), became for many an opportunity to embrace an abstract white middle-class model in its entirety. Whereas our ancestors had abstracted and recombined with great discrimination and care, many of us accepted unthinkingly the images and trends paraded before us. In doing this, we won with ease our centuries-long battle against "discrimination."

But we also disrupted our historical process-of-making a usable identity, and many of us have settled for a simple standardization around the norms, racist and other, of middle-class American life. One advocate of this standardization is Shelby Steele, who sees something heroic in conformity to middle-class norms. Another advocate is Clarence Thomas, whose story about his rise from the outhouses of his youth (*Up from the Outhouse?*) conforms to the middle-class model of heroism, but stops there. It makes all the difference in the world, at least in the storybooks, whether the hero confronts the dragon or joins him. It makes all the difference in the world what is chosen as the basis of the happily-ever-after. Is it the self-making, self-affirming challenges of the quest, or is it the creature comforts of consumerism and conformity? The issue of race aside, does the basis of ultimate security and identity reside in process or product?

If the answer to this question is the former, then perhaps another, very basic question should follow. What, in the nature of a group ethos, or an idiom, have we managed to bring forward from our failures in the 1970s and 1980s? The visible "leaders" of the group are always bemoaning the fact that we are losing our "gains." But beyond those material things that can be measured, what else, of much greater value, have we lost? I believe that we have lost, or are steadily losing, our sense of moral certainty, the ability to distinguish between right and wrong. I believe that this moral certainty once was, among the best of us, an ethical imperative, one passed along as a kind of legacy by our ancestors. This was our true wealth, our capital. The portion of this legacy that fueled the civil rights movement was a belief that *any* dehumanization of another human being was wrong. This moral certainty once had the potential to enlarge our humanity. Beneath it was the assumption that the experience of oppression had made us more human, and that this higher human awareness was about to project a vision of what a fully human life, one not restricted by color, should be. We seemed to be moving, on an ethical level, toward a synthesis of the "twoness"—the merger of the double self into a better and truer self—that was the end Du Bois had in mind.

Because of the complex ways in which the black American idiom relates to the white American essence, there were certain whites who anticipated the projection of a new *human style*, one which finally transcended race, rising from our struggle. This did not happen. What happened instead was that the process-of-making a usable identity was minimalized in its ambition: from the humanly transcendent to the material plane, from an ethic based on possibility to an ethic grounded in property. The historical moment had provided us with a choice between continuing a process of human redefinition of an evolving sense of self, with all its pains and risk and glory, and entry into a prearranged set of social formulas. The choice was between process, which is on the side of life, and product, which goes against the fundamental ends of life. Many of us chose the latter option, and something of very great value in us began to die.

While our slave ancestors would no doubt be proud of us as skillfully crafted copies of white people, they would not really recognize many of us as blood kin, as products of the process they initiated. The very first articulation of language in their idiom, as expressed in their songs, had sufficient vitality to look beyond the trends of the moment and identify with an age that was yet to come. The best of them looked back on their own degraded status from the perspective of a future time when their own process-of-self-making was complete. Denied recognizable human souls by the society that enslaved them, they projected their full souls so far into the future that they became content to look back on their enslavers with laughter, and with pity. This was one measure of their full and self-confident humanity. Where once we shared in their ethical critique of the moral defects in the "other world" of Du Bois's dualism, many of us have now abandoned, or trivialized, this resource. One result of this mass defection is that we now lack a moral center, an independent ethos, a vital idiom. Another result is that the country itself now lacks the moral dimensions once supplied by our critique. It lacks our insights into what is of truly transcendent value. On this essential level of moral abstraction, in those places where *meanings* imposed by the black American group had value far beyond its immediate experience, the group is at risk of losing the catholic dimensions of its ancient ethical struggle for identity.

As a substitute, we now compete with white Americans for more creature comforts. Many of us now eat and dress in extraordinary style. We can lie and lie with greater and greater facility, and can even compete with whites in this enterprise. Back during the late 1970s, the comedian Richard Pryor captured the bleakness of our choice in graphic vernacular language. In one of his routines he portrays a black wino standing on a street corner, humming hymns and directing traffic on a Sunday morning. The wino sees a junkie coming up the street. He says, "Who's that boy? Is that Junior? Look at him. In the middle of the street. Junkie motherfucker. Look at him. Nigger used to be a *genius*, I ain't lyin'. Booked the numbers, didn't need paper or pencil. Now the nigger can't remember who *he* is."

My assertion is that something very tragic happened to a large segment of the black American group during the past two decades. Whatever the causes of this difficulty were, I believe that they were rooted more in the quality of our relation to the broader society than in defects in our own ethos. That is to say, we entered the broader society just at a time when there was the beginning of a transformation in its basic values. The causes of this transformation are a matter of speculation. In my own view, we became integrated into a special kind of decadence, which resulted from what has been termed "false consciousness," one which leads to personal demoralization.

The basic pattern of this erosion was outlined, early in this century, by the Spanish philosopher José Ortega y Gasset, as he contemplated a similar development in his native Spain. "This degradation," he wrote, merely follows from the acceptance of misgovernment as a constituted norm even though it continues to be *felt* as wrong. Inasmuch as what is essentially abnormal and criminal cannot be converted into a sound norm, the individual chooses to adapt himself to the abnormality by making himself a homogeneous part of the crime weighing upon him. The mechanism is similar to that which gives rise to the popular saying 'One lie breeds a hundred.' "

To fully appreciate the implications of Ortega's insight, one would be required to abandon Du Bois's dualism altogether and view black Americans as simply Americans who, like all others, are open to personal corruption as a consequence of living in a corrupt society. We are required to make the same personal adjustments as others in order to ensure our survival. In this broader sense, the movement of black Americans follows the pattern of other inspired movements to raise the moral tone of an oppressor through an appeal to some transcendent principle. Usually, those armed with only the slogans of liberalism, when they actually confront cynical and entrenched power, reach an impasse. After failing again and again to reform that which is incapable of reformation, such movements tend to regroup in such a way as to leave the sacred ideology intact. Whereas once there was an effort to raise everyone to the same level of equality by pointing to the moral failings of the oppressor, those faced with failure in this tactic often fall back on a much more cynical argument. Since it is not possible to force others to behave as they *should* behave, it is accepted that everyone has the right to behave as the oppressors *do* behave. This leaves the old moral ideology intact as a deadly form of cynicism.

But in the case of black Americans, this cynicism is proving to be much more deadly than the cynicism embraced by other groups. A great many black elites, like other elites, rushed to embrace the fashionable public behavior of the 1970s and 1980s. Part of the appeal of the Reagan years was the reemergence of the ideology of extreme individualism—the main chance, the reification of the bottom line, the location of an ethic in ownership, the elevation of individual concerns over the common concerns of the group. Many black elites embraced a public philosophy which helped to justify, for the first time on an inverted scale, our old "crabs in a barrel" mentality: those at the top of the barrel should try to *push down* those trying to climb out. This new sense of irresponsible individualism contributed to the growth in the sale of drugs as the main concern of a new underground economy in the black community.

And then there was the almost religious identification with politics.

Democratized by Jesse Jackson, a crude political style seeped into many aspects of black American life. Lying and manipulation in personal relationships became fashionable. What made these masquerades so pathetic was the shallowness of the lies and the poor quality of the manipulations. It was as if mentors for the development of these skills had been selected from among those whites who were themselves on the margins of an increasingly sophisticated bureaucratic culture. Flabby tricks seemed to have been learned from those whose own political skills had become obsolete. This was a product of our racial marginalization. During the 1980s, whenever I heard a black bureaucrat depicting with pride the trick he had used to manipulate toward some end, I silently compared it with some much more subtle manipulation I had already witnessed on a much higher level of white society. I imagined this seemingly "new" manipulation as the brainchild of some tired and lackluster white bureaucrat now lost in the mists of time. My silent response was always something like "Crafted by John Doe, Assistant Clerk, Water Works Commission, Cleveland, 1913."

I believe that these preoccupations with fashionable individualism and with small-time politics, toward the end of survival during decadent times, invaded the very centers of our lives. In order to make room for these fashions, we tore down, tossed out, and discarded some of our most basic beliefs. But a very high price was paid for this trade-off. The acceptance of one fashion after another tends to draw the fashionable mind further and further away from the sources of its own vitality, its own feeling tones. A preoccupation with public fashions also erodes the unstated values, what the Japanese call "belly language," which provides the foundation for any group consensus. It seems to me that by the end of the 1980s black Americans had become a thoroughly "integrated" group. The trends of public life had successfully invaded, and had often suppressed, the remnants of our group ethic. Our ancient process of self-making had at last found a resting place, a point of consolidation. We were, at last, no better than and no worse than anyone else.

4.

I am remembering now a very serious discussion I had with one of my mentors one rainy night in San Francisco many years ago. He had been after me for my usual crime: speaking my mind to the head of an institution because I thought that what the institution was doing was wrong. My mentor said, "Man, can you afford to *buy* [a certain institution]? Well, *they* can afford to buy integrity a dime a dozen!" After all these years I have reason to concede the truth of my old mentor's assessment. He understood, as I had still to learn, the extent to which ethics and ownership are interrelated in this culture. He was speaking as a learned student of European and therefore American history and culture. And yet, I still think he was not quite right. Something happens to the *meaning* of integrity when it becomes a property. It ceases to be an active agent, its value content is cheapened, if not destroyed, and all that remains is an empty fashion. The authentification of such empty fashions by society leads to moral dandyism—a public moral stance or style without private substance. We learn to feign a serious preoccupation with what is assigned value as a current moral fashion, and we learn to view with watchful contempt that which is outside the prevailing consensus of public concern. The result is integrity by consensus, as opposed to the much more willful, much more meaningful kind. It represents the difference between looking outside oneself for clues to what *should* be a current concern and turning within to some private scale of values. It represents the difference between a shifting value sense dependent on outside verification and a value sense that is self-reifying, one that is beyond the control, or the measurement, of time and place. My old mentor was right. Integrity can be measured at a dime a dozen. But the attempt to encase it in material terms, paradoxically, causes it to become even more rare.

Our slave ancestors were familiar with this distinction. Their very lives depended on the ability to distinguish between moral fashions and meaningful actions. They survived by having sufficient vitality of imagination to pass over the present scene, if its currents were not moving in their direction, and identify their meaning with an age that was yet to come. In this way they kept alive the hope of eventually being able to continue moving toward their own goals. In this way a defeated people kept alive a sense of integrity, a sense of self, even if their bodies were bought and sold. During the worst of material times they provided a standard for the best of material times.

5.

I am painfully aware that I may be much too critical of negative developments that might have been inescapable for all black people, myself included. I sit here in Iowa City in almost complete isolation from the flow of black American life. My telephone and my letters have provided a lifeline during all these years. On the other hand, I read a great many books and magazines, and I talk on a regular basis with selected friends in other parts of the country. I am beginning to sense that, just now, the group is engaged in a search for something that has been lost. Many of us are looking again to the past. Many of the new middle-class people are trying to fill a void in their lives by embracing a connection between the languages and the cultures of African peoples and our old black American traditions. Some of our children are learning to salute African flags. There is among us now the belief that, like immigrants from other nations, we must have a homeland to look back on before we can resume the process-of-making our identity. I have no arguments, now, with the choices being made by others.

But it does seem to me that our slave ancestors resolved this issue many centuries ago, long before most of the immigrants arrived in the United States. In the words of Howard Thurman, our slave ancestors were stripped of everything except what in them was literal and irreducible. Out of this raw and wounded humanity there began to be projected a new people, a people whose only vital lifelines were the roots they planted in the future. All the ancestors who came after them were linkages in the ongoing process of self-making. The present generations are likewise extensions of this same imaginative projection. Many of us have already tried to opt out of this process by attempting to standardize an identity around the norms of middle-class life at a time when the authenticity and the vitality of those norms were questionable. For many, this excursion has proved unsatisfactory. What seems to be gathering strength now is a comparable excursion, this one toward the traditions of ancient Egypt and Africa. Because I am isolated here in Iowa, I think I will sit out this second side trip.

If my years in this place have taught me anything, it is to be even more wary of abrupt shifts in the language and habits that appear around me. I have learned to continue with my own process-of-making, in my own way. I have learned, mostly on my own, that when the lifestyle out of which the idiom of a people grew is changed or altered, the idiom can break down. Such breakdowns provide the excuses needed to abandon a lifestyle based on a meaning that has been called into question by outside reality. But if the idiom has been identified with the essence of one's own life, and the former lifestyle was merely its transitory expression, then the old values at the basis of the idiom *hold* their essence of identification. Sometimes this holding action can go on for years during a period of readjustment. But afterward it is possible for a *new* lifestyle to grow out of the experience of the old values with a new reality. This is how human beings change with the times while remaining themselves.

What was only an abstraction for me became concrete many months ago as I watched the retirement of Thurgood Marshall from the U.S. Supreme Court and the elevation of Clarence Thomas to Marshall's seat. I was interested in Thomas because both of us were raised in Savannah, Georgia, in extreme poverty, and both of us attended the same Catholic school system there. When Thomas publicly thanked the nuns in that school system, I could remember names and faces. But as the Senate hearings dragged on, and especially after Anita Hill's allegations, I found myself identifying less and less with Clarence Thomas, as well as with Ms. Hill. Both of them seemed to me to be captives of ideology. At one of the low points in the hearings, after Ms. Hill had testified, my older sister called me from Connecticut. She said, "James, Clarence Thomas didn't attend the same Catholic school we did in Savannah. If he had, he would have remembered the first thing the nuns taught all the kids." And then she recited the first lines of a poem: "I have to live with myself and so,/I want to be fit for myself to know."

When the lifestyle out of which the idiom of a people grew is changed or altered, the idiom can break down. But if the idiom has been identified with the essence of one's own life, and the former lifestyle was merely its transitory expression, then the old values at the basis of the idiom hold their essence of identification. And afterward it is possible for a new lifestyle to grow out of the experience of the old values with a new reality.

Such a process of continuation and change is an essential part of one's *meaning* as a human being. A reclamation of essential meaning, for black Americans, has very little to do with the other side, the white side, of Du Bois's dualism. But at the same time, considering the white American context of our idiom, it has *everything* to do with it. Once again, we must consider the special interrelatedness of the two groups. Among white Americans, as among black Americans, there is now a desperate hunger for every value once included in the rhetorical category called "ethics." As the responses of "John Doe" to the Thomas hearings must have made clear to a great many people, the current fashion in moral dandyism and lying is about to run its course. The hunger for moral certainties provides much of the appeal of David Duke and Ross Perot. Beneath the open racism of Duke's supporters, one can perceive the first stirrings of a response to the metaphysical problems shared by all people, black Americans included, who have become personally demoralized by living with a false consciousness. For better or for worse, there is now a public lust for moral clarity. This hunger permeates all groups, and transcends the special interests of any one.

I would not advocate a return to a strict religious tradition, but I would hope that the group try again to understand some of the old definitions of the words "truth" and "meaning" and "honesty" and "love" and "integrity." I am grateful to be hearing, these days, much more familiar language working its way through the black American community: "If you want to talk that talk, you have to walk that walk." I consider this first step toward the reassertion of the old idiom downright refreshing. And I am attempting to consider something refreshingly radical: Since every other attempt at "integration" has failed, perhaps we have one last chance to help each other, through our divided black and white vocabularies, work toward some common and solid definitions.

I want to believe that the spirits of our black ancestors, from the safe perspective of their long-imagined bridgehead someplace in the future, would somehow expect this effort on our part as a final affirmation of the self-definition, the process-of-making, they initiated those centuries ago. All I have been struggling to say is this: the implication of Du Bois's dualism notwithstanding, we should remember the uniqueness of our origins and locate, within our own idiom, sufficient courage to affirm this uniqueness as the only possible positive norm. Perhaps we should consider doing this as a way of keeping faith with our ancestors. It may well be that the uniqueness of our uniqueness, along with the implications of that, is our most basic value and is the most meaningful asset we have. If so, we ought to find ways of affirming it.

The Du Boisian Dubiety
and the American Dilemma:
Two Levels of
Lure and Loathing

C. Eric Lincoln

And thou who didst with pitfall and with gin
Beset the road I was to wander in
Wilst thou with predestined evil round enmesh me
And then inpute my fall to sin?[1]

William Edward Burghardt Du Bois was born in Massachusetts in the same decade that slavery was disestablished as America's "peculiar institution," and although Du Bois escaped the direct experience of slavery, the society and the culture in which he was to be immersed

---

Dr. C. Eric Lincoln's primary scholarly contributions have been in the sociology of religion, but he is almost equally well known for his lectures and publications in the sociology of race and ethnic relations. Among his many works are the seminal study *The Black Muslims in America; The Black Church Since Frazier; Race, Religion and the Continuing American Dilemma; The Negro Pilgrimage in America; The Black Experience in Religion;* and *The Black Church in the African American Experience* (with Lawrence Mamiya). Professor Lincoln's novel, *The Avenue, Clayton City,* won the Lillian Smith Award for Best Southern Fiction in 1988; and his collected poems, *This Road Since Freedom,* were celebrated by Boston University with a professional presentation at Symphony Hall in 1991. Many colleges and universities have recognized Professor Lincoln's contributions with honorary degrees, including Carleton College, Boston University, Clark Atlanta University, and St. Michael's College. In 1990 he was named Howard Johnson Distinguished Teacher of the Year at Duke, where he is Professor of Religion.

and to which he was to struggle to relate, did not. In that simple fact lies the answer to much of the riddle of the Du Boisian dubiety, that awesome "double-consciousness," which is assumed to be the critical component of whatever it is that defines (and devalues) African Americans as a class as peculiar as the institution from which the definition takes its descent. Writing from his unchallenged pinnacle as America's foremost black intellect to be born in his century, the penetrating insight and the imaginative prose of Dr. Du Bois demanded and received the interest and attention of three continents. In an America debauched by civil war and preoccupied with a burden of misgivings and apprehensions about the ultimate meaning and consequences of that war, America seized on Du Bois in search of some intimation of reassurance. The war was over, but the national polarity over the wisdom and the quality of freedom for the African had barely begun. The law had made Americans out of Africans, but could the judgments of the law be validated in the flux of social and political intercourse? Who and what was this "African" who had been around for centuries and yet nobody had bothered to know?

The war was over, but whether America had sown the wind and must in consequence reap the whirlwind was still to be determined. While Du Bois's singularity could hardly lend itself to a realistic prognosis of the black experience in a free society, his opinions were considered oracular by a significant audience of Americans, black and white alike. So it was that when Du Bois addressed himself to the nature and the meaning of black identity in white America, while he did not resolve the problem, he did ensure its institutionalization, for his intensely personal experience was inevitably extrapolated to cover the whole universe of black people in America, no matter how disparate the circumstances which shaped their individual perceptions of reality. During slavery it had been unnecessary to see, or to try to understand, the African beyond the blackness which enshrouded him. Now that he had been freed and thrust peremptorily upon a society which knew next to nothing of him beyond his convenience as a chattel, the romantic mysticism in Du Bois's cryptic reference to "twoness . . . two souls, two thoughts, two unreconciled strivings, two warring ideals in one dark body" fixed itself in the American psyche and became a part of the conventional paraphernalia by which "Negroes" were to be evaluated and explained. Du Bois's poignant and compelling articulation of the inner turmoil he experienced as he wrestled with the question of who he was and where he belonged made him the individual counterpart of a society which itself was engaged in an uncertain struggle for identity and validation. But W. E. B. Du Bois was not *Everyman*, not even Every Black Man. His personal turmoil was not necessarily universal in the African American experience, the beguiling romantics of septuagenesis and mystical caul notwithstanding.

The notion of "double-consciousness" articulated so poignantly by Du Bois a hundred years ago has become for much of contemporary America a standard reference to the unresolved quest for "self-conscious manhood" believed to have eluded African Americans in general, leaving them peculiarly vulnerable to the debilitating ravages of cultural schizophrenia. It was not surprising, of course, that Du Bois's personal apperceptions would be seized on and universalized because of his stature as a scholar and intellectual. But more compelling was the fact that America was in desperate need of some way to understand "the Negro" which, in the face of his new freedom, could justify freezing him in a perpetual time warp that would obviate the need to grant to him the full spectrum of human complexity, which demanded a full spectrum of human response. Slavery had been abolished, but there were still formidable obstacles separating the African American from full common participation in the body politic, and the most unyielding of these were the barriers of convention, the reluctance of the human mind to disgorge itself of a prey that defied digestion.

The "lure and the loathing," a romantic euphemism for black self-hatred, is the extrapolation of the Du Boisian dubiety that allegedly commits the African American to unending irresolution and self-flagellation in the fruitless effort to fully realize the "American" component of his being. The clue that such an effort is bound to end in frustration is stated clearly in Du Bois's soliloquy in *The Souls of Black Folks* when he recognizes that the "true self-consciousness" he seeks must always be refracted through "the revelation of the other world." True self-consciousness through such a refraction is of course no self-consciousness at all, but only the reception of external projections which may well be inconsistent with any objective reality. The clue becomes the obvious when Du Bois recognizes that his soul is being measured by "the tape of a world that looks on in amused contempt and pity."

The persistence of the "lure and loathing" syndrome as an extrapolation of Du Bois's personal dilemma is a remarkable measure of the receptivity and staying power of Du Bois's idea as an adequate answer to the riddle of blackness, and the inherent incapacities believed to be associated with it as the primary undergirding of racial prejudice in America. Du Bois, who by a sort of common consensus became in time almost legendary as the most prominent intellectual to come out of the African diaspora, was uniquely equipped by time and circumstance to be cast in such a role. He was born free, and in a free state traditionally sympathetic to the relief of the "African condition." He was born of mixed ancestry at the end of an era that was to define and mold America's self concept and her practical response to the African presence as well. He was born with one foot anchored firmly in a centuries old tradition of American slavery, and the other poised over the uncertain, uncharted ground of a future in which ex-slaves and their erstwhile masters would be "equal."

He was educated in white institutions and black institutions in Massachusetts and Tennessee, and crowned, as it were, with a confirmation at Heidelberg. In an America so lately torn apart over the issue of race and its relevance, and in frantic search for the most painless solutions to the new problems unleashed by a massive reversal of history, it can scarcely be surprising that the wisdom of W. E. B. Du Bois took on an oracular cast, or that his personal struggle with identity was universalized for all black Americans. The problem is that Du

Bois was hardly characteristic of the black Americans of his time, or of this time, and the convenient assumptions of the yearning to be white and the hatred of being black, or some derivative of that sullen syndrome, is clearly untenable. The lure and loathing ascribed to African Americans is neither inherent nor self-evident, and where it functions at all it does so as the projection of a cultural artifact which is more revelatory of contradictions outside the black psyche than within it.

People do not ordinarily loathe themselves. As a matter of fact, human history is replete with numerous instances of peoples who considered themselves *the people nonpareil*, which is to say unique in the creative scheme of things. Certainly it would be difficult to imagine an Ashanti or Yoruba warrior fresh off the slave ship at Charleston at war with himself over his identity; and if Nat Turner, David Walker, or Harriet Tubman had any such anxieties, *even after the experience of slavery*, they were the best-kept secrets of the age. Self-loathing is a counterfunction to survival and to the will to survive. It must therefore be considered abhorrent to any natural human predisposition. In consequence, if people do not come into the world hating themselves, then self-hatred, wherever it exists, must be a learned response, an acquired pattern of behavior, a dysfunctional contaminant from the human flux in which one's primary socialization takes place. Hence, it is reasonable to look for the origins of self-hatred outside the group in which it is alleged to occur, and more specifically, inside any associated group which stands to be convenienced by it.

Self-loathing is the abject internalization of prominent aspects of the caste mentality, and the notion of caste, which is the perfect institutionalization of self-deprecation and subordination to the perceived rights of preference and privilege of some outgroup, does not originate in the group *en caste*. Caste is the extreme projection of ethnicity, which is the normative expression of group preference common to all peoples. But caste is in the making when ethnicity turns aggressive, and one group by one means or another effectively projects its values of self-perception upon a second group, which internalizes them as a part of its own belief system. When this happens the sublimated people have for whatever reasons of incentive or coercion conceded their natural sense of adequacy and worth to an outgroup to which, by definition, they can never belong. A caste has been created, but the lure for "otherness" like the loathing for the self is a cultural imposition and not implicit in any natural predisposition of race or color. For that reason the romanticization of Du Bois's personal struggle and its extrapolation to cover all African Americans as a class must be held suspect as something more than a tribute to his wisdom and insight. Pounced on by a nation still nervous about its own judgment, the Du Boisian dubiety was quickly integrated into the developing arsenal of racialism as a polite explanation for black ineptitude that had been previously taken for granted. In the process, every black individual was reduced from the distinctiveness of personhood to the anonymity of a color class.

The refusal to grant personal distinctiveness to people who are "White," "Black," "Asian," or other serves notice that a judgment of value has already been made, and that it has been made on the basis of some physical feature, which, in America, is to say color. If all Blacks, or all Latinos, "look" alike, it is because the judgment has already been made that they are alike, and therefore predictable in sensibility and behavior. In the face of that prejudgment, an investment in individuation would seem unwarranted, and those who indulge such racial shorthand obviate the necessity of risking meaningful interpersonal encounters in which their private shibboleths may be challenged. This kind of simplistic racial calculus became fixed in American convention quite early, first in the effort to routinize relations with the Indian, and later in the depersonalization of the slave. In each case, manipulation and control were the ultimate objective of the strategy involved. Old habits die hard, and old ideas lurk on in the mind long after the perceived exigencies which occasioned them have been met, or ostensibly abandoned. In consequence we have never developed an effective methodology for dealing with racial and cultural diversity in the absence of a felt need for control or exploitation. This failing bodes no rejoicing as the cosmopolitanization of the American experience moves relentlessly into the twenty-first century. For while color may be the most convenient reference for wholesale manipulation or avoidance, it is also the least reliable index for understanding and interacting with persons. So it was that Du Bois, who if objectively evaluated would have been exceptional in any company irrespective of race, became by conventional reductionism the archetype to an alleged psychosis which disparaged an entire subculture.

Just as the successful projection of ingroup conventions and stereotypes onto associated outgroups exacerbates the fixity of roles, it also encourages the voluntary withdrawal from meaningful social interaction, especially from situations in which the competition for scarce values may be implied or anticipated. During the slave era for example, it was strategic to effective slave management to convince as many slaves as possible that by some implausible sleight of history they were the "sons of Ham" and cursed by God to be perpetual hewers of wood and drawers of water for the sons of Athelstan. Similarly, the convention that to be "African" was to be the subject of an arrested mentality which required "white" control in the best interests of all concerned, weighed heavily against the confidence some black people had in their own leadership, a syndrome that was not fully dissipated until the civil rights movement of post–World War II. In the vernacular of self-censure, "the white man's ice was just naturally colder!" It is the burden of this notion that is sinisterly implicit in the romantic extrapolation of Du Bois's personal struggle as a universal expression of African American identity.

The prevailing values in the culture into which Du Bois was born ran in principle to the equality of persons and the "unalienable rights" of such persons to "life, liberty and the pursuit of happiness." However, principle and practice, even in the most ambitious of human societies, are not always in consonance, and despite its sacredness in the official hierarchy of common values, under stress the understanding conveyed by principle is often tacitly modified to make its meaning more consistent with its actual observance. When this happens the original ideal may remain fixed and burnished in the pantheon of cultural values, but its true function may be reduced to innocuousness. It is relevant and necessary to talk about principle and practice in American culture because the "warring ideals" which troubled Du Bois did not necessarily derive from some sort of personal tragic flaw. There were flaws in the society which mirrored and may well have been the ultimate source of those which troubled him. It is possible to argue that there was nothing wrong with Du Bois, or with those affected by his syndrome, which would not be healed if America herself were healed. This evolving Atlantic civilization, which liked to conceive of itself as a model and a beacon for all future civilizations, was warned early by Alexis de Toqueville that, despite its obvious promise, there were striations of inconsistency in the emerging American national character. A hundred years later those striations had so flawed the national character that Gunnar Myrdal could discern a full-fledged national "dilemma," a society in such fundamental contradiction to the precepts, the creeds, and the principles by which it defined itself as to be constantly grasping for its true identity, the "real" America. In Du Bois's indecision lies the bitter fruit of that dilemma, for in America's failure to find its own true self-consciousness the pattern was set by default. The cryptic disparity between principle and practice, ideal and illusion tinged whatever it touched.

Societies institutionalize their experiences, individuals internalize them. The American dilemma noted by Myrdal on the eve of the Second World War had been a prominent feature of our culture long before Myrdal scratched through the patina of loftiness to a less generous reality underneath. W. E. B. Du Bois was inevitably a child of the American dilemma: a tragic example of a gifted and sensitive progeny born of a house divided against itself. If Du Bois could not determine his identity, it was because his country had been unable to achieve hers, and the identity *assigned* to him by convention was inconsistent with that *guaranteed* to him by the principles upon which the national identity claimed to rest. If there was to be lure and loathing in Du Bois's struggle with the reality he glimpsed so imperfectly through the mesmerism of race, then it was inherent in the contradictions by which he was processed for a future that did not exist. At Fisk University, which had always had a white president and a predominantly white faculty; at Harvard, where even the mere fact of his admission was a monumental waiver of tradition; and at Heidelberg, where his presence and his matriculation could in no sense be considered normative, Du Bois was socialized to be a white man in a society which was not yet prepared to accept him unconditionally as a *person* at any level. His unacceptability made no sense to him. It was a violation of all the orderliness of reason and the sacred mandates of morality with which his socialization had been obsessed. In consequence, his whole life, powered by a formidable intellect and a vision of the redeemability of the principles which undergirded the American Dream, became an unremitting crusade against the illogic and the immorality of the dilemma that held America hostage to her own ideals.

Du Bois's uniqueness as the foremost black intellectual of his time primed him for a destiny he could never fully appropriate, and cursed him for his efforts. A true son of the Enlightenment, he was of course committed to the rule of reason and to the perfectability of human institutions through the logic inherent in the human enterprise. As an American, he was also heir to the Protestant ethic, which called forth the best efforts of human endeavor and blessed them with divine recognition and human approbation. Between reason and religion, how could America fail? Du Bois's prodigious scholarship, his preoccupation with the church, his commitment to civil rights and the rule of law, and his international promotion of the resuscitation and liberation of Africa were all part of a piece. They were all predicated upon the assumption that civilization implies a divinely inspired rule of right, and that to know the right in a civilized, God-fearing society is to do it. Du Bois's whole life was a poignant illustration of the frustration that comes with the eventual recognition that "civilized" societies are not necessarily "logical" in their behavior, and that "religion" and "morality" are as likely to reflect the culture as they are to shape it. His own efforts to overcome the illogicality and the moral repugnance of racialism gradually shifted from scholarship and reason to politics and economics. It all ended in a terminal gesture of nationalism as he chose to die in his African motherland in a final grasping after the peace of mind his American fatherland was unable to afford him. The lure had reversed itself; the loathing had come full circle.

The syndrome I refer to as the Du Boisian dubiety still lives, of course, but it does not have a place of prominence in the ravages of psychic debilitation with which contemporary African Americans must contend. In the first place, few black Americans since Du Bois have been educated to be "white" in a white-controlled society. They know better. There were few precedents for the education of blacks at the time Du Bois was born in 1868, but by the time of his death in 1963, America had delivered to her black children a solid century of separate and unequal education designed from its conception to prepare them for a "place" which had been designated especially for *them* in our expanded order of universal freedom and inclusive citizenship. That message was made quite clear from the beginning. In simple translation it meant that while black citizenship was both genuine and equal, the black citizens were expected to interpret it with the discretion and reservation proper to the station assigned them! Booker T. Washington understood clearly the implications of that *double entendre* and ordered his priorities accordingly, while W. E. B. Du Bois found it so incredible as to spend his life in defiance of it.

The lesson intended was that no matter how conclusive the antecedent circumstances that shut them out from preparation for meaningful participation in the society, African Americans have no legitimate claim whatever on any of the common values America holds in store for its people if those values are preempted by white Americans. Freedom and equality are not retroactive, and the travail of slavery and segregation through which many of those values were amassed, enhanced, or secured counts for nothing. Once America got past the initial shock and the disquieting turbulence of civil rights resistance in the streets, petitions for African American involvement have been routinely denied, ignored, or dismissed as whining appeals for special consideration on the basis of some nebulous notion of "victimization." Obviously, America does not want to hear about victimization, which, if recognized would imply some degree of moral or rational responsibility to help repair the damage. The critical lesson in the rejection of affirmative action is that the *black* holocaust didn't happen, or that even if it did, responsibility died with the mandate that ordained it.

It is a lesson that the spiritual heirs of Du Bois find hard to accept. The "blacks-and-whites together," who marched and prayed and got themselves brutalized in a faithful appeal to the conscience of America are painfully out of step with the realities of post-Reaganism. They have *not* "overcome," and there is scant hope that they will in the foreseeable future. Such "overcoming" as there may be is more likely to inure to an "emergent" class of "new black conservatives" whose operative philosophy is to keep a sharp eye on the weather instead of on the weather report. The variables of the report do not always add up to what they seem, but the weather is always what it is. The so-called new black conservatives are not "new" at all, of course. They are as old as the game of black survival. What is new is that today the game is played with facility and sophistication, avoiding the grace-less intimations of lapsed privileges, battered rights, or convoluted logic which characterizes the civil rights efforts at black participation in the American Dream. The new philosophy is saying that if "rights" are not a realistic option, "resources" are the next best thing. Bread on the table, they say, is better than rights on the books.

In any case it is clear that the critical question for most African Americans has nothing to do with double-consciousness. That question was long since laid to rest by the confirmations of history:

America, you commanded me
And I surrendered up the ancient ways,
The ways I knew before this land became your land,
Before you made your God to be my God.
The ancient ways, the laws I kept, the Gods I knew
are gone. How can I know those ways again
What am I if I am not American?[2]

A more pertinent question than "What am I?" is "How can I be who I am and still hack it in America?" This poses a perplexing issue for all those whose controlling assumptions are that most black Americans have a "Cinderella wish" to be white Americans. This fearsome bugaboo accounts for the national preoccupation with securing the gates and manning the barricades at all costs, with law, economics, religion, social taboo, intimidation, and selective history all thrust into the breach wherever it is perceived to develop. But paranoia has its price, and irony of ironies, the most towering barricades come to naught if there is a crevice in the base. Contemporary demographers predict an America featuring a white minority by the middle of the next century, and they give major credit, and properly so, to changing patterns of immigration and high reproduction ratios common among the non-whites in America, as elsewhere in the world. But little is said about the fact that the browning of America has been an inevitable and unremitting feature of American life from the beginning of the Anglo-African experience at Jamestown, Virginia, almost four hundred years ago. Since that time the widespread dispersion of the Euro-African gene pool in the general American community has become both obvious and exponential, a factor of no little significance to the American dilemma, or to the dubiousness of any allegation of "lure and loathing" that dilemma has produced. Even before the end of slavery it was not unusual for an escaped slave with the right genes to become a "white" man, possibly of power and position, if he could make it to free territory. Ever since the Civil War made every state a "free territory," the countless numbers of "black" Americans who have become "white"

Americans via a simple act of will and a change of scenery cries out for new definitions of what we mean by "black" or "white." In the meantime, given the confidential nature of instant racial metamorphosis, whether it is the push of powerlessness or merely the pull of privilege that trips the button of transition will probably remain forever moot. In the meantime, as more barriers deteriorate and the browning of America moves on inexorably to redefine the horizons which rim our perceptions of racial reality, one wonders if the notion of Du Boisian dubiety will finally become obsolete, or whether even now the software for the more precise calculation of *gens de couleur* and fragments of self-consciousness is being readied for the generation ahead.

Notes

1. Edward Fitzgerald, *The Rubaiyat of Omar Khayyam*, 1879.
2. C. Eric Lincoln, *This Road Since Freedom*. Durham, Carolina Wren Press, 1990.

Primal
Orb
Density

Wanda Coleman

. . . a pimp is really a whore who has reversed the game on whores . . . be as sweet as the scratch, no sweeter . . . always get your money in front just like a whore.

—Iceberg Slim,
Pimp: The Story of My Life

Here I am. I prize myself greatly. I want the world to enjoy me and my art but something's undeniably wrong. I've come to regard myself as a living, breathing statistic governed not by my individual will, even as I will myself to struggle against my own damning analysis, but by forces outside myself. Where do I end and the stats begin? This regard compels me to the podium when I prefer the porch or sitting curbside to watch traffic pass. Who am I but a certain weight, a mass of blood and bone who breaks when dashed to stone? Am I my

---

Wanda Coleman's first book of fiction, *A War of Eyes and Other Stories*, was published by Black Sparrow Press in 1988. Her sixth book from Black Sparrow, *African Sleeping Sickness: Stories and Poems*, appeared in 1990. She received the 1990 Harriette Simpson Arnow prize in fiction awarded by *The American Voice*. *Hand Dance*, her newest collection of poems, will be published in 1993. Her many honors include a residency at Djerassi Foundation and a Guggenheim fellowship in poetry.

people's keeper/griot who sings and in song passes truth along? Could it be my kinkiness/my grade of hair has affected my brain?

Behooved to become adept at articulating pain, through seeing clearly and unapologetically, I am unreconciled in my strivings to overcome the war within and the war without my body; the war in which I measure myself with "the tape of a world that looks on with amused contempt and pity" (W. E. B. Du Bois).

In an attempt to determine my place in this unspeakably brutal reality, I turned to what written works of my forebears I could locate at the time. The one author who singly shed the most light onto my darkness was W. E. B. Du Bois.

Implicit in Du Bois's *The Souls of Black Folk* was the hope that once a successful merging of "his double self" occurred, the strife of the Negro in America would somehow cease. The white America and the black America would eventually become one. His implications were: (1) American society would somehow grasp this transformation of the Negro and recognize it. (2) This unique form of internal fortitude would, almost superhumanly, bolster the Negro against any further physical or emotional onslaught. Du Bois's emphasis was on *faith*, the belief that the obvious wrongs done to the black race would be recognized over time and rectified; that the Negro, by somehow forging his dual identities into one, truly American, would eventually come to assume his rightful place at the table of plenty.

At the beginning of this century, Du Bois could not anticipate that the shape of the table itself would be altered; that perhaps by the time the Negro found his place at it the sumptuous meal would already be devoured; that the souls of black folk might be beset with an altogether new crop of hunger grown on the plantations of a sophisticated technology and an accelerating swiftness in the alternating currents of global affairs.

Du Bois's vision could very well encompass the annihilation of one or two races from the face of the earth; events to arouse a few anthropologists, leaving the rest of Western culture unconcerned. But he could not foresee the computer chip or the arrival of Armageddon at Hiroshima and Nagasaki. He could not anticipate the possible and probable annihilation of the Earth itself; or how facing that probability would affect the souls of all humanity; how these complexities might eclipse the Negro in his struggle; might exacerbate that struggle. However, Du Bois's vision could become seed to and inspire a new generation of "seers."

Contrary to the hope expressed by Du Bois, there is no present-day pity for the plight of black folk on the part of white folk. The "amused contempt" resonates as whites steadfastly deny the realities of black existence in America. Furthermore, the ways in which American social denial takes place have become extremely slick. For example, white denial is manifest in such euphemisms as "hate crimes," a phrase gaining popular media usage in the eighties, designed to mute the powerful images of racism inherent in the action verb phrase "to lynch." It also serves to *reduce* the impact of complaints of racism by blacks-of-slave-origin. This reduction is accomplished by equating violence against Afro-Americans with so-called gender or sex-preference-related violence, or even violence against animals. This false dichotomy ultimately helps to diminish John Q. Public's perception of racism as a national problem. Thus, the language blacks have traditionally used to fight and/or define racism is undergoing deliberate deconstruction.

At the end of this century Du Bois's New Negro faces renewed struggle. Our troubled State of the Race is increasingly expressed in intermittent bursts of urban violence, riots, or unrest. Our struggle is the by-product of a deeper calculated systemic condition endemic to American domestic political apathy and a social denial which has poisoned the American psyche since the atomic devastation of Hiroshima and Nagasaki. Ours is not, nor has it ever been, a nation-specific discourse. Our struggle affects the entire planet and everyone on it. And I must see through to this.

And so I have grown yet another eye, a primal orb density which provides me constant double view. Thus I may observe with such intense focus I become emotionally cock-eyed; so skewed I can't know of any racial incident without relating it to my personal circumstance. It's impossible to read a book or newspaper, watch television or a movie, or listen to music without perceiving the racist ramifications. I even see racism under my bed.

,although he was not a suspect two officers fired multiple rounds from their weapons striking him in the upper torso clad only in his underwear he was pronounced dead at the scene no weapon found

BLACK AMERICA IS UNDER SIEGE

Whose jobs earn the lowest pay?
Black female domestic and health-care workers.

What was begun in the 1920s, and restructured in 1958, was completed with the nullification of the gold standard by President Richard M. Nixon in August 1971, when America's economy (and the world's) essentially became a gigantic currency pyramid scam as an end came to the U.S. commitment to swap gold for dollars in the world money chase.

Domestically, in order for those at the top of the pyramid to remain there (and a chosen few at bottom and middle levels to rise), a strong and solid base of the disenfranchised must be maintained. This base consists of the most minimally stable individuals the nation produces: the lower middle and poor working classes.

I am a member of the latter.

The hellish circle I go around and around in is called the effects of the stock-market indicator on a poor black working-class mother born west of the Hudson River, created in Southern California, raised in the Los Angeles *barrio* of Watts.

During the angel-dust rage, ante-crack, I received googobs of criticism for living in "the boonies." I was stuck there because it was the only area where I could find decent housing at fair rates. Black friends egged me to "return to civilization"; white friends never visited. On one occasion I poured out my survival miseries to an old Maoist revolutionary buddy, an expert on black capitalism. After soundly criticizing my ghetto lifestyle, he suggested I relocate to Jonestown. He had just returned from Guyana and was quite impressed with Jim Jones's little colony and thought it just the cure.

her body was found hanging from a tree in the suburban community she was young and poorly dressed sheriff's spokesmen said there was no obvious indication of suicide

What is Never Never Land?
The place black applicants go to get home loans at higher interest rates.

BLACK STUDENTS, 16 PERCENT OF THE NATION'S
PUBLIC SCHOOL POPULATION, ARE TWICE AS LIKELY AS WHITES
TO BE SUSPENDED, RECEIVE CORPORAL PUNISHMENT,
OR BE CLASSIFIED RETARDED

To further strengthen the pyramid's base and keep it solid (because, remember, if it isn't kept solid the whole structure will become unstable and cave in on itself and virtually everyone will lose, even those on the bottom who've been there all the time and have little hope of elevation), corporations, businesses, and wealthy individuals must be competitive as they operate their variations of economic scam. In the process the worker/employee/flunky becomes more and more modular in nature (the name changes but the game's the same) and significantly less important to the workplace, therefore replaced with minimal if any disruption in the cash flow. This increasing devaluation of the worker includes loss of such benefits as medical and/or dental insurance. Workers are routinely fired as they approach retirement. The age of the full-time wage earner is passing as America not only becomes a nation of service, but a nation of part-timers. In this climate of cutbacks and union busting the traditional work ethic (quality, loyalty, integrity, sincerity) is invalid if not downright disadvantageous. The worker, white-, blue-, or pink-collar, has become devalued or dehumanized. The laws of the streets have become the laws of the boardroom.

With each severe shrinkage of the American economic pie prospects dim for those who have never gotten their bite of a slice.

he was shot and killed they believed he had pointed a gun bystanders said he was unarmed and fleeing a beer in his hand when he was shot in the back of his neck no gun was found

SUBPOVERTY JOBS REPLACE MIDDLE-WAGE JOBS
WHILE NUMBER OF HIGH-WAGE JOBS FALL

The process of worker dehumanization has been aided by the rapid advance of computer technology. Ultimately every participant in the economy not sequestered in wealth, who must earn money to survive, is increasingly forced to obey the dictates of those at the top while having fewer and fewer opportunities of acquiring wealth by his/her own honest sweat. This is the world according to Las Vegas, as society becomes a casino where luck is a matter of fixed calculation and the odds are with the house.

The economic effectiveness of the earnings of those on the bottom of the pyramid are minimized by taxing, in one form or another, the necessities: food, shelter, family, medical care, and the grave. The ability of those at the bottom to transcend their circumstances are minimalized by limited access to education, information, and the media. It is impossible to pull oneself up by one's own bootstraps if one has no boots.

Now factor in race.

Primal Orb Density

FAILURE OF GOVERNMENT TO TAKE POSITIVE ROLE IN ENDING RACISM

To maintain their rarefied places, those at the top of the pyramid, with maximum power, may change the rules of scam with minimum effort (be the motivation religious, political, self-interested, racist, gender specific, class based, or complex combinations thereof). Doing so ensures keeping the bottom the bottom. Because of their powerlessness, those at the base of the pyramid are only effective when able to organize en masse. Their inability to organize is frequently exacerbated by differences in ethnicity, gender, and degree of hunger.

they saw him running it remained unclear whether he actually was the target and police officers involved declined comment the man was not armed and was not a gang member according to witnesses

What is a buppie?
A fictitious segment created to substantiate the illusion of "overall betterment" for the equally fictitious "black mainstream."

I must censor myself to obtain what I need to liberate myself from poverty. This psychological Möbius is numbing in the traversing. In order to establish communication with a sensibility unlike mine I have to gauge the points of potential cultural collisions, then navigate accordingly. This faculty, my primal orb density, like a periscope, enables me to pierce the layerings of social prejudice and steer an intelligent course (dialogue) through its terror-infested waters (assumptions based on ignorance).

In my eye, my frantic scramblings to become substantial, I imagine myself functionally insane, operating within the constraints of a society itself driven mad, made sick by its unresolved history of slavery and ongoing trauma of racism.

"The enemy is aware of . . . ideological weaknesses, for he analyzes the forces of rebellion and studies more and more carefully the aggregate enemy . . . he is also aware of the spiritual instability of certain layers of the population. The enemy discovers the existence, side by side with the disciplined and well-organized advance guard . . . a mass . . . whose participation is constantly at the mercy of their being for too long accustomed to physiological wretchedness, humiliation and irresponsibility. The enemy is ready to pay a high price for the services of this mass." (Frantz Fanon, *The Wretched of the Earth*.)

as she watched television she was rendered brain dead by a single shot to her head she died hours later police call the incident an apparent drive-by shooting no suspects identified at this time

UNEMPLOYMENT OF BLACKS MORE THAN
TWICE THAT OF WHITES

The horrible irony of the Federal Government's passing laws to impose the death penalty on drug dealers is that it, itself, is the granddaddy of all drug dealers; using alcohol to devastate the nation's indigenous population; using the criminal underworld to introduce heroin into the veins of its black underclass.

The death penalty is not meant to eliminate drug usage and dealing. It simply redefines the context under which usage and dealing occur, especially in the black community, where drugs have always repre-sented "the devil's work," the most heinous means of escaping stul-tifying poverty for the circumstantially failed. The death penalty is one more device to keep "certain elements" from rising to the top of the pyramid.

THE AIDS DEATH RATE FOR BLACKS IS THREE TIMES
GREATER THAN FOR WHITES

". . . he's a Negro, he has a right to sell drugs 'cause Whitey makes it impossible for a Black to make enough honest bread." (Charles Mingus, *Beneath the Underdog*)

Drugs have historically proved effective tools of creating and oppressing an underclass as long as the designated freebooters controlled traffic, those designated being members of the dominant culture and allowed to ascend in the pyramidal hierarchy (to schmooze with the pharaohs).

As a result of cultural shift, political developments "south of the border" brought in immigrant drug dealers who went straight into America's ghettos to exploit whomever they found there, mainly us blacks, according to their own needs. Control unexpectedly fell into the hands of a new breed of gangsters-of-color, young black and Hispanic males set on "living large."

responding to a complaint of domestic violence they ordered him to place his hands on his head without provocation they clenched him from behind began to drag him backward began to knee him in the groin and strike him in the face though he was unarmed and offered only natural resistance to the blows to his groin the officer drew a revolver and shot him in the back

What is a choke hold?
Asphyxiation due to wallet restraint for abnormal behavior associated with constant copings with racism exacerbated by a hostile and combative attitude.

THE KILLER OF A WHITE PERSON IS MORE LIKELY TO BE
SENTENCED TO DEATH
THAN THE KILLER OF A BLACK PERSON

I play on racist assumptions to facilitate my daily doings. There is the woman of diverse feelings and capabilities. There is the stereotyped angry young black poet who only gets applause as long as her teeth are bared. It makes life easier on the one hand. On the other, dangers arise if I'm to maintain integrity. How morally strong am I? If I fail how much of myself will I be able to salvage as I scramble for my spot in the pyramidal hierarchy?

Poetry has little monetary value in society and being black compounds the issue.

To paraphrase Justice Thurgood Marshall: A black child born to the most ignorant, poorest black mother in these United States, by "act of breath," has exactly the same value, worth, and rights as a white baby born to the wealthiest, most intelligent white woman.

With the establishment of direct links to the drug source, dominant-culture freebooters, despised because of their raw, unconcealed bigotry, were suddenly unemployed insofar as the dope business was concerned. This was an unexpected circumstance which allowed enterprising black and Hispanic males to claw their way into the pyramid elite, if over the backs of their peers. Therefore, it was incumbent upon those freebooters who hadn't cemented their positions on top to get out of the dope business.

Once the dominant culture perceived dealers were no longer predominantly ethnically white, it was permissible to impose the death penalty since the lives of blacks, Hispanics, and poor whites traditionally remain devalued.

he was wandering in the middle of the street acting bizarre he received three jolts from the taser gun but they had no effect officers employed a swarm technique and brought him to the ground he died as a result of the altercation while being treated in the emergency room a coroner's spokesman said no cause of death had been determined pending outcome of toxicological tests

URBAN BLACK MALES ARE LESS LIKELY TO REACH
AGE SIXTY-FIVE THAN MEN IN BANGLADESH

What is workfare?

Unskilled welfare mothers forced to leave preschool children to go to work yet expected to provide adequate child care on lower than average wages.

Delicious irony is that the political vision of Americans of color is so effectively clouded the majority fail to see how the death penalty is leveled specifically at their own males. Most of our law-abiding voters would, predictably, favor the penalty, failing to understand the sophisticated economic dynamics behind it, and would be rightly unsympathetic to those who feed so destructively on their own kind.

My poet consciousness shattered, I nevertheless armor myself for battle with the secondary me defined by the American conspiracy of circumstance. It is this second self who poses problems/is a barrier I must break through in order to effectively communicate. This barrier self resides in the eyes of those with whom I conduct my daily doings: my attorney, a bank teller, my lover, a child, a grocery-store clerk, and so on. For example, if I want a job, I have to carry myself in a way which is nonthreatening or seen as safe by my white employer. The energy I exert in this barrier-busting exhausts me. My opinions and values must be suppressed. The only place I experience liberty is on the page (within limits of what's salable imposed by the white publishing establishment). I cannot afford to do otherwise in the course of daily commerce without dooming my primary self. The means by which I protect myself have come as gifts from mentors who've taken time to "school" me or "give me game."

the twenty-five-year-old man was hospitalized bruised and comatose after his arrest he never regained consciousness officials maintained he was drunk and died while violently resisting arrest

THE AVERAGE BLACK FAMILY EARNS HALF
AS MUCH AS THE AVERAGE WHITE FAMILY

There's a lot of serious moola in hate: white men experience unfavorable treatment in 27 percent of their job searches while black applicants are treated unfavorably in 50 percent of theirs. White applicants are three times as likely to receive job offers and almost three times as likely to advance in the hiring process over blacks. Fifteen percent of white applicants receive job offers compared to only 5 percent of blacks.

It's all about value. The value of life vis-à-vis money. You are only worth your weight in dollars inherited or earned. When the dollar is devalued so are you. Now what do you do when your skin cripples your earning capacity?

In transmuting the U.S. economy into a pyramid scam, additional phenomena had to take place: an erosion (or politicizing) of the illusive moral underpinnings of the nation, the Constitution and Bill of Rights. The ideals embodied in these documents, fodder for political careers, have to be controlled and the national waters muddied if the financial infrastructure of the pyramid is to be maintained.

These ideals never existed in reality, especially for the slave underclass. Yet these ideals became *dangerous* once black demands for equality and first-class citizenship gained enough leadership momentum to become the civil rights movement with its battle cry of one-man-one-vote. They had to be neutralized by devaluating worker status as well. The era of the blue-collar wealthy was short-lived. Without full realization on the part of the worker his/her prostitution was legalized.

EROSION OF PAST GAINS

My delicious dilemma is language. How I structure it. How the fiction of history structures me. And as I've become more and more shattered, my tongue is likewise and I find conventional forms and dialogues stifling, draining—to be glassed in by language in addition to the barriers of my dark skin and financial embarrassment. Under these contraints I cannot reconcile myself with such dualities: black/white, male/female, mother/daughter, child/adult, friend/lover, worker/artist, street/university, hard/soft, as they kaleidoscopically affect a whole.

"The race problem is not a problem of the facts of biology, of scientific data thoroughly analyzed and systematically taught. It is first and foremost a social problem which can be satisfactorily dealt with by social means of a kind which will require important revisions of some of our present ideas. For until the psychological disturbances which are created in the person by our processes of socialization are modified, the race problem will continue to plague us. Hence, the importance of inquiring into the nature of these processes and the effects which they produce upon behavior." (Ashley Montagu, *Race, Science, and Humanity*)

he played with his prized toy gun all the time he waved it around and would point it at anything residents tried to look out for the 6-foot-tall 180-pound retarded 13-year-old police officers mistook his plastic pistol for a real weapon, drew their guns and fired four shots from their .357 Magnum service revolvers

BLACKS ARE MORE LIKELY THAN WHITES
TO BE VICTIMS OF MAJOR VIOLENT CRIMES AND BURGLARIES

There are moments when I doubt the clarity with which I see the world; say to myself, "This can't be," or dismiss what I've seen as madness. My vision, a second sight, allows me to distinguish between matters of racial prejudice and matters of taste. It also allows me to cope with that strange post-sixties phenomenon in which anyone non-black who personally knows someone black fancies himself/herself expert on the black condition.

Should black Americans of slave origin successfully obtain the social parity rightly demanded, persistently appealing to the so-called morals of a nation (as did the Southern Christian Leadership Conference and Martin Luther King), we would effectively share economic power, would be able to alter the cultural dynamics of the pyramid. The danger of black social parity was foreseen by the pyramid's elite and to date successfully aborted.

But where is the sanity in appealing to the morality of a nation whose economic wealth is rooted in the immorality of slavery and whose growth is predicated on the ongoing, sophisticated process of dehumanization?

she answered a knock at her door was shot as the two men opened fire she died at a nearby hospital her youngest son standing behind her was killed on the spot a sixteen-year-old who wanted to become an actor the two gunmen retaliated for a weekend slaying they believed committed by the older son

NEGATIVE TO ZERO NET PERSONAL WEALTH

If I make an assertion about my particular black experience invariably it will be countered by the experience of another black individual. I have no authority and to use myself as a standard proves valueless in marketing myself to the white literary establishment. No matter how many prizes I win I am still "just another niggah." This stereotyping diminishes the significance of black thought when any and all blacks are considered experts on themselves at a man-in-the-street level.

Should the word of a nineteen-year-old gangbanger carry the same weight as a fifty-year-old university professor? Are we talking UZIs or "Ulalume"? Other ethnic groups are granted their intellectuals but (our) black spokesmen/women seem forever held suspect, ever having to substantiate themselves; one can never have too many credentials or pay too many dues.

If black individuals were allowed to pursue their notion of the American Dream it would mean full black participation in the shaping of America's future, its language, its eco-political terrain. Ramifications would be worldwide, the assumption being that black influence would be so great it would cause familiar terrain to become unrecognizable if not infertile for ethnic others on every level (as in certain contact sports). The game and the name would irrevocably change.

his body was found hanging from a fig tree along with a suicide note testimony from a handwriting analyst claimed the note was not written by him it was determined the hanging death of this young black homosexual was unrelated to the same-night assault on two black men by men in KKK robes

Five easy steps toward the eradication of poverty (token solution designed to counter criticism that all black intellectuals must provide solutions if to merit serious consideration):

1. Minimum-wage increases tied to cost-of-living index.
2. Government subsidized child-care programs.
3. Nationalized medicine and health care.
4. Mandatory education through four years of college.
5. Rigid enforcement of antidiscrimination laws.

NATIONAL CLIMATE OF SELFISHNESS

They come to these shores psyches intact. They know who they are despite oppressive governments and strife. They've never been subjected to the immense cultural negative feedback American blacks suffer. These immigrants, including those of similar coloration, willingly buy into the All-American Lie and isolate themselves from blacks only to the extent they can use our backs to strengthen their own positions economically.

I mean, what do I say when my son's first experience of being called "nigger" is provided by the son of a Nicaraguan émigré.

We blacks remain the lowest, least-integrated underclass in a "nation of immigrants," albeit ours was the forced immigration of slavery. At the end of the 1960s it was apparent that once we achieved full citizenship (ceasing to be wards of the Federal Government or "second-class citizens") then (automatically) what was true for black Americans, of slave origin, would automatically be true for every other oppressed group within society. This recognition gave rebirth to the white women's movement, American Indian movement, Gay Liberation, the Brown Berets, the anti–Vietnamese War activism etc. ad nauseam. The only problem being that racism as it manifested itself on America's political left caused these second-level social "movements" to evolve apart from the thrust of the civil rights and black power movements instead of *in tandem* with them; borrowing strategies, rhetoric, and style.

the fifteen-year-old girl was shot by the foreign-born owner of a liquor store in dispute over a bottle of orange juice when the girl gave it back and tried to walk away the store owner shot the black teenager in the back of the head killing her

COLOR-BLIND SOCIETY

What is a black farmer?

A species it is predicted will be extinct by mid-next-century as they are losing their land two and a half times faster than white counterparts.

Lyndon Baines Johnson's misguided "War on Poverty" bureaucracy reinforced the social evil it arrogantly presumed to eliminate. It failed because the extent to which racism permeates every aspect of the American psyche was underestimated. At the close of the seventies many blacks felt abused by Jews, white women, gays, and anybody else who stood to gain from the January 1964 ratification of the 24th Amendment and the passage of the civil rights bill on June 29, 1964, and from the subsequent push for affirmative action, for that matter, precisely because *skin color* per se was never a major issue for these factions. Thanks to advances in medical science one can alter one's facial features, sex organs, and hair; however the skin-color change has yet to be perfected.

Plus there was an unexpected outcrop of trendy, safe, and sometimes frivolous movements, some rooted in Christian fundamentalism, which allowed many dominant-culture cause-niks to get their protest kicks without exposing themselves to the kind of violence suffered by those at Kent State. These movements served the double purpose of luring the attention of the media, keeping focus off the deeper, more urgent issues of race.

the despondent mother who had been evicted from her apartment fatally stabbed her children then leapt to her death from a thirteen-story building

TWO THIRDS OF CHILDREN IN
BLACK FEMALE-HEADED HOUSEHOLDS
LIVE IN POVERTY

The pathology associated with skin color and how it affects one's ability to survive and/or move from one socioeconomic class to another, was and still is of major significance for those like me who identify as black Americans. Once we began to wield newfound political clout with cries of "Black Power," whites who embraced us during the civil rights phase of the struggle could not understand a fledgling, almost adolescent, expression of a people who wanted long-denied social parity *on their own terms.* This naïve nationalistic rush would not be supported by their philanthropic dollars.

> *someone in a passing car swung through the quiet neighborhood fired two shots at random toward the muted light filtering through kitchen curtains the forty-five-year-old schoolteacher was struck once in the head she was pronounced dead several hours later*

INADEQUATE WELFARE BENEFITS
CONTRIBUTE TO HOMELESSNESS

Not all the pyramid elite are unsympathetic to those at the bottom. During the civil rights movement some channeled money to various groups and causes or underwrote individual leaders. Wealthy individuals, businesses, and corporations could afford to sponsor cause-of-choice and still get a break from the government through certain tax loopholes and deductions. A second step in muddying the moral waters of the nation was in altering the tax structure to close those loopholes and impose new limits on deductions, making certain pursuits less profitable as tax shelters. This effectively cut off major cash flow to the black subculture. The recession and oil crisis of the early seventies polished off the rest.

Once monies, and so-called guilt funds, were effectively dried up, the movements they supported collapsed.

As the seer beyond the veil, as gifted possessor of a primal orb, I am compelled to explain and explain, to join a chorus of explainers articulating the black/Afro-American experience, constantly providing the context in which I will be more clearly understood and perhaps appreciated. Success at this brings on euphoria, failure despair.

*a twenty-one-year-old black man died under mysterious circumstances
after his arrest for reckless driving the coroner's special team reported
unanimously he burned himself out suffering a sudden cardiorespiratory
collapse the result of stress and exhaustion*

AMERICAN APARTHEID

The pyramid scam underscoring America's truly voodoo economics
is maintained by actual human sacrifice, the lives of those at the bottom
of that pyramid; those most vulnerable to changes in the stock-market
indicators; those most likely to be devastated by social ills from drugs
to acquired immunodeficiency syndrome (AIDS). Whenever the
garden-variety all-American Negro accentuates the positive, eliminates
the negative, and latches onto the affirmative in transcending cultural
bias, a countermove is made to mess up any and all progress (failure
to enforce legislation, use of immigration to fuel the underclass while
simultaneously setting back black advancements, deregulation, and
so on).

Socioeconomic factors coupled with the persistence of white prejudice and the layering on of new immigrants compounds fin de siècle
black segregation.

*the thirty-four-year-old bus driver was shot seven times in front of his
home police officers said they thought they heard a sliding gun bolt and
fired after he failed to raise his hands as ordered*

THERE IS NO CHANCE OF BLACKS' CATCHING UP
WITH WHITES BEFORE
THE MIDDLE OF THE TWENTY-SECOND CENTURY

Does the process of making the invisible visible transform the seer
as well as the seen? When does the victim become the perpetrator? A
panel of experts says, a Ph.D. study addresses, a recent poll reveals,
a committee report states, a government report issued says, a national

study determines, a crime survey indicates, and a federal study finds . . .

Some reversal of these oppressive social circumstances must be found if one is to effectively "pimp the system."

The diabolical beauty of the American pyramid scam is that blacks, like any other segment of society, must buy into the lie of white racial superiority if they are to succeed within the structure. And to buy into one's (race's) ultimate self-destruction is pathological.

It is this devastating knowledge that develops my other eye, strengthens my dual seeing. If I am to do more than merely survive it is imperative that I see clearly. I must not allow the fact that I'm born a statistic, a living comment on the hypocrisy of my America, to cloud my vision. Yet I am compelled to wonder where the statistics end and I begin. And if I persist as a statistic have I the terrible fate of dying as one?

The Illusion of
Racial Equality:
The Black American
Dilemma

Robert Staples

Never in the history of *Homo sapiens* has a society brought together so many cultural, religious, and racial groups in one country as the twentieth-century United States. Protestants, Catholics, Jews, Buddhists, Muslims, Italians, Africans, Chinese, Mexicans, Indians, all live together under the same government and operate in the same economy. This diversity is all the more striking when it is noted that none of these groups are at war with each other, that they coexist peaceably. This situation runs counter to the experiences of other countries in the world, where conflicts between ethnic and religious groups are epidemic. In 1986, more than five million people worldwide died as a result of ethnic and religious conflicts.[1]

As a society dominated by people of European ancestry, the U.S.A. appears to have accommodated people of different national origins while European governments are besieged and in danger of being toppled by the small number of non-European immigrants allowed

---

Robert Staples is a Professor of Sociology at the University of California in San Francisco. He has been the recipient of distinguished achievement awards from Howard University and the National Council on Family Relations. Professor Staples has been widely published in popular and scholarly periodicals in the United States and around the world. Among his books are *Black Masculinity*, *The Urban Plantation*, and *Black Families at the Crossroads*.

into their countries. Whereas most countries, in the latter part of the twentieth century, have permitted immigration on the basis of labor demand and personal wealth, American immigration policies have favored the family ties and refugee status of American citizens. Consequently, 85 percent of the legal immigration to the United States for the last twenty years has involved citizens of Latin America, Asia, the Caribbean, and Africa. The white, non-Hispanic population in 1990 was recorded as 75 percent of the American population and, if current immigration and birthrate trends prevail, fewer than half of this country's citizens will be non-Hispanic whites in the year 2080.[2] Further testament to the efficacy of the melting-pot theory is the high rate of intermarriage between these different groups. Most telling is the statistic that shows that Jews, a group that has faced persecution for most of its existence on this planet, have a minority of their members married within the same faith.[3]

It is within the Afro-American community that America's blend of free-wheeling capitalism and political democracy has produced the most startling success stories—or so it seems. Having come to the American continent, first as indentured servants, later as slaves, suffering from the most vicious form of segregation and discrimination in the post-slavery era, they have risen to heights never envisioned for any group that occupied such low status. Jesse Jackson's slogan "From the out-house to the White House" belies the struggle of this nation to keep its black population in a perpetually subjugated condition since their arrival. Having used their labor, destroyed their culture and family life, the American version of apartheid and the caste system was erected after the official end of slavery. The white South created dual public institutions to degrade them, and states outside Dixie used informal rules to establish a ceiling on their aspirations and status. The black condition was best summed up in the saying: "No black shall ever rise above the lowest status of a white man."

Perforce, 1990s America has witnessed a dramatic turnaround of this country's determination to see and treat all black Americans as subhumans. This reversal did not come without a great deal of turmoil for a country whose self-definition is "the world's greatest democracy." It fought a bloody civil war over the issue of black slavery, perverted many of its institutions to protect racial inequality, endured mass demonstrations and protest against Jim Crow over a twenty-year period before officially eliminating the practice, and witnessed its major cities in flames during the 1960s as rebellions by blacks occurred throughout the nation. Because the civil rights movement and urban rebellions transpired during the expansionist and neo-colonial phase of capitalism, the pragmatic captains of industry and government decided that the caste line had to be abolished. Civil rights laws, recruitment of blacks into heretofore excluded positions, affirmative action regulations, loans, scholarships, social programs, set asides, and so on were gradually used to reduce the absolute caste line extant in 1940.

Those measures bore fruit in the 1990s when the world's largest black middle class was created. Overall, black Americans had a total income of $300 billion a year, a figure that equals the income of the twelfth-largest nation in the world. The median household income of black married couples, in 1990, was $33,893, giving them almost the highest standard of living in the world. Blacks also have a median educational level of 12.2 years, higher than most Europeans. More than a million blacks were enrolled in institutions of higher learning in 1991.[4] More than other people of color, blacks appear to be integrated into the institutional life of American society. On the political level, they serve in the president's cabinet as his advisers, on the Supreme Court, as governors of states, as presidential candidates, as the head of the military, and as mayors of the nation's largest cities. In the major sports, amateur and professional, blacks dominate and earn millions of dollars in salaries and commercial endorsements. Three of the five wealthiest entertainers in America are black, the biggest box-office stars and highest-rated TV shows have, in the past, been black, and the largest sales of a record album are by a black performer. Not all blacks in the entertainment industry are performers. In 1991, two dozen theatrical films were directed by blacks, starring black actors and actresses.

One might think that 1990s America is a racial utopia—or close to it. Certainly a black sociologist from Harvard, Orlando Patterson, believed it to be true when he wrote in *The New York Times* that "the sociological truths are that America, while still flawed in its race relations and its stubborn refusal to institute a national, universal welfare system, is now the least racist white majority society in the world; has a better record of legal protection of minorities than any other society, white or black; offers more opportunities to a greater number of black persons than any other society, including those of Africa; and has gone through a dramatic change in its attitude toward miscegenation over the past 25 years."[5] Professor Patterson is regarded as a color-blind neo-conservative, which helps to explain his pollyannaish view of race relations. Another view is held by an Afro-American filmmaker, who has earned millions in the movie industry. Douglas McHenry is quoted as saying, "Today there is probably more segregation and less tolerance than there was. More than ever, there are two Americas."[6]

Ironically, both men are essentially correct. The U.S., with a white majority, has made more accommodations to its racial diversity than any other country largely composed of Europeans. Even South American countries, with their pervasive pattern of miscegenation, have reserved the most powerful and prestigious positions for those most clearly identified as of European ancestry. The Patterson argument is most flawed when it depicts the U.S. as "the least racist white majority society in the world." However one defines racism in the 1990s, this country is more racially segregated and its institutions more race driven than any country outside South Africa. This fact, at least for the Euro-American population, has been disguised by the emerging racial ideology of the "color-blind theory." This theory has as its main premise that after 365 years of slavery and legal segregation, only 25 years of governmental laws and actions were necessary to reverse the historical systematic and legalized segregation and inequality in this country, and no further remedial effort is needed. The net effect of the color-blind theory is to institutionalize and stabilize the status quo of race relations for the twenty-first century: white privilege and black deprivation. Most notable among the proponents of the color-blind theory are the ideological descendants of the theories that slavery was necessary to make Christians out of African savages, that the South could operate separate but equal facilities and Jim Crow could not be abolished because it interfered with states' rights.

The color-blind theory ignores the reality of 1990s America: that race determines everyone's life chances in this country. In any area where there is significant racial diversity, race impacts on where people live and go to school, whom they vote for, date, and marry, with whom they do business, who they buy from or sell to, how much they pay, and so on. This does not sound like the racial utopia Martin Luther King dreamed of. Indeed, it may have been his worst nightmare. Yet there could be a worst nightmare for the prophet of racial equality. How would he have felt if he had watched his former lieutenants endorse the right-wing Ronald Reagan for president in 1980, or the organization he founded, the Southern Christian Leadership Conference, remain neutral on the appointment of Clarence Thomas to the U.S. Supreme Court—a neutrality tantamount to the support provided by Strom Thurmond, Jesse Helms, and David Duke (former Grand Dragon of the Ku Klux Klan). The complexities of race in 1990s America are enough to confuse any outsider who has read the history of race relations in the U.S.

In part, to sort out the contradictions in American race relations, it is necessary to look at the other side of the black success story. Despite the largest black middle class in the world, the average black household income is only 56 percent of white household income. More than 32 percent of black households have incomes below the poverty line. The high income of black married-couple households is a function of multiple workers in those households. Moreover, poverty in the

U.S. is increasingly synonymous with people of color. Only 8 percent of whites are considered poor, and they are disproportionately found among the elderly, women with children, and rural and farm families. Of all Western nations, the United States has the greatest inequality of wealth. According to an international study, poverty in the U.S. is more widespread and more severe: poor families here stay poor longer; and government programs of assistance are the least able to lift families with children out of poverty.[7]

Poverty also is more likely to be spread among the nonelderly households and to be widely distributed across all age and family groups. It is this class of poor people of color that make up a majority. In the more racially homogeneous countries of Europe, Australia, and New Zealand, government welfare programs and subsidies have eliminated the kind of massive poverty found among young households in this country. The tolerance of pervasive poverty, malnutrition, and homelessness can only be related to the perception that it is people of color who bear the brunt of American poverty and the reasons attributed to are their failure to get an education and work hard. When asked if the Federal Government should see to it that every person has a job and a good standard of living, 65 percent of blacks said it should, but only 24 percent of whites thought so. Euro-Americans were more inclined to give support to the idea of "individuals getting ahead on their own," versus government intervention.[8] Surely the racial differences in attitude toward government assistance is linked to the fact that unemployment, for white male heads of households, is less than 6 percent, and as many as 46 percent of Black males sixteen to sixty-two years of age are not in the labor force. Moreover, money is not the only measure of wealth in 1990s America. Noncash assets are easily convertible into cash. They include stocks, bonds, businesses, property, and so on, a total of $10 trillion. Given the concentration of wealth in the U.S., Euro-Americans will control 97 percent of those assets. Most blacks have only their homes and automobiles as assets. Because black homes tend to be located in black neighborhoods, their value is inherently less than those of similar homes in white neighborhoods.[9]

Based on any variable that can be statistically measured, blacks have not achieved racial equality in any area of American life. And they are overrepresented on every negative variable except suicide, itself a mixed blessing since black suicide rates are highest among its young people in contrast to white suicide rates weighted toward its oldest members. And the direction of change in the U.S. has made some conditions worse than in the era before the civil rights movement. In 1950 the black unemployment rate was double that of whites: in 1990 it was triple. Housing and school segregation are worse outside the South in 1990 than in 1950. The inequality of wealth is greater in 1990 than in 1950, when most people earned money from wages. In the 1990s, people earn money, in larger numbers, from stocks, bonds, property, leveraged buyouts, etc. The percent of intact black families vis-à-vis white families was much higher in 1950 than in 1990, as was the lower number of black children born in wedlock. The times they are changing but things remain the same.[10]

For some reason this society documents but does not change many of its discriminatory practices. There are numerous studies, most of them conducted by Euro-Americans, showing the retention of racial discrimination in employment, housing, education, health care, and so on. One study found that 75 percent of black men seeking employment were discriminated against.[11] In another investigation of housing discrimination, it was discovered that blacks face discrimination 56 percent of the time they seek to rent a house and 59 percent of the time they try to buy a home.[12] Other studies reveal black patients in a hospital were more likely to be sent to inexperienced medical doctors and that car dealers were likely to charge Afro-Americans and women higher prices than white males. The number of studies showing racial discrimination in every facet of American life makes a mockery of the color-blind theory and Patterson's claim that this is the least-racist white majority society in the world.

Adding to the scholarly studies of racial discrimination are the TV shows, like 60 *Minutes*, which showed an employment agency using special codes to avoid sending black applicants to employers for jobs. On September 26, 1991, the show *Prime Time Live* showed a nationwide audience what it's like to be black in 1990s America. They sent two twenty-eight-year-old men, Glen Brewer, black, and John Kuhnen, white, to shop in the same stores, attempt to rent the same apartment, and apply for the same job. Here are the results of their experiment in the city of St. Louis:

> At several stores, Mr. Kuhnen gets instant service: Mr. Brewer is ignored except at a record store, where a salesman keeps a close eye on him, without offering any assistance. When they go for a walk, separately on the same street, a police car passes Mr. Kuhnen but slows down to give Mr. Brewer a once-over. At a car dealership, Mr. Kuhnen is offered a lower price and better financing terms than Mr. Brewer. Inquiring about a job at a dry cleaner that has advertised for help, Mr. Kuhnen is told jobs are still available; Mr. Brewer is told, "The positions are taken." Following up a for-rent sign, Mr. Kuhnen is promptly offered an apartment, which he does not take; ten minutes later, Mr. Brewer is told it has been rented for hours.[13]

That program gave Euro-Americans a visual lesson in the mundane indignities that many Afro-Americans experience day after day. Of course, only the most naïve white viewer should have been surprised at the results. Despite the color-blind theory, white claims of reverse racism and preferential treatment for blacks, there is no queue of whites claiming black heritage to qualify for the "benefits" of black membership. The color-blind theory is a smokescreen to mask the persistence of a racial hierarchy in American life. Blacks who buy into the theory are easily manipulated, compare themselves to their poorer brothers on the African continent, and measure their progress by those standards, and a small but increasing number of black opportunists who seek to reap the rewards of catering to Euro-American prejudices. The illusion of racial equality seems real because tokenism begins at the top and slowly trickles down to the bottom. Only a small number of elite positions are available in 1990s America and they are often visible to everyone. Few Euro-Americans make claims on the elite positions albeit they are very desired. Selection or appointment is very subjective and the qualifications ambiguous. Thus, it is easier to integrate the elite positions, such as Miss America or head of the military, involving a few thousand people than provide equal employment opportunities for millions of black and white workers. The blacks see their members in elite positions and take pride in their achievements, although their own situations have not improved—reflected glory. Euro-Americans see those same blacks and can rationalize a dramatic change in the racial character of American society while thinking that the poor, homeless, and criminals could have made similar achievements if they had gotten an education and worked hard.

The illusions of racial equality are best exemplified in the two areas in which blacks appear to dominate: entertainment and sports. While three of the five wealthiest entertainers are black (Oprah Winfrey, Bill Cosby, and Michael Jackson), they are not the wealthiest people in the entertainment industry.[14] Those people are white and own and/or manage record companies, talent-management agencies, movie studios, and so on. Because black entertainers often have unique skills and American society highlights all black entry into elite positions, they have a visibility difficult for Euro-American entertainers to attain. However, there are thousands of Euro-Americans we do not know about earning millions yearly from the entertainment industry. There are comparatively few black millionaires in show business and we tend to know them all. Moreover, even among the wealthy black entertainers, their income is divided up among agents, attorneys, accountants, producers, and so on. In most cases those people are white. There is virtually no white entertainer who shares any significant portion of his/her income with a black person.

It is possible that Euro-Americans take 97 percent of the dollars spent on entertainment produced in this country and distributed to the rest of the world. Thus, black success in the entertainment world is racial tokenism at its worst. And the constraints of race dictate the kind of entertainment product that blacks are allowed to exhibit. Although people of color buy 38 percent of the movie tickets, almost all the blacks starring in movies are men and comedians. Former basketball star Wilt Chamberlain has written, "The movie industry is still back in the 1930's and 1940's. The Eddie ("Rochester") Andersons and Stepin Fetchits of today are the Eddie Murphys and Richard Pryors. Producers give starring roles to comedians and let them make a lot of money, but they never cast people of color in the roles of real heroes."[15] The same is true of prime-time television, where blacks are frequently relegated to scattered token roles or the clownish context of a situation comedy. With the exception of the now defunct Cosby show, most of the prime-time sitcoms featuring blacks portray them in particularly stereotyped roles. One NAACP study found that "No Black executive makes final decisions in the motion picture or television industry, that only a handful of Afro-Americans hold executive positions with film studios or television networks."[16]

Anyone watching the popular American sports on television would have to be impressed with the number of black athletes. In the case of basketball, the starting players are often all Afro-Americans. The sports pages are replete with the million-dollar salaries of professional athletes and their commercial endorsement deals. While the most popular sports, football, baseball, and basketball, are the ones dominated by blacks, those athletes do not necessarily earn the highest incomes. Because of sponsor tie-ins, endorsement deals, and appearance fees, the top ten of the highest-paid athletes are mostly whites in the less popular sports of tennis, golf, and racing.[17] Since those sports appeal to a better demographic group (i.e., higher-status whites), corporations pay more per audience than in the more popular sports. It might be noted that the white-dominated sports have fewer injuries and greater longevity for their participants. As true of show business, black athletes share their incomes with agents, accountants, investors, and so on, almost all of them Euro-Americans. And it is essential that a black player be superior to any white rivals for his position. He will rarely be allowed to be a part-time or reserve player in any sport. Those positions are reserved for Euro-Americans. Few blacks can remain in their sports, after finishing their careers, as managers, coaches, or front-office employees. In sports where the top ten players are all Afro-Americans it was rare to find an Afro-American clerk-typist in the front office of most professional teams.

On the amateur level, the exploitation of black athletes is most blatant. Afro-Americans constitute almost 75 percent of the players in the major revenue sports at the collegiate level. While they ostensibly do not get paid except for tuition and expenses, the alleged advantage of college athletes is a college education for four years' sports performance and a chance to enter the lucrative professional sports arena. Yet only a fraction will join a professional sports team, and 70 percent of black college athletes do not attain a college degree within four years. [18] Adding insult to injury, the revenues received from the black-dominated sports programs are generally used to subsidize the less-popular, Euro-American-dominated sports such as lacrosse, volleyball, baseball, wrestling, and tennis.

Throughout American society the illusion of racial equality is promoted as a reality. Although black political participation increased dramatically, once blacks were permitted access to the voting booths as a result of the Voting Rights Act of 1965, Afro-Americans hold less than 2 percent of all political offices in the United States while comprising 13 percent of its population. [19] As a result of at-large elections and political gerrymandering, black candidates cannot win elective office in political districts where blacks are not a majority. With few exceptions, Euro-Americans vote for Euro-Americans, regardless of the political party, gender, or other variable. Race transcends everything in politics. Until recently, no Afro-American had been elected mayor of a major city with a majority of the Euro-American vote. That explains why blacks rarely win state-wide offices, because no American state has a majority black population. Afro-American politicians are generally dependent on getting 90 percent of the black vote and 20–40 percent of the white vote in order to win elective office. Once they are in office, their appointments are often of Euro-Americans to the most important positions—a tactic designed to reassure the business community of their "color-blindness" and to pacify Euro-American voters worried about black "domination." With a black mayor in charge, blacks lose the right to charge racism in their governance. Seemingly they also lose the desire to change black mayors, as relatively few black incumbents are ever voted out of office by their black constituents.

The structural inequality, based on race, poses a vicious circle for Afro-Americans. A high rate of unemployment creates a class of impoverished blacks, particularly males, who resort to illegal activity in order to survive. While representing less than 6 percent of the American population, Afro-American men comprise 47 percent of the prison population. Almost one of four black men aged twenty to thirty are in jail or on probation or parole. The United States has the highest percentage of its population behind bars of any country in the world, and a majority of them are poor and people of color. Blacks make up 40 percent of prisoners awaiting death penalties. The majority of those death-row black prisoners have been convicted of murdering Euro-Americans. In the last forty-seven years, no white person has been executed for murdering an Afro-American.[20] The inescapable conclusion is that the American legal system, and its participants, place a greater value on white life than on black life.

Other examples abound on racial difference and the question of value. In a bizarre case of a sperm-bank mixup resulting in a white woman's giving birth to a black child, the white "victim" was awarded $400,000 because of the mistake.[21] Imagine the anguish of millions of black mothers who have no choice but to give birth to black children.

Had the situation been reversed, a black woman inseminated with a white man's sperm, the baby would still be considered black, and it is doubtful that a jury would award a black woman $400,000 for giving birth to a biracial child. It is these countless racial insults that make most Afro-Americans feel they live in the United States at the discretion of Euro-Americans, even those most recently arrived. The case of Rodney King, the black male beaten by Los Angeles police officers, certainly did little to reassure Afro-Americans that they have the same citizenship rights as Euro-Americans. His case was not an isolated incident. A commission assigned to investigate the Los Angeles Police Department found over seven hundred racist, homophobic, and sexist remarks typed by officers into the department's car-communication systems over the previous eighteen months.[22] One of the most eloquent testimonies to the legacy of racism is the number of prominent blacks stopped and abused by police officers in this country, ranging from famous athletes to singers and movie stars. Comparable situations with Euro-American celebrities are almost unheard of.

Racial indignities affect the black middle class the most. They have played by the rules, achieved some degree of success, and find they are still below the lowest-ranking Euro-American. As one Afro-American woman was quoted, "Life in general requires a lot of psychic energy for Black people on racial things."[23] A professor of philosophy wrote an article entitled "In My Next Life, I'll Be White." He speaks of the fact that black men rarely enjoy the public trust of Euro-Americans, that they are always regarded as possible thieves, criminals, violent and dangerous until proven innocent. The essence of his argument is that while white males have committed more evil cumulatively than any other class of people in the world, a suit and tie suffice to make one of them respectable.[24] Black women, while regarded as less dangerous, encounter the same suspicion that they are shoplifters or morally loose. The important point is that being denied the public trust leaves a deep psychic scar of discrimination, which festers and becomes the fountainhead of low self-esteem and self-hate for those who have no emotional salve.

Those Afro-Americans who do not have their self-esteem destroyed often suffer from a quiet anger at their treatment. This anger is currently being manifested in a racial chauvinism almost as virulent as its white counterpart. It is expressed in a kind of dysfunctional racial solidarity that has left the race victim to a series of charlatans and racial demagogues. Any black who yells racism when accused of misconduct is assumed to be innocent without being required to prove that innocence. This anger and this racial solidarity reached their most extreme form in the nomination of black jurist Clarence Thomas to replace Thurgood Marshall on the U.S. Supreme Court. Nominated by the titular head of the Republican party, the party which had captured the presidency of the nation largely through its use of racial appeals to white voters, Thomas had a record considered so anti-black that one black political scientist called him a "racist by proxy."[25] Another columnist wrote, "Stripped of his color, Clarence Thomas is just another Republican conservative apparatchik come to Washington to seek his fortune by protecting the already powerful from the weak and disenfranchised."[26]

That Thomas had the support of former and current arch segregationists, such as Strom Thurmond, Jesse Helms, and David Duke, seems not to have mattered or was not known to his black supporters. When Professor Anita Hill, an Afro-American woman, accused him of sexually harassing her, the low-esteem, angry black population rallied to his defense, representing 60 percent of the blacks polled on the matter.[27] White Southern Democrats claimed their vote to appoint him was from fear of black anger if they did not. Observers of the situation speculate that Thomas's anti–civil rights record will be reinforced by his anger at black groups for attempting to derail his appointment. Meanwhile, the party of Strom Thurmond, Jesse Helms, and David Duke is talking about a massive defection of blacks from the Democratic party because of their support of Clarence Thomas.

One black leader's explanation for this weird marriage between blacks and the leaders of American racialism, Roger Wilkins, says, "Blacks have been terribly deprived throughout our history and we've been deprived among other things of symbols of pride occupying high places. So that when a Black is presented for such a position, there is an instinctive reaction to support that person."[28]

The controversy over Clarence Thomas revealed some widening splits in the Afro-American community and the Euro-American political strategies for the twenty-first century. Those splits are along gender and class lines. Gender lines are dividing because some black men feel that black women are given preference over them, that white men like to put black women in between themselves and black men. Many blacks accused Anita Hill of acting as a tool for white men to ruin the life of a black man at the peak of his career. That many black leaders did not share that view is reflected in the statement of Jesse Jackson that Anita Hill will rank in history along with civil rights pioneer Rosa Parks.[29] Representative Craig Washington put it best when he said, "It is not Black women who have lynched Black men. It is white racism that has been tolerated for so long by many of Judge Thomas's supporters. It is a problem that will not be addressed by attacking and demeaning Black women."[30] Thomas's claim that he was the victim of racism was the real irony. Most of the racists in America were his supporters, and the white supporters of civil rights were his opponents.

Class divisions are a more serious matter. Since the desegregation of public facilities and the rise of racial tokenism, blacks have been less united as a race on many matters that affect one class more than the other. Younger blacks have become ahistorical and simply want to enter mainstream America. The Republican party has been in power for eighteen of the last twenty-two years, by controlling the White House. They attained power by developing a political strategy to appeal to southern whites resentful of the civil rights gains in the 1960s. In the 1980s the Republican presidents Reagan and Bush both had past histories of publicly supporting racial segregation. As the party of white America, there was little room for blacks, except those who supported the racist and classist views of the Republican party. Clarence Thomas was an opportunist who decided to jump on the Republican bandwagon at exactly the time this bandwagon was crushing millions of Afro-Americans into deeper economic misery. One columnist noted: "Thomas has spent a lot of his life seeking to please people who hate him, currying favor with the man, being available as a token and symbol."[31] Thousands of other blacks, hungry for some political power, will join the Republican party because the line for political participation is shorter. Race traitors are in short supply, even in 1990s America. If the Republicans believe that replacing white overseers with black ones will make blacks accept slavery, that may be the greatest illusion of them all.

The double-consciousness that Du Bois wrote about still exists, except that the racial identity of blackness threatens to overtake the national identity of Americans. White America is imposing this choice upon many of its black inhabitants. Being human—also American—seems beyond the pale of consideration for people of African descent. For all the progress that has been made on so many fronts, it is still true that Afro-Americans have their worth measured by the darkness of their skin, not the content of their characters. In a society where there is no scarcity of decent jobs, housing, and education, nonracial factors may become the criteria for the perception and treatment of black Americans. Du Bois also recognized that the class factor was intertwined with the racial factor. It is unlikely that the problems of race and class will be resolved in this generation's lifetime. Until the problem of class division is resolved, the problem of the twenty-first century will continue to be the problem of the color line.

Notes

1. Report says five million died in wars during year of peace. *San Francisco Chronicle*, June 18, 1987, p. A-1.

2. A. Carlson, "Collapse of Birthrates in Industrial Democracies," *San Francisco Chronicle*, May 14, 1986, p. A-4.

3. Paul Spickard, *Mixed Blood: Intermarriage and Ethnic Identity in Twentieth Century America*. Madison, WI: University of Wisconsin Press, 1989.

4. U.S. Bureau of the Census, *The Black Population in the United States: March 1990 and 1989*. Washington, D.C.: U.S. Government Printing Office, 1991.

5. Orlando Patterson, "Race, Gender and Liberal Fallacies," *The New York Times*, October 20, 1991, p. A-15.

6. Quoted in Greg B. Smith, "Director's No. 1 Hope for House Party 2," *San Francisco Examiner*, October 23, 1991, p. D-1.

7. Arch Parsons, "Poverty in U.S. Worse than in 7 Western Nations," *Oakland Tribune*. September 19, 1991, p. A-8.

8. F. Harris and L. Williams, "JCPS/Gallup Poll Reflects Changing Views on Political Issues," *Focus*, vol. 14 (October 1986), p. 4.

9. "Wealth, in Black and White," *The New York Times*, July 24, 1986, p. A-1.

10. U.S. Bureau of the Census, "The Black Population in the United States: March 1990 and 1989," op. cit.

11. Manning Marable, "The New Racism: The Etiquette of Racial Prejudice," *The Oklahoma Eagle*, October 10, 1991, p. 26.

12. "Housing Survey Shows Bias Against Blacks, Hispanics," *San Francisco Chronicle*, August 31, 1991, p. A-2.

13. Walter Goodman, "Looking Racism in the Face," *The New York Times*, September 26, 1991, p. B-5.

14. "The World's 40 Highest Paid Performers," *Parade Magazine*, November 10, 1991, p. 28.

15. Quoted in Liz Smith, "Wilt's Claim Sounds like a Tall Tale," *San Francisco Chronicle*, October 17, 1991, p. E-1.

16. "Study Says Hollywood Still Shuts Blacks Out," *San Francisco Chronicle*, September 24, 1991, p. A-2.

17. Michael Hiestand, "Blacks Popular but Scarce as Product Endorsers," *USA Today*, December 19, 1991, p. 9-C.

18. Jim Myers, "Whites Still Get Most Athletic Scholarships," *USA Today*, December 18, 1991, p. 4-C.

19. U.S. Bureau of the Census, *Voting and Registration in the Election of November 1988*. Washington, D.C.: U.S. Government Printing Office, 1989.

20. Alan M. Dershowitz, "Justice Isn't Color Blind," *San Francisco Examiner*, October 8, 1991, p. A-15.

21. "White Woman Who Had Black Baby in Sperm Bank Mixup Awarded $400,000." *Jet Magazine*, August 19, 1991, p. 6.

22. Manning Marable, "The New Racism: The Etiquette of Racial Prejudice," *The Oklahoma Eagle*, October 10, 1991, p. 26.

23. Delores Watson quoted in Ronald Smothers, "South's New Blacks Find Comfort Laced with Strain," *The New York Times*, September 23, 1991, p. A-1.

24. Laurence Thomas, "In My Next Life, I'll Be White," *Ebony*, December 1990, p. 84.

25. J. Owens Smith, "Clarence Thomas's Nomination Unveils Crisis Among Black Intellectuals," *California Black Faculty and Staff Newsletter* 16 (September-October, 1991), p. 2.

26. Bill Mandel, "Truth, Justice and the American Way," *San Francisco Chronicle*, October 18, 1991, p. A-4.

27. "New Polls Show Most Americans Favoring Thomas," *San Francisco Examiner*, October 14, 1991, p. A-9.

28. Roger Wilkins quoted in Peter Applebome, "Despite Talk of Sexual Harassment, Thomas Hearings Turned on Race Issue," *The New York Times*, October 19, 1991, p. Y-7.

29. Teresa Moore, "Jesse Jackson Gives Hill a Spot in History," *San Francisco Chronicle*, October 14, 1991, p. A-2.

30. Representative Craig Washington quoted in "Black Caucus Decries Thomas Racism Defense," *San Francisco Chronicle*, October 16, 1991, p. A-9.

31. Alexander Cockburn, "Democrats Let Thomas Off the Hook," *San Francisco Examiner*, October 21, 1991, p. A-21.

Patriots

Anthony Walton

*When an individual or a party is wronged in the United States,
to whom can he apply for redress? If to public opinion, public
opinion constitutes the majority; if to the legislature, it represents the majority, and implicitly obeys it; if to the executive
power, it is appointed by the majority, and serves as a passive
tool in its hands. The public force consists of the majority under
arms; the jury is the majority invested with the right of hearing
judicial cases; and in certain States, even the judges are elected
by the majority. However iniquitous or absurd the measure of
which you complain, you must submit to it as well as you can.*
— Alexis de Tocqueville,
Democracy in America

_____

I.

On a particularly bleak and blustery morning early last March, a school
crossing guard, thirty-five years old, white and male, pulled an au-

_____

*Anthony Walton has published poetry and essays in publications as diverse as Callaloo and
The New York Times. He is the author of Mississippi, and the co-editor, with Michael S.
Harper, of The Little-Brown Book of Contemporary Afro-American Poetry, both to be published
in 1993. He lives in Brunswick, Maine.*

tomatic pistol from his raincoat and fired several shots at Clinton Drake, a middle-school student, aged thirteen, black and male. The student's offense, according to the crossing guard, was that the boy had taken to walking to school and back, passing through the guard's jurisdiction at Cumberland Street and Washington Avenue next to the 7-Eleven, in the company of another youngster, twelve years old, white and female, a fellow student at Lincoln Junior High. The boy and the crossing guard had argued the propriety of this association the day before, and on the morning in question the guard shouted, "Nigger, I said leave her alone! She's white! She's white!" before emptying the clip of his weapon in the general direction of the children. Miraculously, the boy and the girl and another young friend (thirteen, white, and male) walking with them were unhurt. Police later carved several slugs from an exterior wall of the 7-Eleven and from an auto parked nearby. This incident is by now a dusty file at the police department in Portland, Maine, where it occurred, a town not otherwise noted for racial conflict among the citizenry. It happened several blocks from my own home in Portland. I'd like to don a mask of easy cynicism and declare that there is nothing that white folks can do that would shock me, a thirty-year-old black man, but that would be a lie. The State of Maine, in the person of the Superior Court, judged the assailant sane and capable of standing trial, which he did, and he was found guilty of attempted murder, among other crimes, and sentenced to forty years in prison. If the boy had been killed, the ramifications would have been, more than likely, national news, another Emmett Till or Yusuf Hawkins case; as it was, it was merely another happenstance of a cold day on a side street in the provinces.

II.

Very early in the morning of another March night at the other end of the empire, another young black man was pursued through the Pacoima section of the San Fernando Valley in Los Angeles, his car eventually curbed by a force of police from the Los Angeles Police Department and the California Highway Patrol. This force, to corral one automobile containing three black men under no criminal suspicion, consisted of twenty-one officers, thirteen cars, and a helicopter.

One of the young men, Rodney King, who had been speeding and driving erratically, was ordered by loudspeaker to exit his car along with his companions. What happened next is disputed; King says he did nothing, did as he was told; police officers claim King refused orders and lunged at them. What is clear is that Rodney King was shot twice in the chest with a Taser stun gun by the highest-ranking officer present, Sergeant Stacey Koon, and subsequently beaten with nightsticks and batons by officers Theodore Briseno, Laurence Powell, and Timothy Wind. As described by the report of the Independent Commission on the Los Angeles Police Department.

Koon acknowledged that he ordered the baton blows, directing Powell and Wind to hit King with "power strokes" [an LAPD term]. . . . Finally, after 56 baton blows and six kicks, five or six officers swarmed in and placed King in both handcuffs and cordcuffs restraining his arms and legs. King was dragged on his stomach to the side of the road to await arrival of a rescue ambulance.

This event might have passed in the national consciousness as quietly as the shooting in Portland, an anonymous conflagration in the urban night, but for two types of high technology that indisputably recorded aspects of the arrest, altering the very reality of the situation by making it unavoidably, irrefutably true. The proceedings were videotaped with a camcorder, by a Los Angeles citizen, George Holliday, from his living room, producing a tape that played over and over again on local, national, and global television, sickening and shocking virtually all who saw it. The police officers themselves also recorded damning evidence of their attitudes and culpability on their police communication computers. Just before beating King, Officers Powell and Wind sent a computer message to other officers, saying that a domestic dispute between a black couple they'd just broken up was "Right out of *Gorillas in the Mist*"; after the beating they sent this message to a colleague: "I haven't beaten anyone this bad in a long time." The colleague answered, "Oh not again . . . why you do that . . . I thought you agreed to chill out for a while . . ." During the beating one of the officers was heard to shout, "Nigger."

Rodney King survived the beating with twenty stitches, eleven skull fractures, permanent brain damage, a broken ankle, a crushed cheek-bone, kidney damage, and a burn on his chest. His right eye was suffused with blood, shining pure red.

III.

How does it feel to be a problem? W. E. B. Du Bois asked that question ninety years ago in *The Souls of Black Folks*, and it echoes louder today: *How does it feel to be a problem?*

Watching the Rodney King beating on videotape, I pictured the policemen riding through the Los Angeles dark after the beating, sending their computer messages and breathing heavily, greedily, but happily, "We beat them till our arms was tired . . ." running through their minds. But what was it, I wonder, that they were beating, what were they trying to subdue, what demon were they exorcising from the early spring? Was it merely Rodney King? Or was there some spiritual darkness, some sickness there surging through the night? These questions link with others in my imagination: Why did that Portland crossing guard feel so threatened by the guileless associations of children? Why was Yusuf Hawkins shot down like a dog, on his knees and begging for his life, shot because he was merely, and only, peacefully present on a public sidewalk? Why does Willie Horton still linger in some remote and sulfurous corner of the national psyche, ready to frighten and divide? Why is the Nazi, the Klansman David Duke, thirty years after Selma, embraced and championed by a majority of the whites in Louisiana, and who knows how many elsewhere? Will black Americans ever feel completely that America is their home? Why are blacks the national scapegoat? What are whites, when they use that scapegoat, running from? The questions are endless, but the sum of that infinity can be expressed in one sentence: How does it feel to be a problem?

Black Americans have been a problem, *the* problem, from the very beginning of this country, the American Revolution. In 1776 Thomas Jefferson, speaking for the Continental Congress and American patriots such as John Hancock, Samuel Adams, John Adams, Robert Morris, Samuel Huntington, and Benjamin Franklin, wrote these words: "We hold these Truths to be self-evident, that all Men are created equal, that they are endowed by their Creator with certain unalienable rights, that among these are Life, Liberty, and the Pursuit of Happiness. —That to secure these Rights, Governments are instituted among Men, deriving their just Powers from the Consent of the Governed, that whenever any Form of Government becomes destructive of these ends, it is the Right of the People to alter or to abolish it." It has become a commonplace to observe that "all men" were not in fact "created equal," at least not in the eyes of Jefferson and the Continental Congress or any number of succeeding generations of Americans, but here lies the first tangle from which entwined our current dilemma. Though the first man to fall in Boston in 1770 was a black man, Crispus Attucks, the patriots didn't want black soldiers to fight for independence (thus earning a place in the new land) and didn't allow them to until the British began enlisting escaped slaves and promising emancipation. When, after the war, the patriots were enjoined to form a new government and a constitution which enumerated rights and freedoms heretofore never seen by common citizens anywhere in the world, blacks were again a problem. How to guarantee rights of travel, free speech, freedom from search and seizure, and so on, when chattel labor was a linchpin of much of the economy? And how to keep the southern states from gaining political advantage by counting enslaved blacks in their populations when determining representation?

The solution was to declare those with dark skin less than persons, by extension less than human, from the beginning, right there in Article I; "Representatives and direct taxes shall be apportioned among the several States which may be included within this Union, according to their respective numbers, which shall be determined by adding to the whole number of free persons, including those bound to service for a term of years, and excluding Indians not taxed, three-fifths of all other persons." So the nation was measured by "free persons," "Indians not taxed," and "three-fifths of all other persons," with "all other persons" meaning those bound in "the peculiar institution." These euphemisms were the preferred way of discussing blacks and black issues in official circles; "slavery" was not mentioned in the constitution until 1865, when it was abolished. But the problem of what to do with all those who were not created equal was solved, and the nation has lived out the implications and determinations of that decision to this day.

IV.

Here, then, is where we find ourselves, those residents of the United States who are both black and American, early in the third century of the Union, late in the second millennium of the Christian Era: we are the distance between what America, the best attempt that the species has made thus far to live together under laws, is and what it has stated it desires to become. When we read the words of Jefferson, Lincoln,

Douglass, and Martin King, when we are inspired by the achievements and possibilities of America's citizenry and institutions, we have only to assess the lives of the oldest "minority," the slaves, colored, Negroes, blacks, and African Americans, to understand the progress and status of that attempt, the American Dream, the promise of a free and good life that so much of the world still longs for. Taking the temperature, so to speak, of black America is a shortcut to assessing the internal health of the Republic.

In late 1991, the prognosis is not good. From the framing of the Constitution through the *Dred Scott* decision, the Civil War, the Emancipation, *Plessy* vs. *Ferguson* and *Brown* vs. *Board of Education* to the Voting Rights Act, the story of African descendants on this continent has been tragic, but on an upward arc of progress, things getting better little by however little. No matter how cold we were it was a little warm somewhere just ahead. And we felt as an article of faith that someday somebody, some of us, would get into the brick house where that warm fire was and sit in big chairs right next to the hearth. A promise isn't much to live on, but it was enough. It had to be.

The word "patriot," meaning "one who loves his country," is rooted in the Latin *patria*, or fatherland, and *pater*, or father. In this etymology is implied the notion of a country as a family, a group claiming common descent and sustenance, in this case from lands and ideas. It is my fear, when looking at America, the land where I was born, that the various constituent members of the society are giving up on the promise of building the first republic where *all* men and women are created equal. As the economy shudders through what is probably an epochal and historic contraction, it seems beyond the elected political leadership and most ordinary citizens to envision an America where there is room for all who wish to earn a place within it. In this vision of reality, blacks again exist as a problem in the nation's attempt to become itself. "Oh, if it weren't for these blacks," they imply, "we could become great again." This story ignores historical truth for the mythological past, a past in which blacks are the enemy, the other, *la bête noire.* Perhaps there is something in the human heart that requires this enemy, this *raison d'être*, this organizing principle. American Caucasians would not be *white* without *blacks*; they wouldn't know who they are. They wouldn't be "up," they wouldn't be "on top." I suspect these sorts of things are very important to certain classes of whites.

But I digress. If I say that white Americans have given up on the hope of an America that lives up to its founding documents, what I really mean is that they have decided to stop pretending that they ever believed in such a thing. I think many white Americans, particularly in the working and middle classes, sincerely believe that they are losing ground, that the American Dream is failing them, too, and they need someone to blame. If this country was once perceived as being rich, powerful, and with limitless horizons, whose fault is it if none of that seems true any longer? Who has been the problem from the beginning?

Something that disturbs me more is my fear that large numbers of black Americans are giving up as well, weary of four hundred years of tragedy and burden, exhausted from being left in the cold one day too long. This is not a simple statement to make, nor an easy one; there are so many things better for black Americans than ever before, with the promise of more, but these signs are counterbalanced by the signs of no progress in some quarters and even backward motion in others. Perhaps it also seems contradictory to delineate and dissect four hundred years of white oppression and then question black resolve, but if we follow Camus and agree that "the point is to live," then we've got to find a way to do our best, for everybody. Fannie Lou Hamer put it the best I've ever heard: "We didn't come all this way for no two seats when all of us is tired." These are the best and worst of times for American blacks, and things seem sometimes, some days, to add up to zero, malaise.

Many whites and a group of blacks loosely referred to as "conservative" have taken to criticizing the more affluent sufferers of this malaise as malingerers, negative fantasists. "How can you, an attorney, a doctor, a Yale man," they say, "possibly feel persecuted?" The trouble with this analysis, putting aside for the moment its inadequacy, is that it overlooks the totality, in the group sense, of the black experience, its involuntary interrelatedness, the fact that every black person on the continent, precisely because he or she is black, is a factor in the life of the country and part of "the problem." Black Americans are tied to each other in ways that the majority cannot begin to presume to understand, which is not to say that blacks are any more or less monolithic or individual than whites, Hispanics, Asians, Native Americans, or any other group. But within that human individuality lies the seed of our ongoing political and economic defeat. We are, to begin with, greatly outnumbered in all circumstances; that is complicated by the fact that, as individuals, we all also have a right to our own thoughts and choices, which makes unified action unlikely.

I wonder if white Americans experience anything equivalent to this: I may, for example, be able to ride the Metro North commuter train to a suburban home in Fairfield County, Connecticut, but when that train emerges from the Grand Central tunnel at Ninety-sixth Street I must look down from the trestle to the tenements below and wonder why I'm at IBM or Time-Warner or some big law firm, and why the black people "down there" are trapped in that ghetto, blighted by drugs, AIDS, crime, and indifference.

Justice Clarence Thomas would say that I'm on the train because I deserve to be there, that my grandfather and father worked hard in fields and factories to purchase stability and opportunity. These sacrifices, he would say, allowed me to rise, on their backs, through American society. All that is certainly true. What is also true is that they, and I, were lucky, through genes or fate, to surge through the maelstrom of dashed hope and denied opportunity to grasp a tenuous piece of the American Dream. When we discuss racism in American society, especially its contemporary effects and consequences, we seldom if ever take measure of the cumulative damage of the past, the millstone of history that grows heavier and more onerous with each generation. We have now uncounted generation upon generation of

American blacks who have been subject to every kind of physical and psychological deprivation yet cataloged by humans. How can those blacks—and I hate to use this term speaking of human beings but it seems accurate—the detritus of four hundred years of social crime, technological change, and historical disadvantage be expected to compete in the current information and digital economy? (Increasing numbers of whites are also unable to compete.) There have been five or six generations of blacks since slavery. How much time, in the real scale of things, is that? How many generations were in slavery?

Black Americans have been victims from the beginning of the American experiment: one could say that, along with the Native Americans, we have been *the* victims. To say that is not to bask in "victimology" as the conservatives might have it, or to engage in "who has suffered the most" sweepstakes. It is simply to annotate accurately and completely American experience. We have been, again, the principal means of white self-identification and self-justification; we have also been among the first to suffer and the last to profit as the nation ratcheted its way toward the more perfect union. We have helped raise America's children, died in America's wars, plowed and harvested its fields, built its roads, and stoked its mills and factories. We have been, in a word, *patriots*. Still, by actions and sometimes words, we are told that there is no place here for us. We are neither citizen, in the fullest sense, nor aboriginal; what must we do to earn a place in America?

V.

Had it pleased heaven
To try me with affliction, had they rained
All kinds of sores and shames on my bare head,
Steeped me in poverty to the very lips,
Given to captivity me and my utmost hopes,

Patriots

I should have found in some place of my soul
A drop of patience. But, alas, to make me
A fixed figure for the time of scorn
To point his slow and moving finger at!
Yet could I bear that too; well, very well.
But there where I have garnered up my heart,
Where either I must live or bear no life,
The fountain from the which my current runs
Or else dries up—to be discarded thence,
Or keep it as a cistern for foul toads
To knot and gender in—turn thy complexion there,
Patience, thou young and rose-lipped cherubin!
I here look grim as hell!

—Shakespeare
The Tragedy of Othello
IV, II, 57–80

How does it feel to be a problem? I have, for most of my adult life, wondered what, exactly, is the stain we black Americans carry, what is it about our mere presence, our mere existence that can inflame such passion, embroil the nation in such histrionics for so long a time? In a *Time* article dated July 22, 1991, writer William A. Henry III states plainly, while discussing all-white golf clubs, "The highly visible act of excluding people from prominent community institutions based on skin color serves as a powerful and disturbing symbol that racism is tolerable in the nation's top social echelons. . . . In addition, in almost all cases, the private clubs bring together a community's business, professional and political elites and thus perpetuate patterns of unequal opportunity."

At a less rarefied economic pitch, but with the same intent, is the Colony Beach Club in New Rochelle, New York. As reported in the October 4, 1991, *New York Times*, New York Attorney General Robert

Abrams filed suit against the club, accusing it of systematically excluding black applicants from membership. The furor was initiated when a female white member was told that her black babysitter would have to wear a uniform when on the premises because white members "want to know the difference" between members and their employees. A subsequent investigation revealed that white applicants were routinely admitted to membership upon payment of a fee while black applicants were routed through a circuitous process, which required, among other things, the sponsorship of a current member, and were often counseled that there were no spaces or even applications available. One black test applicant reported that after meeting with the club manager she asked to tour the grounds; when she returned to the clubhouse she found that the doors were locked, the windows and shutters closed, and only the pool boy to tell her no one else could see her that day. The club, however, was not above renting the facilities in the off-season winter months to black families and organizations for social events.

I couple such news stories with the results of two polls taken in the spring and summer of 1991. A *Washington Post*–ABC News poll found that 50 percent of whites questioned believed that an equally qualified black is less likely to be hired than a white competitor. Fifty-eight percent stated that equally qualified blacks are less likely to be promoted. But 59 percent of these whites believed that correcting any such biases took jobs from whites, and 88 percent felt that in no case whatsoever should racial preferences be considered in hiring, promotion, or college-admissions decisions. I read these numbers to mean that white Americans do in fact support racial preferences, but for *whites*, and they are increasingly willing to say so plainly. And this poll was conducted in the white working-class neighborhoods of southwest Chicago, where, I think it's safe to assume, there are not too many whites of the sort that can be expected to shed many tears over the plights and prospects of black Americans. These people, from their moment of arrival on these shores, have seen blacks as their chief economic rivals. Yet a certain percentage of them will admit to a stranger that blacks may not be getting a fair deal. They just don't care, or, to be fair, they care more about themselves, and blacks are an easily identified target.

An even more disturbing poll was reported by Louis Harris. Six percent of whites polled stated that blacks are incapable of learning under any conditions, and another 25 percent thought that black children could learn, but that society would never be able to motivate them to do so. Eleven percent felt that blacks are genetically less intelligent, whereas, in a strange and revealing turn, 55 percent felt that blacks and other minorities didn't have commensurate educational opportunity. Interestingly, large majorities of whites said they would be in favor of increased social spending to ameliorate the social ills beginning to swamp the nation, and felt it was in their self-interest to do so.

These surveys are, of course, random samplings, but their numbers are revealing as to the schizophrenia of the country on racial matters. On one hand, blacks are some sort of lepers, inferior and infirm beings that threaten the comfort, peace, and prosperity of whites. "Freedom of association," the whites cry, then they use that freedom to conspire against the freedom of others and avoid any unnecessary contact that might contaminate them. Then, on the other hand, whites acknowledge that blacks have been mistreated, and even that something needs to be done about it, but when actually confronted with choices, the group seems to run aground on the rocks of privilege. It seems impossible for our society, and whites control that society, to draw a line connecting "how whites have viewed and treated blacks" and "how large numbers of blacks live today." Is it too much to say that white Americans seem to want blacks out of sight and mind so as not to sully collective imagery of what this society is and is not, but to simultaneously "straighten up and fly right," become peaceful and orderly productive members of the same society? How are blacks to do that if they aren't allowed to the table? And, since the table is currently construed as a zero-sum game, meaning that whites must lose for others to gain, will there ever be peace?

VI.

In light of the foregoing, one can doubt in sincerity whether or not it is possible for a black person to be an American. I do not think the question is correctly formulated as either/or; rather, one should question what one should *do* if one should find himself or herself both American and black. Why not embrace our fate? Speaking for myself, I can imagine no other life for myself than within "the veil," as a Negro, an other, a blackamoor. I'm glad to be an American, and more glad to be on the margin, an outsider, a cowboy if you will, that most American of persons, aware and observant of society, but never quite in.

This is, of course, an individual existential choice. But I'd rather be conscious, suffering, *human*, than sleepwalking, supercilious, and thoughtlessly privileged. These seem to be the choices in every developed society throughout the world, and they are not necessarily allocated by racial group. Don't those things that, when we as black Americans live up to them, make us most human—spirituals, the blues and jazz, the great art of Romare Bearden, Ralph Ellison, and Alvin Ailey—spring from our experience? And, strangely enough, aren't these arts and artists among the most American the continent has produced?

I think that what we as blacks have to do is embrace, understand, and communicate what has happened to us here these last four hundred years. Then we have to figure ways of transmitting that awareness to every single black child that is born. Race is not a person's defining characteristic, but a person is forced to live out the implications of who he or she is within the context of a culture. In our culture, skin color is an extraordinarily large factor, and there needs to be some method of equipping each and every black child with a story that will enable him or her to negotiate the obstacles those children will face living out that fate.

To even discuss this will be difficult. Black Americans are the tribe that is not a tribe; there are multiplicitous ways of being black, and beyond that, American. Cohesive groups in this culture are united by ideas, not physical characteristics. To illustrate: An Asian can be a Mormon, but a Mormon is not necessarily an Asian. American Jews, for example, are often organized around an idea or several ideas— Judaism, Israel, the Holocaust, the simple idea of being Jewish. A black or a Hispanic can be a Jew, and some are. American blacks are organized around the melanin content of their skin, a physical fact. I came across this quote several years ago: "You were born a Jew, your task is to remain a Jew. The rest is up to God." To say, "You were born a black, your task is to remain a black . . ." does not make sense (with very few exceptions). What can unite blacks? Religion? Politics? Black individuals run the ideological gamut, to simplify, from Walter Williams and Shelby Steele to Cornel West and Molefi Asante. Thomas Sowell and Amiri Baraka probably wouldn't agree on much more than "We were once slaves down in Egypt," but there is the thing that truly unites us as blacks—history—and if we could begin to teach that history, accurately and with some dimensional perspectives, blacks might better develop a consciousness of who they are, where their ancestors have been, and what, exactly, it means to be black, to occupy this mythological space in the nation's imagination.

We are mythological figures in this society. In so many ways no one, including, sometimes, us, *sees* us. Americans, black and white, see things in their imaginations, then project those ideas and emotions onto specific individuals, thus denying those individuals their selves. We aren't teaching significant numbers of our children how to live with Du Bois's "twoness," Ellison's "invisibility," and in this failure we are denying them the tools they need to master their society psychically. Our children need to reconnect to their experience and history so that they can accurately place themselves within the continuum and matrix of world, Western, and American history.

We need, in Joseph Campbell's terms, a myth. We need to tell our young people that surviving as a black in this culture involves more than dashikis, cufis, kente cloth, and Malcolm X hats. We need to help every black child learn, as a matter of course, that being a black American involves a way of looking at the world, a philosophical position. We need a new story—and this doesn't involve politics or religion—that gives them a teleological place to exist in the here and now. Then we'll need to deemphasize if not destroy the current dominance that youth culture and its vapid disregard for the future, its materialism, religion of instant gratification, sexual permissiveness, and unrelenting violence, is visiting upon black communities. Too much black life is run by children, largely as a result of black men's abandoning theirs. This trend of youth culture and abandoned families is sweeping through the entire society, but as with most negative societal trends, it exacts its highest toll from blacks. These are areas under black control, and of concern to blacks of all beliefs. These children, and by children I mean twenty-one and under, are dying, and we have to begin telling them the truth, which is that dignity and survival have been possible for blacks in the *worst* of times, which they are not today unless you let them be. This is not to say every black person enjoys the opportunity to become an investment banker, just that we are going to have to start somewhere. We must take control where we can, and if not our children, where? They must be told that they live in a society where Darwinism has become attached to Calvinism in such a way that human life is not only seen as survival of the fittest, but that the fittest are seen as deserving, even being destined, to survive.

Let us, blacks, grant that white folks are eye-deep in blood, guilt, and responsibility for what has happened to blacks in America. Now what? As lawyers say, "You've got a judgment, now you have to collect." We aren't going to collect, ever. In fact, we are in danger of becoming superfluous people in this society. With the exception of the military, popular music, and professional athletics, all of which could have done without us, we probably *have* been superfluous since World War II. We are not essential or even integral to the economy. White folks don't need us to pick cotton, stoke foundries, or bolt on fenders anymore. They don't need us as maids and nannies either. In the coming economy, there will be plenty of displaced, near-superfluous whites for those jobs. (See Germany since unification.)

So blacks have got to get about some economics as well. Building black small business is crucial, with expansion to ownership in industry and finance possible and needed. Property is the way up in America, with capital accumulation and business ownership a step behind. Using whatever credit and capital sources are at hand, government, private, church, and community, and working with all those in the larger society that wish to work with us, we've got to become capitalists in the mainstream economy with a vengeance. This is self-defense for blacks, the only defense with a probability of working. If current trends continue, the welfare state as we know it will no longer be fiscally supportable or supported. The political consensus for this is already breaking apart, and, as can be seen in the exurban and edge-city movements, wealthy whites (and blacks) will in ever greater numbers withdraw into taxing districts wherein the revenues will not have to be "shared" with the urban poor. Blacks need, in a word, to buy into the culture. I think this is within our grasp. If we're going to be here in Rome, and, realistically, where else are we going to be?, we have to, as a group, become Romans.

VII.

How does it feel to be a problem? Clinton Drake, Rodney King, and I can be described as problems in the American scheme, but we are also Americans. I am an American. Such a simple statement, and so complex. And I would say that I am an American before I am a black, though the conjunction of those twin fates creates a third that exists in the ether, unto itself. In some ways a black American is a prisoner who carries his cell, his skin, around with him; it is just as true that he is the freest black man on the planet. Who is harder, in truth, on black people, Bush of America, or Mobutu of Zaire? Moi of Kenya? Mengistu of Ethiopia? I am also American because I love things— cars, guns, privacy, the blues—that most Americans love, and that most blacks love. I think of D. H. Lawrence's remark: "The essential American soul is hard, isolate, stoic and a killer." Doesn't that describe Robert Johnson? Jack Johnson? Miles Davis? Frederick Douglass? I think it also describes my father, though he might not think it a compliment.

I claim America, for the black Americans who died helping create it, and for those living here today in whatever circumstances. And I'm mindful of Alexis de Tocqueville, who said in 1831, "I do not believe that the white and black races will ever live in any country on equal footing. But I believe the difficulty to be still greater in the United States than elsewhere. An isolated individual may surmount the prejudices of religion, of his country, or of his race; and if this individual is a king, he may effect surprising changes in society; but a whole people cannot rise, as it were, above itself."

As black Americans, we have to internalize, for survival, contradictory impulses. America is home, and we love it. We are the bastard children, and must be on guard. As I write, I have before me the cover of the February 27, 1991, issue of *Time*, depicting the liberation of Kuwait City by American troops. As an American I'm proud, and relieved; as a black man, I'm even more proud because most of the marines in the photo holding up the flag are black. I nod in respect, *patriots*. But then I wonder where those men are now, what happened to them after the parades and after they'd taken off their uniforms. If they like to golf or swim, can they join a club? If they're from Louisiana, what are all those pro-Duke folks saying to them? Did they survive

Kuwait to die in South Central, Robert Taylor Homes, Bedford-Stuyvesant? And what of their comrades, the black boys who also crouched in the sand for six months, but didn't make it back alive? Thinking of those fallen brings to mind other dead, several more, the playmates of my childhood, all of whom, except for my brother, are dead. Drugs, AIDS, suicide, murder. I am thirty-one years old, black and American, filled with thoughts of all those dead boys, those lovely boys. O America.

Du Bois's Dilemma
and African American
Adaptiveness

Ella Pearson Mitchell

Many years ago, my godmother, Emma Benson Wallace (also Ruby Dee's mother), attended Atlanta University as an undergraduate. She had the good fortune to study under the incomparable W. E. B. Du Bois. Few treasures of her life ever came close to the satisfaction of having sat at his feet, although she often conceded that his delivery was as "dry as dust." So Du Bois has always been one of my heroes, from early youth on; and my husband and I spend a lot of time footnoting and affirming his brilliant insights.

With all due respect for his genius, however, it is time to reconsider a bit of Dr. Du Bois's wisdom, as it applies to the purposes of contemporary life among African Americans. To be more specific, it is now necessary that the African American community rethink what is probably his most famous saying: "One ever feels his twoness,—an American, a Negro; two souls, two thoughts, two unreconciled strivings; two warring ideals in one dark body, whose dogged strength alone keeps it from being torn asunder."

Ella Pearson Mitchell teaches courses in homilectics at the Interdenominational Theological Center in Atlanta. She edited the first two volumes of *Those Preachin' Women* and is the author of *Women: To Preach or Not to Preach*. Her articles have appeared in several publications, including the journal *Religious Education*. In 1989, she received the honorary Doctor of Humane Letters degree from Talladega College.

Our rethinking of this dual identity and biculturalism must be done in the light of the tremendous adaptiveness of recent graduates of African American colleges and other institutions of higher learning, as well as the admirable adjustment and psychic wholeness of many without such training, whose mother wit has shown amazing multicultural sophistication and survival skills. It would appear that at least a substantial minority of African Americans are no longer plagued by these "two warring ideals in one dark body," or by his "two unreconciled strivings." There must be some form of solution to Dr. Du Bois's dilemma already in fairly wide practice.

One might describe that solution in the terms of a stimulating paradigm, expressed in life by the Apostle Paul, and recorded in theory in his first letter to the church at Corinth (I Corinthians 9:22): "I am made all things to all persons that I might by all means save some." A related declaration appears in his Second Epistle to Timothy (1:5–7): "When I call to remembrance the unfeigned faith that is in thee, which dwelt first in thy grandmother Lois, and thy mother Eunice; and I am persuaded that in thee also. Wherefore I put thee in remembrance that thou stir up the *gift of God*, which is in *thee*. . . . For God hath not given us the spirit of fear; but of power, and of love, and of a sound mind."

If one were to think of the predicament of the Apostle Paul in the terms of Dr. Du Bois's statement, it might read thus: Paul was "trapped" in a world where his ethnic culture and identity were assigned the same low standing as that assigned the "Negro" of Dr. Du Bois's day. Yet Paul considered all his cultural and intellectual equipment to be a gift from God. So he felt no great conflict between them, and thought people in his situation ought to take full advantage of their multiple cultures and working identities.

Paul was the son of a Jewish mother and father, the latter being of the tribe of Benjamin. How his father gained for himself and his son the status of citizens of the Roman Empire we do not know. Living and functioning in a majority Greco-Roman culture and workaday world, Paul was nevertheless deeply indoctrinated in the things pertaining to his family's Hebrew tradition. Indeed, he would have had every right to cry out, in parallel with Du Bois, "I am divided; my spirit is rent asunder. Who shall deliver me from this crisis of identity?"

Instead of this, one reads Paul's solution, as found in the midst of his answer to charges made against him by a church that he had founded in the city of Corinth. He had been unjustly accused of seeking silver rather than souls. As he engaged in rebuttal he dealt at some length with his call from God, and his serious sense of vocation. Then, as was the case with much of his writing to the problem-ridden mission churches, he burst forth with a brilliant insight that might never have emerged had he not been accused. He declared his call and capacity to serve with or without salary, and went on to say that he was prepared to relate to Jews as well as Gentiles; to those under the law as well as those outside the law; to those who were weak, as well as those who were strong. Then he said, in the words cited, that he was made by God to be all things to *all* persons that he might by all these cultural patterns be used to save some.

Few passages have more relevance for life on the planet Earth today than this one. It declares a gift not adequately treasured in America: multicultural competence. But it is a gift more and more essential to effectiveness and even survival, as the world gets smaller, because of the ease of worldwide communication and travel.

To be sure, such a cultural competence is formed in a crucible where identity is always at serious risk. But the decade of the nineties, more than any previous decade, *demands* such competence in a world whose rate of change leading up to the year 2000 will exceed even our present change rates. The risk of failing to broaden our cultural competence is even greater than the risk of psychically divisive exposure in depth to competing identities and cultures. In this light it becomes apparent that one of the most unheralded strengths of African American schools and churches has been the bestowal of a firm identity and dual cultural competence on sizable numbers of the oppressed whom they serve. Often unaware of their subtle achievement, they have helped solve the problems of identity and launched into the service of God and their communities persons of impressively multicultural competence and of psychic and spiritual wholeness.

What was it that Paul had; what is it that these schools and churches give?

Paul's early formation was in a supportive environment, even in the diaspara or dispersion of the Jews across the Greco-Roman world (= "up North"). Whatever Hellenistic culture in Tarsus may have done to erode his self-esteem as a "Hebrew of the Hebrews," it was offset by his study of the tradition, probably at Jerusalem. In addition to learning so intensively about his roots, his Hebrew culture and identity, he was well equipped to debate with the best Greco-Roman thinkers at places like Athens. He could reach out with power and creativity to other cultures and identities.

Likewise, African Americans have developed increasing awareness of the strengths of their culture and identity. Institutions of higher learning once miseducated African American students in the supremacy of Western culture, giving them the ambition only to prove their competence in it equal to that of whites. In the process, they imparted a sense of ethnic inferiority to even their best students. Now many such schools are known for freeing late adolescents and young adults to focus on the best of their own culture, as well as the best of other cultures, without the need to fight off the assaults on black dignity which are so common in white academia.[1]

Indeed, academic choices of African American students today would suggest that the personal grounding offered in the best of the predominantly "black" schools is far more important than any other value to be gained, for instance, in Ivy League schools.

As one observes the African American communities of the North and the West of the United States, one sees over and over again that people with black college psychic nourishment and ethnic formation provide the leadership. It is a risky but often evident generalization that those whose local formal education has not been so blessed seldom seem to provide their share of the leadership of inner-city communities. For one is not likely to be a leader even in one's own sight when one has been nourished only in an atmosphere of hostility, or of limited acceptance at best.

Now all of this relates to Du Bois's twoness at the point where it suggests a mature self-esteem which does not require or even seriously consider the approval or disapproval of America's ethnic majority. It is my strong conviction that Du Bois's anguish over his twoness was born of the lack of such fundamental emotional independence. Brilliant as he was, as profound as were his insights, and as sure as he was of his gifts, he was still the child of Great Barrington, Massachusetts, where he had to fight for minimal recognition, solely because he was African American. There was little in his experiences in Germany and at Harvard to help overcome his childhood deficit. The scars never left his soul, nor did more than a few African Americans of his day ever escape the need to know that they had met the "enemy" on his own cultural terms and equaled him. Too many still feel the need to know that this enemy fully recognizes their equal competence.

At this point it is interesting to go back to the Apostle Paul's multicultural competence and secure identity; there was no want of excellence in either culture. Many African Americans have paralleled Paul at this point of competence. As far back as autobiographies of escaped slaves (1830–60), one finds the same impressive bicultural competence. This genre, called "slave narratives," was great political literature and effective antislavery propaganda. Look for instance at Austin Steward's penetrating analysis of the chronic vulnerability of even a comparatively good master, to say nothing of the decadence inherent in the rearing of masters' children.[2] Here is an enslaved African engaged in incisive observation, no doubt well before his escape from slavery. His wisdom and articulate expression are the result of a mastery of two cultures, achieved through self-confidence and a mind self-liberated to engage in analysis. It was an impressive but not unique accomplishment.

Likewise, although people seldom think of it in these terms, the apostle Paul was a phenomenal achiever. Here in one person was most of the theology of the early Christian church. He wrote more of the New Testament than any other single author. Yet he started with a simple faith dominated by rural folk, country people like Peter and Andrew, with no training whatsoever. He bridged from that profound and simple folk religion across to the mightiest minds of Greco-Roman culture. Indeed, Paul provided the intellectual basis on which the Christian mission to the whole world depended. It sprang from a tiny, insignificant Jewish folk cult to become a major religion of the known world, largely on the wings of Paul's interpretations.

Paul was able to do this because he had mastered both the culture of Christianity's origin and the culture to which the faith was to be sent. In addition to this, by a kind of providential synergy and serendipity, one culture cross-fertilized the other. In Paul's magnificent mind, there emerged timeless insight, partly because his frame of reference was not restricted to any *one* culture, and because he was free to utilize all his gifts.

Thus it was that Paul was able to sell a strange idea like the *resurrection* to cynical Greek intellectualism, in a theological masterpiece which was based not on some abstract Greek notion but on a figure called a seed! He went on to say with telling logic, "You don't know where a new plant comes from because the seed out of which it comes is already dead; in fact, it won't ever spring forth *until* it has died. And if you don't know what is happening to that seed, why should you assume that you would know what's happening when this body dies." (I Corinthians 15:35–38.) I still marvel at the forceful manner in which this genius fused Greek philosophical speculation with good old countrified mother wit.

What can be said of Paul and of our slave ancestors can be said on a wider scale of many people in our day and age. Graduate after graduate has been able to go out into the world and bring about near miracles in community after community. And all because of that same combination of solid identity and that extra insight born of intellectual competence in two cultures. I think of names like Marva Collins (founder of Chicago's West Side Preparatory School) and Benjamin Carson (internationally recognized Baltimore neurosurgeon), and I can't escape the conviction that their matchless contributions were born of dedication/motivation and of this genius due to cross-cultural competence and serendipity.

What, then, what does all of this say to us who ponder Dr. Du Bois's very impressive and widely quoted statement about twoness?

The first thing this says is that one need not necessarily lament being born and having to live among two cultures, of which one's own is considered the lesser. Even in a position of being oppressed, it is in fact unquestionably advantageous to have access to and become competent in two or more ethnic groups and cultures. This is true especially if one has a firm grip on one's primary identity. Even when, with Paul, one is able to identify with a variety of ethnics, one can be psychically healthy only when one knows which one is the authentic core being, the "real me."

Even with a childhood in isolation from great communities of African Americans (as was the case with Du Bois), one can still get a great deal of identity affirmation from an intentionally supportive small group or nuclear family. With proper focus during early nurture, one can grow into a secure being who is unapologetically African American at the core. All else will be valued on its merits, but those merits will include the capacity to blend with and serve the purposes of the primary identity.

For some this may seem to be extreme—an ethnocentric ultimatum of dangerously narrow dimensions. As a matter of fact, it is only a healthy and normal approach. To do less is to downgrade oneself, and to engage in naïve assumptions about the objectivity of the members of other cultures and ethnic groups. One is not prepared to make a contribution to one's own race or to any other race until one is, at the core of being, healthily affirmative of one's own identity and needs. Only then can one develop the psychic and spiritual surplus out of which come the kinds of creativity that bless the world at large. The most rigorous ethical standards of the Christian faith require that one love one's neighbor only *as* one loves oneself, not more than (Matthew 19:19). One need no longer feel torn by "two unreconciled strivings," because one has set them in proper working priority and sequence.

The "two souls" of which Du Bois spoke are a reality only if one has engaged in the suicidal enterprise of equal identification with two or more groups and their worlds. It is one thing to understand and be competent and fluent in two or more worlds. It is quite another thing to attempt to be affectively linked with all of them at the core of one's very being. The use of the term "suicidal" above is more than mere rhetoric. One can actually become schizophrenic as a result of such an effort. And more than one African American has engaged in self-destruction upon finding the task utterly impossible. This among a people generally noted for a far less than average rate of suicide.

The inner turmoil of these people and, to some extent even of Du Bois, comes from a deep need to be accepted by the power group. Two responses come to mind. One is that the Euro-American power group has a few marvelously open and unprejudiced people in it, but the vast majority are not ready yet. And it will be decades and maybe even centuries before the biases die. Slow as is the ethnic assimilation process since slavery, it may be faster than the rate of permanent change away from racism in this country. To peg one's security and psychic health to such an eventuality is indeed self-destructive.

A second and more risky response to this deep inner need occurs in the context of our numerous visits to Du Bois's grave in Accra, Ghana, in the wall of the old Christensborg castle. It grows in part from our conversations with those who knew him in his last years and days.

Although Du Bois went all the way to Africa to do his final works of writing and editing, he was not really happy there either. The acceptance for which his soul cried was not easily found among even his own people. His liveried servants, limousine, and other accoutrements all seemed to suggest a longing utterly different from mere human-to-human warmth. The elitist and even aristocratic lifestyle on which he insisted marked him not only as a far from authentic Communist; he was an awesome intellect incapable of any real warmth toward any group, all because he had not experienced that warmth in his formative years.

What can be hazarded here in connection with Du Bois may be far more widespread among *all* African Americans than is sensed by more than a tiny core of African American scholars and therapists. As a once widely active worker with preschool children, primarily African American, I dare to advance the notion that no single need among growing, forming African American children is nearly so important as the ability to accept oneself in all details: roots, ancestry, intellect, and physical features. And all this relates to Du Bois at the point where he, too, failed fully to form as a joyous, creative soul because of the scars of subtle rejections, which made his own self-acceptance less than adequate. And the tragedy is that these scars were lifelong, robbing him of the benefits and joys due one who did so much for a whole race.

For all these reasons, the internal war of "ideals" and identities of which Du Bois spoke was real. He did indeed feel spat upon, seeing himself "through the eyes of others." My word in response is that this need not be so today, however inevitable it may or may not have been in the days of that amazing human being, W. E. B. Du Bois. The goal toward which all our African American homes, schools, and churches must strive in our time is to become persons who are fully competent and fluent in every necessary culture, and able to identify effectively with them all. But this African American will be able to do all of this only if fully aware of and secure in her or his own African American primary identity.

Notes

1. *Chronicle of Higher Education*, vol. 35, issue 33, April 26, 1989, pgs. A1–A28ff. Denife K. Magner, "Blacks and Whites on Campuses: Behind Ugly Racist Incidents, Student Isolation and Insensitivity."
2. Austin Steward, *Twenty-two Years a Slave and Forty Years a Freeman*. Reading, Mass.: Addison-Wesley Publishing Co., 1969, p. 72. (Originally published in 1857 by William Alling, Rochester, New York.)

Ambivalent Maybe

Wilson J. Moses

Two souls dwell, alas, in my breast.
The one wants to separate itself from the other.

Two souls, two thoughts, two unreconciled strivings;
two warring ideals in one dark body, whose dogged
strength alone keeps it from being torn asunder.

I am increasingly uncomfortable with clichés about double-consciousness, even when they issue from the pens of such literary giants as J. W. Goethe or W. E. B. Du Bois. The two-souls paradigm is essentially reductive, for even a man as unremarkable as myself must have more than two souls. To reduce oneself to two souls is almost like reducing oneself to two dimensions. The personality of every

---

Wilson Jeremiah Moses is Professor of English and History at Pennsylvania State University. His publications include *The Golden Age of Black Nationalism, Black Messiahs and Uncle Toms, Alexander Crummell,* and *The Wings of Ethiopia.* He has edited the forthcoming *Destiny and Race: Sermons and Addresses of Alexander Crummell.* His articles have appeared in *The Journal of Black Studies, Phylon,* and *American Literature.* He is currently working on a book which received a National Endowment for the Humanities Fellowship for University Teachers.

human being is complex and contradictory. It is true enough that my feelings as a black man have sometimes been in conflict with my sense of American nationality. But over the years I have become resigned to the fact that my interests, so far in this life, have always been inseparable from those of the United States.

I am restless and vulnerable, here at home. But in Europe or in Africa I have never felt any less vulnerable or alienated. Much of this certainly has to do with being black, but a portion of it simply derives from the human predicament. We must all feel lost and lonely and threatened by inevitable doom. Every age in the history of mankind has been an age of anxiety.

In order to explain myself it is necessary to explain not one but several sets of contradictions that I believe to be perpetually irreconcilable. I have to be specific about the several contexts in which I have experienced my raciality and other dimensions of my personality. I find it necessary to say something about my parents, about my ambiguous class background, about the regions where I grew up and where I presently live, about my religious background, about the university I attended, and—within the bounds of taste—about my marriage.

I grew up in Detroit, a city where geographical common sense is contradicted by the fact that Canada is due south, separated from Detroit by a river that is not a river. The Detroit River is actually a mile-wide strait connecting Lake Saint Clair to Lake Erie. Lake Saint Clair is small enough to be forgotten on some maps, and yet it stretches to the horizon, and standing on its shore can be like standing on the shore of the ocean, so that Detroit has sometimes the feel of a coastal city.

My father was employed by the Detroit Water Works so he spent a lot of time on the river. One day while he was out on the river taking water samples a man jumped to his death from the Ambassador bridge, narrowly missing my father's boat. My father was interviewed by the police and his name was given on the radio. But he never mentioned the incident until my sisters and I heard about it from the corner grocer and came bursting into the house with questions.

During the summers he liked to fish on the river, and sometimes he took me along. Once or twice we were joined by his friend Sterling Wilhite, one of the smoothest, darkest men I have ever known. His speech was sometimes clipped and ironic, at other times soft as the bittersweet poignancy of Scott Joplin's "Elite Syncopations." Like many black men of his time, he was that sharp juxtaposition of high culture and jazziness that one saw and heard in Count Basie and Duke Ellington. He lived on the west side with his graceful, pretty, almost-white wife, and his two daughters, who were friendly but very gentle and refined. I would listen to the quiet conversation of the two men, until I dozed off with the rocking of the boat. They had cool Atlanta University accents, and their language, while always free of profanity and solecism, could be hard and serious. I think they had the quality that is called *negritude*.

Downtown Detroit is laid out like the spokes of a half-wheel, with Jefferson Avenue, its base, running along the river, and Woodward Avenue, its main street, running north by northwest; the other two spokes of the half-wheel, Grand River and Gratiot avenues, fan out to northwest and northeast. The old black ghetto, Paradise Valley, is on the near east side. That was the side of town where Malcolm X preached, and where Joe Louis and later Diana Ross grew up. During the 1950s the fashionable black bourgeoisie began to move onto the west side, but it was the east side that could boast of the most interesting history, and the most local color. I grew up on the east side, although quite a distance from Paradise Valley. Our family lived in a "changing neighborhood," where white ethnics were being displaced by black working-class people. But Paradise Valley was still the center of black life in Detroit, usually referred to as Black Bottom or simply "the bottom."

The bottom was where my father went to the dentist and to the barbershop; it was the center of the black business community. In the

bottom were colorful storefront churches, as well as the mighty dome
of Ebenezer Baptist Church. There were exotic rib joints, where you
could see the sportin' crowd, with their "processed" heads and Cadillacs
parked out front. There were bars, where hardened factory workers
with scarred faces drank whiskey and listened to "gut bucket" blues.
There were also the offices of tough-minded lawyers, dignified old
black men, who used big words and tolerated no nonsense. There were
colorful costumes, barefoot prophetesses, and men wearing fezes. There
were fish markets, and vegetable stands with giant black round wa-
termelons, and little grocery stores, where people gossiped, joked, and
told the greatest lies on earth. The Great Lakes Life Insurance Company
was in the bottom, and so was the *Michigan Chronicle*—always printed
on green paper. The fraternity houses of Alpha Phi Alpha and Kappa
Alpha Psi were in the bottom, and so was the lodge of the Prince Hall
Masons.

During the 1950s a new black district was developing. Prophet
Jones had his palatial mansion on Arden Park, a fact that provoked
much clucking and head shaking among the respectable working class,
and roused the indignation of those middle-class people who were
forced to be his neighbors. During the years of my young adulthood,
much of the black business and church activity expanded out of the
bottom and onto the west side. The Nation of Islam, which had
flourished in the bottom during the 1930s was relocated on the west
side. The Shrine of the Black Madonna was established on the West
Side by the late sixties. With middle-class blacks settling along Lin-
wood and Twelfth streets, and into the Jewish neighborhoods out
Dexter Avenue, synagogues were converted into churches. Elsewhere,
the sacred tradition in music flourished, with Aretha Franklin singing
in her father's choir. Some of the black churches were big on Handel's
Messiah, and at St. Paul's AME Zion, the future Metropolitan Opera
tenor George Shirley sang, at Christmastime, "Comfort ye. Comfort
ye, my people."

The east side/west side division strongly affected the social lives of black teenagers, because there was a false, overly simplistic distinction between west side "elites" (pronounced E-lights) and east side "hoods." The topic of "E-lights and hoods" was discussed at Reverend Albert B. Cleage's Sunday-afternoon Youth Fellowship, which met in his elegant west-side home. Most of the people on the east side were not hoods, however. I, for example, was not a hood, but a lot of the E-lights never could get that straight. There were a few E-lights on the east side, but I was not an E-light, because I was socialized outside the values of the "black bourgeoisie," and did not attend Fellowship. And, not only was I a Catholic, I went to the wrong kind of Catholic school.

The Catholic schools of Detroit were divided into two classes, those outside the parish system, styling themselves prep schools, like University of Detroit High School or De La Salle Collegiate, and those that were parish-based, like Nativity of Our Lord and St. Catherine's. The prep schools were usually single sex, and had pretensions to classiness that were not always founded in fact. Their graduates were supposed to go on to Catholic colleges like the University of Detroit or Marygrove. The parochial schools often, but not always, had a more working-class character than did the Catholic preps. Nativity of Our Lord, which I attended, was lower-middle-class. The kind of people who went to Nativity lived in single-family houses on quiet streets. The mothers were usually housewives; the fathers were mostly semi-skilled workers, or small businessmen and white-collar workers. The boys stayed out of trouble, played sports, and avoided use of the "F" word. I always assumed all the girls were virgins. They wore crisp navy uniforms with white blouses.

I shall never forget the day my father brought me to the dark old building, with the words over the door "The truth shall make you free," and deposited me in the classroom of Sister Lydia. My stomach was constantly tied up in knots from the time I started to Nativity in 1952 until I graduated in 1960. Attendance at mass was compulsory, and we marched back and forth between church and school in straight lines. Nativity, like most of the older Catholic churches in Detroit, was a gigantic red brick structure. Its style was eclectic—mighty pillars, Roman arches, and lofty coffered ceiling. It was an inspiring vision to witness all those virgins, with their blue beanies, navy uniforms, and white blouses, beneath the stained-glass windows, in procession to the communion rail, while César Franck's "Meditation" played in the background.

The Catholic schools were very good at what they did. They stressed neatness, cleanliness, chastity, discipline, and obedience to authority. In those days, Catholic schools did not encourage the matriculation of non-Catholics. Pupils were expected to make their first communion in the first grade and to be confirmed in the fifth grade. Since there were few black Catholics in the city of Detroit, there were not many black youngsters in the Catholic schools. I was alone in my class of seventy from the fifth to the eleventh grade. But starting in the eleventh grade there were two of us—me and Ronald Mosely. Ron was a little fellow, who played football a lot better than I did and performed well academically, graduating in the upper third of the class. He was a good friend, who stood by me and gave me heartening pep talks, but about a week after graduation he disappeared. His family suddenly moved out of the neighborhood, and to my continuing sadness, I never learned what happened to him.

The rest of my classmates were mostly Italian and German, with a sprinkling of Irish and Poles. I must admit that, in light of the social conventions of the times, the other pupils dealt with me rather kindly and rarely took advantage of my racial vulnerability. I thus view the entire experience with nostalgia. On the other hand, there were occasions when I had to stifle tears, and I daily experienced queasiness and pain in the pit of my stomach when I walked to school.

Thomas Murrell was my friend, and it was he who introduced me to science fiction. He was also interested in music and art. I talked him into taking art-appreciation classes at the Detroit Institute of Arts, and we both made use of the collection of classical recordings at the Mark Twain Library.

I suppose I should have worked a lot harder during the years at

Nativity, but I have neither excuses nor apologies to offer. Religion, History, and English were the only subjects I cared for, and even in these I did not prepare my daily homework assignments, nor did I seriously prepare for examinations. I regret that I squandered the opportunity to develop a solid grounding in Latin grammar, but I found it impossible to study. It was those knots in my stomach. On one point I wish to be definite, however: I was never made to feel that my abilities were in any way inferior to those of the white children. In fact, the nuns constantly admonished me for not working up to my abilities, and warned that someday I would regret wasting my talents. They were right.

On the other hand I read constantly. I read frivolously. Mostly, I read fairy tales, mythology, and science fiction. I loved Shakespeare, but I foolishly neglected to complete my assignments for English classes. I listened to Tchaikovsky, Mendelsohn, and Mozart on old 78 rpm recordings (Vivaldi had not yet become fashionable), and wasted a lot of time strolling around in the Detroit Institute of Arts. Nativity church was itself a kind of museum, and I have idyllic memories centered in my fascination with the medieval character of the Catholic ritual. I never knew Catholicism as a social experience, but I appreciated the Church greatly for its music, architecture, dogma, statuary, and incense. I still appreciate the cultural heritage of Catholicism and feel, in a cultural sense, more Catholic than African.

Of course, I accepted the agenda of Catholic education, for the most part. I hadn't started drinking, but I occasionally smoked a cigar. Sexually, I was a good boy. I discovered a collection of *Playboy* magazines, owned by a friend's older brother, when I was around sixteen, but *Playboy* was comparatively chaste in those days, and I never saw a page of hard-core pornography until I was in college. I did not think much of sex as sex, because I believed it a sin to keep impure thoughts in my mind. Following the injunction of the Baltimore catechism, I committed no sins of impurity, neither alone nor with others, and I had never seen a condom. My youthful fantasies were of romantic love, derived from the few sonnets of Shakespeare, Petrarch, and Michelangelo that I had memorized. My view of women was largely controlled by women, and it was completely ethereal and idealized. I was, in short, a chaste and often solitary nerd.

For four years, I played football, astonishing my teammates with a clumsiness and ineptitude that evoked something bordering on awe. I had a high tolerance for pain and was pretty strong, but I was not agile; I was not deft; I could not sense the drift of a play. I believe I fumbled every single pass that was thrown to me in the entire four years. I had my nose smashed, got my shins bruised, and missed every single tackle that came my way. Finally, in my senior year, I overcame my lack of talent, and *earned* a letter in football. I was allowed to start in several games, and once won the praise of our handsome backfield coach, Gino D'Ambrosio, whom we all passionately adored. Athletically gifted people may find it difficult to understand what I am saying, but I am prouder of that letter than of almost any other accomplishment in my life.

During my high school years, I did not, of course, know the term *cultural relativism*, but I certainly received a basic introduction to the principle, if not the concept. I developed respect for two pantheons of heroes. At school, I idolized the English martyrs, Saint Alban, Thomas à Becket, and Thomas More. Isaac Jogues and Thomas Aquinas, the angelic doctor, were also among my favorites. I also learned black folklore. My Aunt Mary believed that God had sent the iceberg to sink the wealthy bigots on the Titanic. My friend Marvis Lee Butts told me that the Bible predicted the black man would rule the world someday. I realized that certain people in the neighborhood corresponded to stock figures in the African American Carnival of Animals, Brer Weasel, Brer Bear, Brer Snake, and the Signifying Monkey. I also got to know Pepper and Mustard, the Jack Leg Preacher, and Shine.

One day, my mother asked me if I knew that there was a Negro national anthem, and when I said I did not, she sang it for me on the spot. Someone was always singing around our house. If I began humming the barcarole from *Tales of Hoffmann*, Mom would pitch in and harmonize. We especially liked snappy spirituals, like "I want to be ready to walk in Jerusalem, just like John." Another favorite was "Ezekiel saw de wheel, way up in de middle of the air." From early childhood, I was fascinated as much by the language and the lyrics as I was by the rhythm and the melody. We almost always spoke standard English at home, but we enjoyed speaking dialect, as well. We always knew that whenever Mom spoke in dialect she was ready to go on the warpath. Dad wasn't so much into dialect, but he could talk like a preacher when he wanted to—humorously, and with an artful quaver in his voice.

It had always been taken for granted that I would go on to college after high school, but little discussion was given to the question of where. The sisters at Nativity had warned us about Wayne State University, a citadel of atheism and communism, and encouraged the brighter ones among us to think in terms of the University of Detroit, which was operated by the Jesuits. But the University of Detroit was on the other side of town and much more expensive than Wayne State. I sometimes wonder if I might have been happier at the University of Detroit, but at the time I was in rebellion against the Church, and furthermore, I had romantic notions that I would be happier at a school with a large black enrollment. Just to be safe, I applied to Highland Park Junior College, where I was pretty certain I would be admitted.

This was before affirmative action. Still my grades were okay and I was a Michigan resident. I suppose my chances for admission to East Lansing or Ann Arbor would have been perfectly good, but I never even thought to apply. In 1959 lower-middle-class kids who wanted to attend college had to learn the ropes on their own. My family thought scholarships were only for gifted athletes and impoverished geniuses. Since I couldn't play football or improvise on the piano and my father had a job, I didn't think of myself as deserving a scholarship, so I didn't apply for any. In retrospect I can see the need for the various supportive structures that later developed in American universities. Black students have not been the only beneficiaries of such structures. There have been many indirect benefits for all working-class students. The trickle-down effect of equal opportunity and affirmative action programs on public attitudes in such areas as counseling, student aid, and campus employment have benefited all young people. White students have often been better positioned to exploit the indirect benefits of affirmative action than have the mass of black students, who must still overcome poverty, violence, naïveté, and racial prejudice in order to leave their home communities for the university. In any case affirmative action had not yet been invented, and my high school did not have a guidance counselor to show me the ropes.

Wayne State University was in a period of rapid physical expansion, and its enrollment grew from thirty to forty thousand students during the 1960s. Tuition was cheap, and there was no distinction between day and night school, although a large number of courses were offered in the evenings to accommodate working students. The student body included wealthy matrons, returning to college after their children were grown, and chic young women who worked as secretaries in the College of Liberal Arts. There were businessmen, studying the humanities as a hobby, schoolteachers, meeting the requirements for advanced certification, children of Grosse Pointers who for various reasons had not gone off to Dartmouth or Bryn Mawr. I encountered Jewish students of all varieties, for the first time including both the devoutly orthodox and the suavely atheistic. And there were black students, most of us from unsophisticated but aspiring families, children of factory workers and civil servants, working part time, and taking the bus to school every morning.

One of my professors, George Naknikian, told us he had been brought up in the Armenian Orthodox Church, but he called himself an atheist. I remember one student's walking out of class when he criticized the Catholic Church. Milton Covensky and Jason Tickton always insisted on referring to their Jewish religion and culture in lectures, and their lectures were all the richer because of this. I am glad that I was not instructed by generic de-ethnicized white folks. Within a year of matriculating at Wayne State, I first ate meat on a Friday and stopped attending Sunday mass. The opera buffa that was my young adult life opened with my denunciatory sisters calling me Jeremiah the Apostate, and leaving for church singing, "Oh, sinner man, where yah gonna run to? On de jedgement day."

My intellectual life at Wayne State was focused almost exclusively on European culture. That was how I wanted it. During my undergraduate years, I took only two courses in American literature, and none in American history. I loved opera and must have seen at least fifty between 1960 and 1968, most of them during the Metropolitan Opera's annual visit to Detroit. I made an annual pilgrimage to Stratford, Ontario, where I saw perhaps twenty Shakespeare plays, and where I met my future wife, Maureen Connor, a stunning Irish redhead from Minneapolis.

My intellectual and cultural life had absolutely no relation to my formal academic work. I continued to read frivolously and I listened to Schumann and Brahms, but my performance in terms of grades and courses went from bad to worse. In the summer of 1963, I was working at the Chevrolet Gear and Axle Plant in Hamtramck, Michigan, and doing very poorly in college. I found it impossible to study, and had little idea of what I wanted to do with my life.

The turning point in my academic career came when I was married in the fall of 1963. On June 3, 1964, my first son was born, and my grades began to improve. I read British literature, heard German and Italian music, and studied classical mythology.

Gradually, I gained some exposure to the writings of black Americans. The Miles Modern Poetry Room at the university library was next door to the music listening room, where I spent inordinate amounts of time. There I discovered Langston Hughes's *The Ways of White Folks* and *I Wonder as I Wander*. By the time I graduated from college in 1965, I had read Lerone Bennett's *Before the Mayflower* and

Rosie Poole's anthology of Afro-American verse, *Beyond the Blues*. I could never bring myself to finish James Baldwin's *Another Country*—absolutely boring. I found Richard Wright's *Native Son* powerful, but I thought the final courtroom scene embarrassingly naïve. I found Wright's *The Outsider* a far more satisfying and truthful depiction of the mind of the black man. I was impressed by Booker T. Washington's *Up from Slavery* and I discovered Du Bois's *The Souls of Black Folk*, which I consider the greatest piece of writing by a black American. Du Bois's *The World and Africa* was my first experience with what we now call Afrocentrism. It was my encounter with Du Bois that led to my career in African American Studies.

In 1968 I read Harold Cruse's *The Crisis of the Negro Intellectual* which I consider the most important theoretical work in the field of black studies. For an American it must be even more important than Fanon's *The Wretched of the Earth*. I am perplexed by the present dependency of young African American intellectuals on French theorists. Perhaps this is because I preferred German to French in college, or perhaps it is only because I am growing old. But I do not believe that any French theorist—even Fanon—can teach us as much as Cruse can. Fanon's *Black Skins, White Masks*, although a fascinating book, will never be as significant to me as Cruse's *Rebellion or Revolution?*

Not long after reading Du Bois and Cruse, I abandoned British Literature for African American Studies. I left the English Department at Wayne State for the doctoral program in American Civilization at Brown. My original intention was to write a dissertation on Du Bois, but around that time I became aware of William Wells Brown's little book *The Black Man, His Antecedents, His Genius, and His Achievements* (New York: Thomas Hamilton, 1863). This book contained an excerpt from one of Alexander Crummell's speeches that I found poetic and forceful.

Amid the decay of nations, a rekindled light starts up in us. Burdens under which others expire seem to have lost their influence upon us; and while *they* are "driven to the wall," destruction keeps far from *us* its blasting hand. We live in the region of death, yet seem hardly mortal. We cling to life in the midst of all reverses; and our nerveful grasp thereon cannot easily be relaxed. History reverses its mandates in our behalf: our dotage is in the past. "Time writes not its wrinkles on our brow"; our juvenescence is in the future.

This was the same prophecy, although more formally expressed, that was boisterously proclaimed by some of the boys in the neighborhood. This was the prophecy that Ethiopia would soon stretch forth her hands, the prophecy that the black man would rule the world someday! It was the confident message of black messianism and black nationalism, on which I had secretly fantasized since childhood.

"Who was this Alexander Crummell?" I soon learned that he was the great black nationalist conservative of the nineteenth century, who had devoted his life to the cause of Pan-African nationalism. He had been educated in classical and biblical languages at the University of Cambridge and had served the cause of Liberian nationalism for almost twenty years, between 1853 and 1872. He had founded the American Negro Academy after his disillusionment with Liberia and return to the United States in 1872. Du Bois had met him, and described their first encounter in Chapter XII of *The Souls of Black Folk*.

I spoke to him politely, then curiously, then eagerly, as I began to feel the fineness of his character,—his calm courtesy, the sweetness of his strength, and his fair blending of the hope and truth of life. Instinctively I bowed before this man, as one bows before the prophets of the world. Some seer he seemed, that came not from the crimson Past or the gray To-come, but from the pulsing Now. . . .

In Howard Brotz's anthology, *Negro Social and Political Thought, 1850–1925,* I found additional excerpts from writings of Crummell and other black nationalists of the "Golden Age," including Henry Highland Garnet and Martin R. Delany. Hollis Lynch's biography, *Edward Wilmot Blyden: Pan-Negro Patriot,* convinced me that there was more to black nationalism than the black-power advocates of the sixties realized. Dorothy Porter's anthology of early black American writing contained the nineteenth-century writings of Maria Stewart, which anticipated the most impassioned jeremiads of Malcolm X. I was fascinated by the genius and power of Marcus Garvey's program, but hostile to the racial chauvinism contained within it. Years passed before I came to appreciate the importance of Harold Cruse's insights on Garvey, and especially Garvey's emphasis on economic power as the basis of intellectual independence.

Inspired by Cruse's injunction that black intellectuals ought to concentrate on the internal dialectic of the black American experience, I focused on the irony that black nationalism had historically functioned as a vehicle of assimilation. This contradiction became the subject of my doctoral dissertation, which was published as *The Golden Age of Black Nationalism, 1850–1925.* I came to believe that any work in African American studies must be solidly grounded in a thorough study of primary documents by the major black authors of the nineteenth century. I devoted a chapter to Crummell in *The Golden Age of Black Nationalism,* and I eventually made Crummell the subject of a lengthier work.

The furies that pursued Crummell during his life continue to plague black intellectuals in these times, and yet black intellectualism seems to be completely out of touch with any sense of its own history. In an American culture that is obsessed with newness for its own sake, we seem unable to create any sense of a black intellectual tradition. The American penchant for planned obsolescence favors innovation, rather than continuity, and black studies is inescapably American in its adherence to the cult of newness. Innovation has its negative as well as its positive consequences. It often destroys an environment in the name of progress and growth. But growth may be either healthy or cancerous, and the growth that is taking place in the black studies movement may not be all to the good.

College professors are not supposed to compete with professional athletes, movie stars, and talk-show hosts. Our agenda should be defined by what is good for our students. We should be in the business of convincing young people of the value of spiritual and intellectual struggle, and the inevitability of tragedy. Most of our students, baptized in the inanities of Ronald Reagan and the profanities of Eddie Murphy have been taught a profound contempt for the spiritual. We, their parents and teachers, must share blame for their apostasy, if we have, in the words of Du Bois, "worshiped the whores of Hollywood."

But Hollywood is seductive, and I admit I sometimes dream of a motion picture called *The Adventures and Travels of Alexander Crummell*. It begins with the clatter and splash of a horse-drawn buckboard over the filthy gutters of New York in 1834. The times are rough and so are the people. This is the summer of a great race riot, and the bespectacled fifteen-year-old black boy driving the wagon is suddenly pelted with rotten vegetables by a gang of young toughs. We cut to the chase, as the gang pursues the cart through the narrow, jolting streets. But in later scenes we witness Crummell's travels through the idyllic English countryside and his sojourn among the stately towers of Cambridge University. We follow him to Africa, where he sees elephants and hippos, howling monkeys, exotic birds, gorgeous foliage, beautiful, bare-breasted native women, and puritanical missionaries, suffering from heat stroke. The movie would portray the horror of Africa's first military coup and the public lynching of E. J. Roye, Liberia's president and Crummell's friend. It would conclude with the struggles of Crummell's later years, his fire-and-brimstone sermons, his friendship with the young W. E. B. Du Bois, and a deathbed denunciation of Booker T. Washington.

Two souls? All thinking people have more than two souls. Alexander

Crummell was an Afro-American, and an Americo-Liberian, a black chauvinist, and an Anglophile, a black messiah and an Uncle Tom. Many struggles took place in his soul, and certainly there was more than one dialectic. The same was true of Du Bois, who was both a revolutionary and a traditionalist, an aristocrat and an egalitarian, a democrat and a totalitarian. Goethe, too, had more than one war waging in his breast; his classicism struggled against his romanticism, his cosmopolitanism against his nationalism, his traditionalism against his inventiveness. The "fashion of our life," in Crummell's words, "fills us with perplexities and breeds constant anxieties, but these are the heritage of all God's spiritual creatures . . . created for the unending, the everlasting ventures and anxieties of their spirits in the deep things of God."

It is the job of the black intellectual to teach our young people the importance of this inner struggle. Our youth are at some times disturbingly credulous, at others skeptical to the point of cynicism. Our task is to hearten them in their internal warfare against both credulity and cynicism. And our obligations are not limited to black students. Black scholars today often find ourselves teaching predominantly, or even completely, white classes. It is not uncommon for us to feel that we are ambassadors for the race, and that we must achieve by our examples the mighty task of racial vindication. We feel that if we reveal small human flaws we will provide excuses for discrimination against all black people. We fear that any mistakes we make, any deficiencies we reveal, will reflect poorly on our black colleagues, or make the path worse for black students. We have an irrational dread that, if we are mediocrities in our profession, we will hold back the progress of the entire race.

Many black spokesmen speak mainly to white audiences. We do not have to apologize for doing this, any more than Malcolm X had to apologize when he lectured at Harvard and the London School of Economics. We should, however, be honest enough to admit that our perspectives arise out of the rather milky conditions in which we live.

E. Franklin Frazier recognized fifty years ago that the black liberal intellectual, immersed in the bohemian-proletarian culture of his white peers, is often incapable of intellectual independence. So thoroughly have some of us caught the thought and speech of postmodern intellectualism that the spectacle of a desperate and abandoned black youth in the squalor of a Chicago tenement, naïvely attempting to find God's truth in *The Protocols of the Elders of Zion*, evokes more of indignation than of pity. Even those of us with the sincerest intentions have not learned how to reach that black youth, and it seems unlikely that we will reach him so long as we teach in predominantly white classrooms.

Twenty-five years ago Martin Kilson sniffed at black studies and thought he "smelled a rat." More recently John Hope Franklin said that "most African American scholars went into so-called black studies, not by choice but by the force of racism that dictated the nature of scholarship, as it did in virtually all other aspects of American life." There is no question that I, too, have sometimes smelled a rat and wondered if I should have "retreated," as Franklin puts it, "to the study of Negroes."

In one of his visionary poems, "Children of the Moon," Du Bois invented the story of a self-sacrificing demigoddess, who, "in time's weird contradiction," brings to the "children of the moon, freedom and vast salvation." The salvation of a race is a lofty goal and an educator who aspires to it should beware the pitfall of hubris. The "weird contradiction" is something that we have all known. Internal contradiction and ambivalence are part of the human condition, and African Americans, no less than other human beings, are destined to confront them as long as we are human.

Deep Sight and
Rescue Missions

Toni Cade Bambara

I.

It's one of those weird winter-weather days in Philly. I'm leaning against the wall of a bus kiosk in Center City brooding about this article that won't write itself. Shoppers unself-consciously divest themselves of outer garments, dumping woolly items into shopping bags. I'm scarfed to the eyes à la Jesse James, having just been paroled from the dentist. And I'm eager to get back to the 'Hood where I've been conducting an informal survey on assimilation. The term doesn't have the resonance it once had for me. I'm curious as to why that is.

At the moment, gums aching, I'm sure of only four things: ambivalence still hallmarks the integrationist-vs.-nationalist pull in

---

Born in Harlem and raised in New York, *Toni Cade Bambara* is currently based in Philadelphia, where she operates as a media activist. Her books include the anthologies *The Black Woman* and *Tales and Short Stories for Black Folks*; the short-story collections *Gorilla, My Love* and *The Seabirds Are Still Alive*; and the novel *The Salt Eaters*, recipient of the 1991 American Book Award from the Before Columbus Foundation. Her film works include the award-winning documentary *The Bombing of Osage Avenue*, which she scripted and narrated. She is working on a novel based on the Atlanta missing and murdered children's case, and *Yeah, But Not Under Capitalism*, a collection of short stories. She is currently the coordinating writer for the four-part documentary on Dr. W. E. B. Du Bois.

Amero-African political life; social and art critics still disrespect, generally, actual differences in pluralistic United States and tend to collapse constructed ones instead into a difference-with-preference sameness, with White as major and People of Color (POCs) minor; media indoctrination and other strategies of coercive assimilation are endemic, ubiquitous, and relentless as ever; and the necessity of countering propaganda and deprogramming the indoctrinated as imperative as ever. I'm sure also that I am not as linguistically nimble as I used to be when interviewing various sectors/strata of the community, for I've just blown a gab fest on identity, belonging, and integration at the dentist's through an inability to bridge the gap between the receptionist, a working-class sister from the projects, who came of age in the sixties and speaks in nation-time argot, and the new dental assistant, a more privileged sister currently taking a break from Bryn Mawr, who speaks the lingo of postmodern theory.

Across from the bus stop is a new luxury high rise, a colossus of steel and glass with signs announcing business suites for lease. I wonder who's got bank these days to occupy such digs. Philly is facing economic collapse. Paychecks for municipal workers are often weeks late. The hijacking of neighborhoods by developers, who in turn are being leaned on by the banks, which in turn are being scuttled by the robber barons, who in turn are being cornered by IRS investigators working for the Federal Reserve, whose covers have been pulled off by black and Latino task forces, who in turn are harassed by Hoover's heirs. And while many citizens are angry about the S & L bailout being placed on the backs of workers one paycheck away from poverty and obscurity, they are even more distressed by cuts in social services that have pushed homelessness beyond the crisis point. I roam my eyes over the building, wondering if the homeless union would deem it media-worthy for a takeover.

In the lobby of the high rise is a sister about my age, early fifties, salt-'n'-pepper 'fro, African brass jewelry, a woolly capelike coat of an

Andean pattern. She's standing by a potted fern, watchful. She seems to be casing the joint. I get it in my head that she's a "checker," a member of a community group that keeps an eye on HUD and other properties suitable for housing the homeless. A brisk-walking young sister emerges from the bank of elevators. Briefcase tucked smartly under one elbow, coat draped over the left Joan Crawford shoulder pad, hair straight out of a Vidal Sassoon commercial, the sister strides past the visitors-must-sign-in information counter, and the older woman approaches her. I search for a word, rejecting "accosts," "buttonholes," "pounces," and "confronts," but can't find a suitable verb for the decisiveness and intensity of the older woman's maneuver. Obviously strangers, they, nonetheless, make short shrift of amenities and seem to hunker down to a heavy discussion forthwith, the older sister doing most of the talking. She's not panhandling. She's not dispensing literature of any kind. She doesn't reach over to pin a campaign button on the Armani lapel. But she's clearly on a mission. What kind of scam, then, could it be? And if not a scam, what?

I now get it in my head that the older sister is Avey Johnson, sprung from the pages of Paule Marshall's 1983 novel *Praisesong for the Widow*. Avey, having rejected her deracinated life of bleached-out respectability in White Plains, New York, fashions a new life's work, taking up a post in buildings such as the high rise to warn bloods of the danger of eccentricity and to urge them to (re)center themselves and work for the liberation of the people. I'm so certain it's Avey, I move away from the wall to go get in it. My daughter's voice chimes in my ear: "Mother, mind your own business." I head for the curb, muttering my habitual retort: "Black people are my business, sugar." A young-blood on a skateboard zooms by. His bulky down jacket, tied around his hips by the sleeves, brushes against my coat and stops me. The No. 23 bus is approaching. So is rush hour. And who knows how swiftly and mean the weather will turn any second. I board.

From my seat, I watch the briefcase sister spin out the revolving doors onto the sidewalk. She seems preoccupied, unsure, but not about whether to put on her coat. She walks to the corner. Her gait is no longer brisk. Her suit has lost its crispness. She swivels around, though, like a runway model and looks through the glass of the lobby. The older woman has a brother backed up against the newspaper rack. She's taken a wide-legged stance, coat swept back from her hips, fists planted on the rise of the bones, neck working, mouth going. He holds his attaché case in front of him with both hands as though to fend her off. The light changes and the bus moves on.

In *Praisesong*, it's the power of a handed-down tale that rescues Avey from an inauthentic life, from the bad bargain she made early on, surrendering up cultural authenticity in exchange for separate-peace acceptability. Through the tale's laying-on-of-hands potency, Avey undergoes a process of reading the signs and codes, a refamiliarization with blackness that releases the power of Nommo and grounds her, so that she can adopt a responsible life. The tale is still told today in the Georgia and Carolina Sea Islands. The self-same tale informs, too, Julie Dash's 1991 screen masterpiece *Daughters of the Dust*.

In the opening of the independent black feature film, a boat glides into view. The terrain looks tropical. Dragonflies hover over the green-thick water. At the prow of the boat stands a woman in a large, veiled, creamy-white hat. She wears a long, heavy, creamy-white dress. This image is straight out of a million colonialism-as-fun movies. But this woman is standing hipshot, one arm akimbo, cocked chin, all att-ti-tude. These ebonics signal the spectator that Sister Dash has appropriated the iconography from imperialist entertainment for an emancipatory purpose. The boat pulls into the shallows, where a carving of an African, a figure once attached to the prow of a slaver ship, bobs close to shore. The boat docks. A legend appears on screen: "Ibo Landing, 1902." Thereafter, the handed-down tale of the Ibos unfolds as part of the film's complex narrative.

When the boat brought the Ibos from the slaver ship, the story goes, the Africans stepped out onto the sand in their chains, took one look around, and with deep-sight vision saw what the Europeans further had in store for them, whereupon they turned right around and walked all the way home on the water to the motherland. In *Daughters*, various members of the Peazant family, gathered on a Carolina island for a final reunion picnic before migration splits them up, react to the tale in different ways. Several characters, urged by Nana, the family head, to remember, to resist amnesia, to take with them on their journey away from the ancestral place the faculty for deep-sight vision, draw strength from the story, as does Avey Johnson in the novel. "My body may be here," Avey's great-great-grandmother had said, passing along the tale, "but my mind's long gone with the Ibos." *Daughters*, like *Praisesong*, invites the viewer, the reader, to undergo a process to liberate the imperialized eye.

The No. 23 bus, heading for Chinatown, first cuts through a district that community workers call The Zone of Diminishing Options. In the three-block area around Race and Ninth streets are pawn shops that also sell used clothes, labor-pool agencies advertising dishwashing jobs in the Atlantic City casinos, a very busy blood bank, a drop-in shelter, the Greyhound terminal, an army recruiting office, and a hospice center. While draft counseling in the Zone, I'd often think of opening a gun shop, if only to disrupt the perverse visual gag. And while in the Zone, I caught a third of a provocative independent black film called *Drop Squad*. A community worker, cassette in hand, persuaded a pawn-shop owner to play it on a set in the window.

Written by David Taylor, produced by Butch Robinson, and directed by David Johnson, *Drop Squad* is a satire about hijacking the hijacked. A nationalist organization puts the snatch on an assimilated corporate blood, straps him down in a chair in a red-black-and-green-draped community center, and proceeds to try to deprogram him. "You need to reacquaint yourself with you, brother," they tell him, assigning him to read Toni Morrison's *The Bluest Eye*. They take turns chanting a roll-call reveille: Soul Train, Garvey, Eleanor Bumpers, Revolutionary Action Movement, Biko, Fannie Lou Hamer, W. E. B. Du Bois, Sharpeville, Billie Holiday, Frantz Fanon. They argue, threaten, cajole, insist, are determined to wake the brother up. He counters with equal passion for the individual right to be whatever and whomsoever he pleases. Frequently his arguments are sound, momentarily stumping his captors. But they are relentless in their campaign to call the brother home, to reclaim him for the collective mission of race recovery. Privileged as he has become through people's struggles, they argue that he has a debt both to himself and to his community blasted by drugs, violence, joblessness, homelessness, lack of access, and the politics of despair.

I reach Germantown. The Hawk, out now and bold, blows me toward the greengrocer on Chelten. Worker Khan Nguyen has been discussing assimilation for me with her customers, especially Vietnamese and African and East Indian Caribbeans new to the U.S. She reports that assimilation is synonymous with citizenship training. It's her take that while folks know that the intent of the training is to "domesticate" them, the emphasis on democracy and rights makes them "wildly expectant." Khan winks. She has not been tamed by the process. "It may be naïve of me," she says, warming to the subject, but the fact that "new immigrants take democracy more seriously" than it is generally practiced in a society built on theft and bondage, riddled by a white-supremacist national ideology, motivated by profit and privilege, and informed by fascist relations between classes, races, sexes, and communities of various sexual orientations, cultural heritages, and political persuasions "means that, in time, they will become unruly." She leans on the phrase "in time," because I am frowning. I ask about citizenship as a bribe contract: We'll grant you citizenship, and in return you drop your cultural baggage and become "American," meaning defend the status quo despite your collective and individual self-interest. She repeats the phrase "in time," putting her whole body into it to drown me out. I stumble out of there, hugging a bottle of Jamaican vanilla extract (excellent wash for cleaning/deodorizing the refrigerator, by the by), hopeful.

I run into a young friend, Anthony (Buffalo Boy) Jackson, graffiti artist and comic-book maker. I ask for his help, easing into the topic by explaining "assimilation" as I first encountered it in Latin (the changing of letters to make them sound in accord with letters nearby, i.e., *absimilare* in Latin becomes *assimilar*, *eccentricus* in Medieval Latin or *ekkentros* in Greek becomes *eccentric* in English), and *bio* (the process by which the body converts food into absorbable substances for the maintenance of the system). Before I can get to the sociopolitical meaning, Anthony is off and running with "system," recounting a middle-school field trip to a marsh in the New Jersey Pine Barrens to study ecosystems. He loses me, but I chime in when I hear usable things like "symbiosis" and "parasites," and finally the ability of the amoeba to give alternate responses to its environment because of its shape-shifting ability.

"Hold it, Anthony, are you saying amoebas can transform the system? I mean, err rahh, are they capable of collective action or are they basically loners?"

My friend is dancing and laughing at me. "The amoeba shall overthrow, right?" Big joke.

I walk him toward Burger King 'cause now he has an idea—the amoeba as mantua, shape shifter, ninja—and the tables are big enough to spread out on. I bring him back to my needs, and he tells me the issue is rip-off, not assimilation.

"Everything we do," he says, meaning breaking, scratching, rapping, dressing, "gets snatched up and we get bumped off." Which is why, he explains, he admires Spike Lee, because of Lee's control over the films and especially over the spin-offs that come out of 40 Acres and a Mule—CDs, books, T-shirts, mugs, caps, jackets. He ducks inside and shakes his head about me. I'm old enough to know what the deal is, and the deal is rip-off.

Down the block, toward Wayne Avenue, is a produce truck where people frequently gather to talk over the news of the day. Trucker Mr. Teddy, a blood from Minnesota, tells me that only Europeans were invited to become truly assimilated. "And assimilation went out when

Roots came in and busted up the whole melting-pot con game." According to him, nobody's been melted—not Norwegians, not Germans, not Japanese, and definitely not Africans. He talks about the Swedes in the Midwest who, in reclaiming their heritage, particularly their seventeenth-century socialist tradition, have rejected assimilation. "Hmm," sez I and venture to ask if these unmelted Amero-Europeans he speaks of reject as well their race/skin privileges, the socio-eco-political and psychic profits derived from U.S. apartheid. "Now that would be un-Amurrican." He chuckles and slamdunks a cabbage into my bag.

Across the avenue in front of the newsstand where folks are lined up to buy lottery tickets, the daily floor show is in progress. It features an old white guy who shuffles along the strip panhandling from the newsstand, past the wall bordering the Super Fresh, past the Woolworth, to the area near the bank where vendors line the curbs all the way down to Germantown Avenue, where I got off the No. 23. Some black people derive great pleasure from helping a down-and-out white person. The same pleasure, I suspect, that film-buff friends of mine enjoy watching a wrecked Chet Baker fall totally apart on screen in the docu *Let's Get Lost*. There are always folks about, fingering the videotapes on the tables—today "Highlights of the Clarence Thomas–Anita Hill Hearings" is selling for $8—who crack on the generous-minded who give money to panhandling whites. "Christian duty my ass! Let that ole cracker beg in his own neck of the woods." But the consensus notion is that Old Whiteguy is pretty much in his neck of the woods, that he lives, in fact, in posh quarters on Wissahickon Avenue. Should anyone voice that, they are charged with being pro-racist, at least stereotypic in thinking that all white people are well-off. "Well-off or not," someone is saying as I reach the performing arena, "he's getting fat off black people." That remark triggers a mention of jim crow, talking low, and slavery. So a few people make a point of jostling the old man. Should anyone object and call the behavior racist, as in reverse racism, that provokes still another discussion: that some in the race seem to live outside of history and don't appreciate the fact that a race war is going on and that it wasn't bloods who declared it; whereupon statistics are ticked off about infant mortality, life expectancy, illiteracy, unemployment, and other aspects of the war. Meanwhile, Old Whiteguy is steadily collecting loose change, wending his way toward a sister who vends around our way only occasionally.

I don't know her name yet, but I admire her titles: Sam Yette's *The Choice*, Chancellor Williams's *The Destruction of Black Civilization*, and everything that Angela Davis ever published. Should a youth bedecked in gold try to get past her, she'll beckon her/him over and give a mini workshop on black miners in South Africa, apartheid, and the international gold trade. Should a youngblood stroll by in a Malcolm T-shirt (*By Any Means Necessary*) she will get very generous with her wares. Old Whiteguy is another matter.

"You want a what—a quarter!?!" she says. "I'll give you a quarter." Images of Old Whiteguy tied to two horses being lashed in opposite directions flood my dentist-traumatized brain. She looks him up and down and says quite seriously, "Hey, you used to be a young peckerwood, so why ain't you president?" He grins his drooly grin, hand still stuck out. Book Sister turns to the incense seller in a crocheted cufi at the next table. "Come get this clown before I'm forced to hurt him."

Before dark, I reach home, a coop whose comfy lobby I'd thought would ensure me neighbors enough for a roundtable discussion on this article. But the lobby's empty. I drop in on my neighbor Vera Smith. She takes a hard line on both aggressive assimilationists and seemingly spaced denialists, folks quick to call behavior manifested by Book Sister and jostlers as racist, folks who swear that things are all right, or would be all right if Black people weren't so touchy, mean, and paranoid. I say something like "consciousness requires a backlog of certain experiences." Vera ain't going for it. From day one, she says, there's enough evidence around to peep the game and resist. "So it's a decision to be like that," she says. "And it takes a lot of energy to deny what's obvious." Denialists don't want to see, don't want to belong, don't want to struggle, says Vera, putting a pin in it.

We talk into the night about a lot of things. A first-generation U.S. Bajun, she shares with me her plan to have dual citizenship, from the U.S. which she automatically has, and from Barbados also. I'm profoundly pleased for her, and for us, for whenever a Brer Rabbit slip-the-yoke operation can be achieved, it puts another plank underfoot at home *base*.

I ride the elevator, thinking about people I've known growing up (not that all these years aren't my formative years) who worked tirelessly to maintain a deep connection with the briarpatch and its ways of being. No matter where they journeyed in the world or what kinds of bribes they were offered to become amnesiacs, they knew their real vocation was to build home base, sanctuaries, where black people can stand upright, exhale, and figure out what to do about the latest attack. And so they kept faith with the church of their childhood, or the UNIA or Father Divine movement (both alive and well in Philly, by the by), or the family farm in Alabama, or the homestead in the Islands, sending money, cement, clothing, books, lumber, weapons, certain that home base is not where you may work or go to school, but where the folks are who named you daughter, daddy, mama, doctor, son, brother, sister, partner, dahlin', chile.

I rinse my ravaged mouth out with warm salt water and hit the keyboard. As my young friend said, the issue is rip-off. Invisibility is not a readily graspable concept for a generation that grew up on MTV, Cosby, Oprah, Spike Lee, Colin Powell, and black folks on soaps, quiz shows, and the nightly news. Not only are black folks ostensibly participating, so what the hell does invisibility mean?, but what is generally recognized at home and abroad as "American" is usually black. A hundred movies come to mind, but not their titles, sorry. For instance the one about two lost young Euro-Ams who find themselves in what they think is a time warp, the terrain woefully fiftyish, but discover that they've landed in a Soviet spy school, in an American village erected for the purpose of training infiltrators to pass as "American." The two are enlisted to update and authenticate the place and the curriculum. Everything they present as "American"—music, speech, gesture, style—is immediately identifiable, certainly to any black spectator, as black.

As for alienation, or as Dr. Du Bois limned it in numerous texts, double-consciousness and double vision, people coming of age in a period hallmarked by all-up-in-your-face hip-hop and an assertive pluralism/multiculturalism as well don't see barriers as a policy as old as Cortez, as deadly as COINTELPRO, as seductive as the Chris Columbus hype chugging down the pike, and more solid than the Berlin Wall, given the system's monstrous ability to absorb, coopt, deny, marginalize, deflect, defuse, or silence.

I don't know what goes on in classrooms these days, but in informal settings the advice of the Invisible Man's granddaddy, "Undermine 'em with grins," is inexplicable Tomism. The paradoxical paradigm of the Liberty Paint Factory episode in Ellison's novel, the necessity of mixing in black to concoct pure white, is just a literary joke thought up by some old-timey guy on an equally old-timey typewriter. The three aspects of alienation as traditionally experienced and understood by my elders, my age group, and the generation that came of age in the sixties—alienation from the African past (and present—Was there ever an American airline with direct flights to the motherland?), alienation from U.S. economic and political power, alienation from the self as wholly participating in history—don't register as immediately relevant.

I spend a fitful night fashioning questions to raise with myself in the morning. What characterizes this moment? There's a drive on to supplant "mainstream" with "multicultural" in the national consciousness, and that drive has been sparked by the emancipatory impulse, blackness, which has been the enduring model for other downpressed sectors in the U.S. and elsewhere. A repositioning of people of color

(POCs) closer to the center of the national narrative results from, reflects, and effects a reframing of questions regarding identity, belonging, community. "Syncretism," "creolization," "hybridization" are crowding "assimilation," "alienation," "ambivalence" out of the forum of ideas. A revolution in thought is going on, I'm telling myself, drifting off. Modes of inquiry are being redevised, conceptual systems overturned, new knowledges emerging, while I thrash about in tangled sheets, too groggy to turn off the TV.

It drones on about Maxwell, the publishing baron who allegedly went over the side of his private yacht at two in the morning. All commentary reduced to the binary, as is typical of thought in the "West": suicide or homicide? I smirk in my sleep, sure that Maxwell used a proxy corpse and is alive and chortling in, say, Belo Horizonte, Brazil. Jim Jones, no doubt, is operating, courtesy of the CIA's answer to the Witness Relocation Program.

Still half-asleep, I rummage around in dualisms which keep the country locked into delusional thinking. The Two-Worlds obsession, for example: Euro-Ams not the only book reviewers that run the caught-between-two-worlds number into the ground when discussing works by Maxine Hong Kingston, Leslie Marmon Silko, Rudolfo Anaya, and other POCs, or rather, when reducing complex narrative dramas by POCs to a formula that keeps White World as a prominent/given/eternal factor in the discussion. Two-Worlds functions in the cultural arena the way Two-Races or the Black-and-White routine functions in the sociopolitical arena. It's a bribe contract in which Amero-Africans assist in the invisibilization of Native Americans and Chicanos in return for the slot as *the* "indigenous," the former slaves who were there at the beginning of the great enterprise called America.

The limits of binary opposition were in evidence in a manuscript I'd been reading on the way to the dentist's office. Articles that called black cinema "oppositional cinema" to Hollywood totally ignored practitioners operating in the independent circuit, and focused instead on Spike Lee, Matty Rich, John Singleton, Joe Vasquez, and Mario Van

Peebles—filmmakers who take, rather than oppose, Hollywood as their model of filmmaking. The articles reminded me of the way the establishment press during the so-called Spanish-American War labeled the gung-ho, shoot-em-up, Manifest Destiny-without-limits proponents as imperialists, and the let's-move-in-in-the-name-of-hemispheric-hegemony proponents as anti-imperialists. Meanwhile, only the black press was calling for a genuine help-liberate-then-cooperate-not-dominate anti-imperialism. All that is to say, there are at least three schools of black filmmaking in the U.S.: that which produces within the existing protocol of the entertainment industry and may or may not include a critique (Fred Williamson, for example); that which uses enshrined genres and practices but disrupts them in order to release a suppressed voice (Spike Lee, for example, who freed up the B-Boy voice in his presentations, not to be confused with interrogations, offering a critique of U.S. society but not rising above its retrograde mindset *re* women and homosexuals in order to produce a vision); and that which does not use H'wood as its point of departure, but is deliberate and self-conscious in its commitment to building a socially responsible cinema, fashioning cinematic equivalents for our sociopolitical/cultural specificity and offering transformation dramas (Julie Dash, Hailie Gerima, Larry Clarke, and other insurgents of "La Rébellion," who, in the late sixties, drafted a declaration of independence in the overturning of the UCLA film school curriculum).

The limits of binary thinking are spooky enough, I'm thinking, as the birds begin, but what are the prospects for sound sense in the immediate future now that conglomerates have escalated their purchase on the national mind? Since the 1989 publication of the Chomsky-Herman tome *orechestraing* and the fall 1991 issues of *Media Fair*, which drew a scary enough picture of media control by white men of wealth, the noose has tightened. And today seventeen corporations own more than 50 percent of U.S. media—textbook companies, newspapers, magazines, TV stations, radio stations, publishing houses, film-production companies. And computerization makes it all the easier to expunge from available reference material those figures, movements, and lessons of the past that remind us that radicalism is also a part of the U.S. tradition. Without models, how does any citizen break out of the basic dualism that permeates social, educational, political, economic, cultural, and intimate life in this country? I refer to the demonic model abridged below:

We are ordained	You are damned
We make history	You make dinner
We speak	You listen
We are rational	You are superstitious, childlike (as in minor)
We are autonomous and evolved	You are shiftless, unhinged, underdeveloped, primitive, savage, dependent, criminal, a menace to public safety, are needy wards and clients but are not necessarily deserving
We live center stage, the true heroes (and sometimes heroines)	You belong in the wings or behind the scrim providing the background music
We are pure, noble, upright	You are backward, fallen, tainted, shady, crafty, wily, dark, enigmatic, sly, treacherous, polluted, deviant, dangerous, and pathological
We are truly human	You are grotesques, beasts, pets, raisins, Venus flytraps, dolls, vixens, gorillas, chicks, kittens, utensils
We were born to rule	You were born to serve
We own everything	Even you are merely on loan to yourself through our largess
We are the dicks	You are the pussies
We are entitled	You are obliged

I slap the alarm clock quiet and roll over, pondering my own journey out of the lockup. Pens crack under me, paper rustles. When in doubt, hew close to the autobiographical bone, I instruct myself. But my own breakout(s) from the lockup where black/woman/cultural worker in the binary scheme is a shapeless drama with casts of thousands that won't adhere to any outline I devise. I opt instead for a *faux* family portrait to narrate what I can't essay.

2.
Split Vision and America the Beautiful

José Feliciano is on the radio singing "Ohhh beautiful for spacious skies." Everyone holds still, alert to meaning in each stressed note, breath, and strum. Elbows on the table, Aunt Clara studies the pattern of kernels in her corn-on-the-cob as Feliciano builds, reining in his passion then unleashing it. Cousin Claude, the barbecue fork his baton, stands on tiptoe to hit the high notes. "America, America" comes out in preposterous falsetto, but nobody laughs or complains. Fragments of the tune, raspy and offkey, snag in the throat of Granddaddy Daniels. He leaves off singing to say that nobody lets loose on "America" like Aretha or Ray Charles. It takes a blood to render the complex of longing, irony, and insistence that characterizes our angular relationship to this country.

The song over, Cousin Claude forgets he came indoors to take orders; he drifts around the living room while the burgers burn out back. Aunt Clara makes pulp of her corn on the cob; the attack has less to do with food, more with what a hunger the song has stirred up. Granddaddy Daniels clears his throat, spits phlegm into a hanky, then makes a big production out of folding the paper and backing it to the crossword puzzle. The youngsters on the floor doing homework lean in the old man's direction. Clearing the throat is usually a prelude to storytelling, but his pencil point keeps piercing the newsprint, a signal that he's not in a storying mood about, say, why he never rises when "The Star-Spangled Banner" is sung at the stadium, but will shush everybody and strain forward when a "cullid person" is doing the hell out of "America, the Beautiful." Eventually he bobs his head up and down and says that the Latino brother kicked much butt.

Cousin Claude waltzes into the kitchen and dances one of the Moten sisters away from the chopping board. He's humming the last few lines of the song, his lips tucked in and "brotherhood" growling in the throat then richocheting off the roof of his mouth, the final notes thin and trailing out to sea as, the dance over, he bows and heads through the door. The Moten twins, "healthy" women who cook in their black slips and stockinged feet, resume arguing about whether or not hard-boiled eggs are going into the potato salad this day, goddamnit.

Cousin Claude goes down the back steps one at a time like a child. He ponders aloud the mystery and history of Africans in the U.S. The elders, squinched together on the back-porch glider, call out, "Shut up," "Preach," or "Your food's on fire, sugah," depending on how worked up they wish to get on the subject. When the call-and-response reaches a pitch, drowning out the DJ on the radio overhead in the kitchen window, Cousin Claude tries, without success, to lure the elders into a discussion of his childhood days when the household wars between the Danielses and the Motens threatened to split the family up and drive all the children crazy.

War One: Assimilation vs. Transformation

It was Great Aunt Zala, a Daniels, who would shake us awake when Mr. Paul came calling. We'd scramble up and brace ourselves against each other in order to reach our assigned-by-age positions on the horsehair couch that my daddy, a Moten, went and bought anyway during the 1930s Don't-Buy-Where-You-Can't-Work campaign in

Harlem. Legs stuck out, heels hooked in the welting that edged the cushions, we'd manage not to yawn, suck our thumbs, or otherwise disgrace ourselves in front of a race man or race woman, who always seemed to come in the night to do their talking.

Some of the grownups didn't think children should be privy to conversations about the state of the race—our struggles, our prospects, our allies, our enemies. They kept us away from Speakers Corner, union halls, poetry readings, outdoor rallies, tenant meetings, and even our own basement, where longshoremen—"Negroes," West Indians, Puerto Ricans, and Cubans—would meet to strategize against the bosses, landlords, merchants, union sellouts, cops, the FBI, the draft board, Immigration, Murder Incorporated, and other white forces in easy collusion when it came to keeping colored folks down.

The less the children know, the easier it'll be for them to fit in and make their way, seemed to be the thinking of half the household. They lobbied for lobotomy, in other words, convinced that ignorance was the prime prerequisite for assimilation, and assimilation the preferred path to progress. But Great Aunt Zala went right on opening the door to Robeson, Du Bois, Claudia Jones, Rose Garner, J. A. Rogers, the Sleeping Car Porters and Maids, the dockworkers, and members of the Ida B. Wells clubs. The woman would just not let us sleep.

War Two: Repatriation vs. Self-Determination

Cousin Claude entered high school the year of the World's Fair in New York. Grown, to hear him tell it, he had the right to join the Garveyites collecting signatures on a petition demanding reparations from the government and rematriation to the motherland. On April 24, 1939, the petition, signed by two-point-five million African souls, was introduced into Congress. Claude's mother, Aunt Billy, let it be known that she wasn't going no damn where on account of (a) she was part Narragansett on her father's side, (b) she was grandchild of many an enslaved African whose labor had further purchased her place in this land, (c) what was the point in going over there when the thing to do was to fight the good fight over here and change the government's policies that made life here and there and everywhere unbearable for colored people.

By freeing up this country from the robber barons and their brethren in sheets, the argument went, we'd free up half the world. So the first thing was to work hard and develop a firm base here from which to challenge the state. Forget this place, was Uncle Charlie's position; in Africa, we could build bigger armies with which to defeat colonialists and imperialists. Yeah, tell it to freedmen in Liberia slaving on Firestone's plantations, Aunt Billy would say right back. The children were drawn into the debates. Posters made from board-of-education oaktag filled the halls of the brownstone: BACK TO AFRICA *vs*. SELF-DETERMINATION IN THE BLACK BELT AND THE REST OF THE PLANET. Arguments waxed hot. Kinship loyalties frayed. Even after Congress tabled the bill and turned its attention to the war raging in Europe, there was no sleeping in that house.

War Three: Swing-Vote Politics vs. Independent Formations

After what the black press called "Fighting the Two Hitlerisms" at home and abroad, the Cold War chill set in, which we, in Harlem, experienced as heat—HUAC ushering in a new Inquisition. Patriotism against Hitler made the blacks-as-inferior line too blatant, as Gerald Horne points out in his work on Du Bois, *Black and Red*. Blacks-as-subversives became the new line. We experienced a crackdown on thinkers, speakers, writers, organizers, and coalition builders. Independent thought was a threat to national security, the state mouthpieces said at the Smith Act trials.

The household split into ever-shifting factions over the 1948 presidential election. Play ward politics for local spoils and concessions and never mind the "big picture" *vs*. hitch our collective wagon to the NAACP and bloc vote *vs*. Up the Party! and Down with HUAC!

vs. build the American Labor Party and campaign for Henry Wallace *vs*. establish an independent black national party and to hell with all this switch hitting that only keeps us locked into other people's tournaments.

An insomniac at twenty-two, Cousin Claude began reading everything he could get his hands on, haunting the Michaux Memorial Bookstore on 125th street and Seventh Avenue and haunting us too, day and night. He took to quizzing his less-than-peers at the kitchen table: Did we know about Palmares, the sovereign nation self-emancipated Africans in Brazil created? Did we know about the maroon communities in the Sea Islands off the Georgia and Carolina coasts? Did we know that Oklahoma was going to come into the union as either an "Indian" state or a "Negro" state? Did we have any idea how stupid we were? If we weren't going to improve our minds, would we kindly change our names?

Cousin Claude was reading Du Bois as well, who in 1948 had just been bounced for the second time in fifteen years from the NAACP. Cousin Claude took to waking us up at night for our opinion of Dr.'s divided-self proposition: should we invest our time, energy, money, and African genius struggling to become first-class citizens in an insanely barbarous country whose majority despises both us and our efforts to humanize the place; or should we gather our genius together and create a society of our own, in this country or someplace else? Not an elder yet, Cousin Claude could be told to get lost and let us rest. But being a Daniels, he never did.

3.
White Sight and the Bee in the Hexagon

When I first ran across Dr. Du Bois's passage as a girl, I had a problem straightaway. It conflicted with what I'd learned early on through

Eldersay, namely, that the seventh son (or seventh son of the seventh son) who was born with a "veil" (some said "caul," which I heard as "call" as in having a calling) was enhanced by it, was gifted, not afflicted (unless the parents or godparents failed to perform particular rites with the caul, in which case the cauled might see ghosts; but that seemed to me no big deal, for a people who've come through the Middle Passage are surely predisposed to see ghosts, right?).

Second sight enabled the person to see things others couldn't see. Persons born with the veil were, if not clairvoyants, at least clearseeing. They could see through guise and guile. They were considered wise, weird, blessed, tetched, or ancient, depending on the bent of the describer. But they were consulted in the neighborhoods, occasionally revered. It was a vice-versa thing too—that is, people in the community known for unusually imaginative good sense were said to have been born with second sight, born with a veil, even if the sayer had not been present at the birth or could otherwise verify the existence of a gauzy membrane surrounding the eyes of the newborn.

When I came to the bit about looking at your own self all the time through the eyes of people who either pity you or hate you, that did not sound like the second sight I'd heard of. That sounded like white sight, the way your eyeballs roll around in a sea of white when you've totally lost track of yourself because of drinking or some other foolishness. My classmate Kyoto had a name for the condition where a lot of white is visible between the bottom round of the pupil and the eyelid, *sanpaku*. The person is disoriented, out of touch with self, surroundings, the universe. In this disconnected state, the person lacks vitality, lacks precision in thought and movement, has poor instinctual self-preservation reactions, and is very prone to accidents. *Sanpaku* is considered a state of serious physical and spiritual imbalance. You need a doctor, preferably a Japanese doctor, preferably one who can start you on a macrobiotic diet.

Kyoto's family were in the U.S. concentration camps during the forties. He used to say that many of the inmates suffered from white sight. Several, to prove their loyalty to America, enlisted and helped kill Japanese and other members of the Axis powers. I can't say for sure whether he said those volunteers manifested the gravest forms of white sight or not, because we mostly liked to talk about the Japanese American battalions and African American units that liberated the German concentration camps and how the State Department was determined to keep the participation of colored people secret. So in the newsreels we only saw white heroism. It was propaganda designed to promote white sight, we instructed each other.

Frenchy, a neighborhood friend whose bio homework I used to do in exchange for safe passage through the neighborhood, especially through Morningside Park, was a member of the Chapmans and used to refer to a moment in gang rumbling as white sight. Say you've been cold-cocked from behind. Your eyeballs commence to roll up in your head like they're seeking asylum in the mass of neuromelanin surrounding the pineal gland. You definitely need to get to Sydenham or Harlem Hospital. You could have brain damage. You could die.

According to Dear Diary, I'd been at camp shortly before reading the passage in *Souls of Black Folk*, and bees were very much on my mind. So while I was reading about the affliction of viewing the self from an outside and unloving vantage point, Dr.'s "veil" began to take on the look of one of those wood-frame screens beekeepers slide down into the apiary so as to collect the honey from the caged-up bees. Dr.'s seventh son sounded like he needed to see a healer, a seer, someone whose calling was to pierce that screen that somebody, who clearly does not wish the seventh son well, shoved down split the self, because they wanted his sweetness. And his eyes.

By the time I read the passage again, I had experienced enough to know that I needed my eyes, my sweetness, and my stingers. I did not know, though, that I'd already become addicted to the version of the world and my community as promoted by Hollywood movies. I merely noticed that race movies, like race records, were no longer on the scene. But I did not fully appreciate that my celluloid jones made me as up for grabs as a sleeping bee. I interpreted "twoness" as the split-vision struggle I thought I was valiantly waging to stay centered in the community's core-culture perspective and at the same time excel in the schools' and various chump-change workplaces'. I got poleaxed. I got sandbagged and *sanpakued*. I got stuck in the mask. I lost my eyes. I became unmoored.

But blessed, as many of us are, I never left the gaze of the community; that is, folks did not avert their eyes from me. And so I did not stay caged up long in secondary consciousness (Dr. says second sight) or false consciousness (as opposed to primary consciousness, or what Dr. calls true self-consciousness); at least not chronic not-consciousnesshood. For in the community, then as now, were at least four discernible responses to the way in which we are positioned in the U.S.: accommodation, opportunism, denial/flight, and resistance. Long before I learned to speak of these responses as "tendencies," I encountered the living examples, neighbors.

Accommodationists recommended that I read (not to be confused with analyze) white we-are-great books and Negro we-too-are-clean-so-please-white-folks-include-us-in works, and that I speak good English and stay off the streets. Opportunists taught me how to move through the streets and capitalize on the miserable and gullible, 'cause what the hell, the point was to beat Whitey at his own game, which was, don't you know?, taking off black folks. The I-have-never-experienced-prejudice-in-the-all-white-school-and-church-I-attend types urged me not to regard as belligerent every racial encounter, for there were good white people if I looked hard enough and overlooked some of their ideas. All of which was helpful for "breaking the ice" at camps, integrating ballet schools, "proving" we were not what Dem said we were. Of course, many of us did not understand then how dangerous a proposition proving could be. James Baldwin put his mighty mouth on it a bit later, though talking to Dem: "If I'm not who you say I am, then you're not who you say you are. And the battle is on!"

While others saw in me an icebreaker, a lawbreaker, or a potential credit to the race, neighborhood combatants saw something else and spent a great deal of time, energy, and imagination encouraging and equipping me to practice freedom in preparation for collective self-governance (the very thing Hoover and the Red Squads called a danger to the national security—black folks thinking they had the capacity to rule themselves). I became acquainted with black books that challenged, rather than mimicked, white or Negro versions of reality. I became acquainted with folks who demonstrated that their real work was creating value in the neighborhoods—bookstores, communal gardens, think tanks, arts and crafts programs, community-organizer training, photography workshops. Many of them had what I call second sight—the ability to make reasoned calls to the community to create protective spaces wherein people could theorize and practice toward future sovereignty, while at the same time watching out for the sharks, the next wave of repression, or the next smear campaign, and preparing for it.

Insubordinates, dissidents, iconoclasts, oppositionists, change agents, radicals, and revolutionaries appealed to my temperament and my earliest training at home. They studied, they argued, they investigated. They had fire, they had analyses, they had standards. They had respect for children, the elders, and traditions of struggle. They imparted language for rendering the confusing intelligible, for naming the things that warped us, and for clarifying the complex and often contradictory nature of resistance.

Through involvement in tenants' actions, consumer groups, and other community-based activism, I began to learn how and why an enterprise prompted by an emancipatory impulse might proceed in the early stages as a transform-as-we-move intervention, but soon take on an assimilationist character. The original goal might be to oust the slum landlord and turn the building into a coop. But soon rank-and-file men are complaining about the authority exercised by the women officers. Founding members are opting for historical privilege, arguing

TONI CADE BAMBARA

that their votes and opinions are weightier than newcomers'. More
solvent members begin objecting to the equal-shares policy of the
association and start calling the less than solvent chiselers and free-
loaders. Finally, everybody's got it in for the elected chairperson. And
nobody trusts the treasurer. Then there's a purge, a splintering, or the
hardening of factions. And each falls back on the surrogate lingo:
"Same o, same o, niggers just can't get it together."

The situation, in some respects, is worse in these days of *Dallas* and
Lifestyles of the Rich and Famous. Bigger-is-better and grassroots-ain't-
shit drive many a budding organization to grab any ole funding in
order to enlarge. Say a community organization comes together in
response to a crisis government agencies ignore. For a while folks
operate in the style of the neighborhood culture. But soon they begin
to duplicate the very inequities and pathologies that gave rise to the
original crisis: Setting up hierarchal structures that cut less aggressive
members out of the decision-making process. Underdeveloping the
staff in favor of the stars. Deferring to "experts" whether they live on
the turf, share the hardships, and understand the conditions or not.
Devaluing the opinion of the experienced because they are less articulate
than others. Smoothing over difference and silencing dissent in the
name of unity.

Sometimes the virus in the machine is the funding, or a clique with
a hidden agenda, or the presence of agents provocateurs, or media
seduction. Most often the replication is the result of the failure to
build a critical mechanism within the organization, the failure to
recognize that close, critical monitoring of process is necessary in order
to overcome the powerful pull domination and demonizing exert in
this society. That is to say, we often underestimate the degree to which
exploitative behavior has been normalized and the degree to which
we've internalized these norms. It takes, then, a commitment to an
acutely self-conscious practice to be able to think and behave better
than we've been taught by the commercial media, which we, addicted,
look to for the way we dress, speak, dance, shop, cook, eat, celebrate,
couple, rear, think, solve problems, and bury each other.

Fortunately, a noncommercial media exists. Independent-minded students, teachers, parents, fundraisers, spectators, readers, theoreticians, programmers, curators, and practitioners are increasingly drawn to the independent media movement—the films and video, in particular, produced outside of the industry structure. The Independent Black Cinema Movement and now the Independent Multicultural Media Movement are generally made up of progressive-minded POCs who wage a battle against white sight, disconnectedness, indoctrination, assimilation.

POCs, for example, who have challenged white privilege over language have been producing in the last fifteen years books, films, videos, radio formats, poetry, performance art, sculpture, paintings, audio programs, criticism, theory, dramas, at a rate not previously recorded. It is more than a "heritage of insult," as Dr. often phrased it, that draws POCs together to organize neighborhoods, devise curricula, convene conferences, compare notes, collaborate on projects, or form coalitions. Frequently the moves are motivated by acknowledgment of multiple cultural heritage or biraciality. Sometimes they are compelled by a hunch that the answers to questions of identity lie in another's culture. Sometimes alliances are sparked by a determination to understand what is going on in this country that doesn't reach the nightly news or the campuses. As David Mura, Amero-Japanese writer in Minnesota, has frequently said, POCs find in the cultural work of other POCs what they can't find in the Saul Bellows and Updikes, or in Descartes and Plato.

Unfortunately, it is not always easy to locate independent film programs mentioned in the quarterly *Black Film Review*, the Asian *Cinevision* newsletter, *Independent Film & Video* journal, or the publications put out by the Latino Film Collaborative and the Native American Broadcasting Consortium, or the National Black Programming Consortium's *Take One*. It's no simple task to locate the periodicals themselves, *Independent* the only one that is found with any regularity in well-stocked book and magazine stores.

What's particular about this new crop of films and videos? For one, they don't flatten out cultural specificity in favor of "crossover." What is observable about them of late is the awareness that POCs are part of the authenticating audience. What might that mean in the future should artists of, say, the Chicano/Chicana community direct their work with Native Americans readers or spectators in mind? For one, it would probably mean the end of victim portraiture, the kind of characterization the downpressed frequently engage in when addressing "the wider audience," as is said, based on the shaky premise that if only Dem knew the situation they would lighten up. Victim portraits are an insult to those struggles. Victim portraits send a dispiriting message to one's own constituency. What might happen if, say, Amero-Africans pitched our work toward Pacific Islander readers and spectators? We'd have to drop the Two-Race delusion, for one. What is and can be the effect of this swapmeet, now that one out of every four persons in the U.S. is a POC? A reconceptualization of "America" and shift in the power configuration of the U.S.A.

Race,
Science, and
Identity

Kenneth R. Manning

African Americans have struggled to strike a balance between being
"Negro" on the one hand, "American" on the other. While W. E. B.
Du Bois may not have been the first to identify this double-consciousness, he was one of the earliest to portray its social and psychological
impact. His pioneering work, *The Souls of Black Folk* (1903), captures
just how deeply this split consciousness—bordering at times on the
schizophrenic—permeated the lives of black Americans. Du Bois recognized that no perspective on American history and culture would
be complete without an understanding of the ways in which this
dynamic, ever-changing consciousness evolved, found expression, and
perhaps ultimately (though not in his lifetime, or ours) saw resolution.

Of all the historical and cultural forces that have shaped what it
means to be both black and American, science is one of the most
powerful. This essay will explore how the double-consciousness identified by Du Bois was forged and influenced by science. I shall trace

---

Kenneth R. Manning is the Thomas Meloy Professor of Rhetoric and of the History of
Science at Massachusetts Institute of Technology. Professor Manning's biography, *Black
Apollo of Science: The Life of Ernest Everett Just*, was a finalist for the Pulitzer Prize and the
National Book Critics Circle Award. Professor Manning is currently working on a book-
length social history of blacks in the American health professions.

how science has been used to create, substantiate, promote, and disseminate certain negative views of blacks; how these views became entrenched in the culture, shaping not only how whites think about blacks but also how blacks think about themselves; and, finally, how blacks pursuing careers in science have related their work to their own consciousness of self as black Americans, and have attempted to resolve the inevitable conflicts and tensions.

Du Bois's appeal in *The Souls of Black Folks* was a political one—for whites to recognize the contributive potential of blacks and for blacks to seize whatever opportunities might exist to participate more fully and equitably in the social process. The book is soul-stirring, laced with inspirational rhetoric. Its aim was to make whites feel more comfortable about blacks and to promote among blacks a better self-image. Uppermost in Du Bois's mind were the so-called "Talented Tenth," the cream of educated black society. These were the people with perhaps the severest identity crises, the ones who needed most to find self-recognition and to be recognized as part of the American social mainstream.

In struggling with the insecurities and feelings of inferiority of a race of people, Du Bois aimed to develop a sense of fullness of self. Therein lies the truly innovative aspect of his work. But, by focusing so closely on the internal psychology, Du Bois glossed over important external truths: the imposition of real inferiority on a race. A prime culprit in this was science. Nineteenth-century science found in the Negro a ready (if not willing) subject for study, and its conclusions pointed to a supposed inherent inferiority in the Negro. Science essentially defined race, and was subsequently abused in the promotion of racism in America.

The "pride in Africa" concept raised by Du Bois did not acquire a solid basis in science until well into the twentieth century, with the work of the anthropologists Franz Boas and Melville Herskovits. Before then, the most painful aspect of "being a Negro" in this country—the stigma of inherent inferiority—took authority perhaps more from science than from any other field. As a supposedly objective enterprise, science stood apart from religion or art or music, and a range of other humanistic endeavors, to present an unemotional, detached assessment. That assessment, as it related to the nature and potential of the Negro, was almost universally damning, and its social and psychological impact was devastating. The authoritative aura encircling science's cold, hard methods—the gathering of data, the analysis, and the interpretation—rendered the assessment apparently incontrovertible. There were few mavericks like Du Bois with the courage to move beyond the stultifying intellectual framework of the time to chart out a more positive perspective.

The theoretical basis for racial inferiority came originally out of theology, not science. In Christianity, for example, the subjugation of one race to another was put forth as part of a preordained, hierarchical framework of institutional and spiritual allegiances. Hence, in America, the overwhelming support by the clerical establishment for the institution of slavery. In the nineteenth century, however, the onus for buttressing slavery—and, in its wake, the peonage of a race—fell to science as much as to religion. As its practitioners advanced increasingly authoritative statements about the origins and nature of humankind, science grew rapidly in stature to rival religion for control of how people thought about themselves, about others, about the world, and about the shaping of social institutions. Science may have undercut some of religion's precepts and methods, especially after Darwin's work in the middle of the century, but one assumption that they held in common was the superiority of whites over blacks on the great chain of being.

Nineteenth-century models of racial classification had their basis in the work of the eighteenth-century naturalist Carl Linnaeus. The founder of scientific anthropology, Johann Friedrich Blumenbach, broadened Linnaeus's classification scheme to include—along with color—hair, skull, and facial features. The great naturalists of the nineteenth century—Georges Cuvier, Charles Lyell, and Charles Darwin

—were the intellectual progeny of Linnaeus and Blumenbach. All three believed, in varying degrees, that the black race was inferior. Each either pursued bits and pieces of research in this area or made remarks that left little doubt about where they stood and that became part of the lore passed on to succeeding generations of students and disciples. Darwin and Lyell thought in terms of a hierarchy within the human species, in which the Negro was something of an intermediate step between monkey and Caucasian. Cuvier minced no words when he labeled blacks "the most degraded of human races, whose form approaches that of the beast." Louis Agassiz, the Swiss-born American naturalist and professor at Harvard University, apparently considered Negroes a separate species. In observing "their black faces with their thick lips and grimacing teeth," it was difficult for him "to repress the feeling that they are not of the same blood as us."

Although such opinions were impressionistic, based more on assumptions and prejudice than hard scientific research, they entered the mainstream of scientific thought partly because of the status accorded these scientists. Other scientists, both European and American, specialized in the study of race differences, using anatomical and other measurements to "scientifically" establish and reinforce notions of black inferiority. In America, for example, the early nineteenth century saw the rise of craniometry, or the measurement of the brain. Samuel George Morton, a distinguished Philadelphia anatomist, collected skulls to measure cerebral characteristics. Based on his observations, he developed a scheme of racial ranking. His *Crania Americana* (1839) identified a chain of being with whites at the top, Indians in the middle, and blacks at the bottom.

The American Civil War saw the rise of anthropometry—the science of body measurements—as a means of exploring the human physical, mental, and moral condition. The U.S. Sanitary Commission undertook anthropometric investigations of Federal troops, white and black. Over 180,000 blacks were inducted into the Federal Army. The Commission thus had a captive sample, unprecedented in scale, with which to study racial differences and to render comparisons. Influenced by

European methods, especially those of the Belgian philosopher Lambert Quetelet (as popularized by Sir John Herschel), the Commission began what turned out to be an inadequate job of measuring physical dimensions and personal characteristics with instruments like platform balances, calipers, and calibrated tape. Both living and dead human specimens were measured. In addition to raw recruits and seasoned soldiers, scientists pored over the results of autopsies performed on casualties of the war. Sanford B. Hunt, an army surgeon, compared the brain weights of 24 dead white and 381 dead black soldiers, determined from his sample that the average Negro's brain weighed five ounces less than the average white brain, and thus "proved" through hard physical evidence that Negroes were less intellectually endowed than whites.

By the end of the war, whatever was being measured in the Negro was found wanting, different from the American norm. The more "Negroid" you were, the more inadequate were your physical and mental attributes. One typical report proclaimed that "the difference between the mulattoes and the full blacks is here very conspicuous . . . the blacks in their turn falling below the Indians, and these vastly below the whites of whatever class." Hunt's evidence showed that a mulatto's brain weighed more than a pure black's but less than a white's. Such medico-anthropometric methods became standard in the studies of racial differences by private researchers, military investigators, hospital personnel, and a host of others interested in the topic. The work of the Commission was paralleled, for example, by that of J. H. Baxter, a physician who prepared a "statistical, medical, and anthropological" analysis based on a questionnaire circulated among military doctors. The data of Hunt, Baxter, and others allowed late nineteenth-century American scientists such as John Fiske and Edward Drinker Cope simply to assume the relative smallness of the Negro brain. Among the explanations advanced for this "phenomenon" was that the Negro brain stopped growing at puberty, in contrast with the fully grown brain of a true American.

Practicing physicians played a vital role in developing a science-based analysis of the Negro and in disseminating a uniformly negative portrayal. Although not scientists in the "pure" sense, medical practitioners often employed scientific methodologies in their clinical and investigative work. Where they differed most from scientists was not so much in how they approached their work as in their greater access to, and influence on, just about all segments of society. The role of physicians as repositories of expert information on most matters of health, indeed on fundamental questions of life and death, gave their views an authority rivaled only by those of the minister. While these individuals had no special scientific training (as a matter of fact, their training as clinical practitioners was suspect in most instances), they had a remarkable influence on ways of thinking about the broadest questions of life and culture.

As a race, blacks were interpreted "scientifically" on the basis of work carried out by physicians in the context of familiar social institutions. The life-insurance industry, for example, depended for risk assessment and actuarial premises largely on data (death, vitality, and morbidity statistics) compiled and supplied by physicians. The expenses of the U.S. Sanitary Commission's survey, which employed physicians and solicited data from the medical community, were defrayed in part by insurance companies seeking to establish statistical averages. Furthermore, physicians often owned or helped establish companies, served as managers or board members, and earned wages or stipends as "medical directors." Positions with insurance companies were the most common type of institutional affiliation listed by medical practitioners in late nineteenth-century editions of *Polk's Medical Directory of the United States and Canada*. Invested with the power to establish who was a good risk, and who was not, physicians gathered and used data to create quasi-scientific stereotypes of blacks and to promote racially exclusionary policies. This trend compelled blacks to set up their own mutual-benefit associations and self-interest groups. Thus, the insurance industry in the nineteenth century served as a microcosm of racial separateness. While physicians did not initiate the trend, they helped make it an essential feature of the American social fabric.

Nineteenth-century physicians frequently discussed the condition of the American Negro in their journals, at conferences, and in the transactions of their professional societies, as well as in popular newspapers and magazines. They postulated that Negroes were more prone to disease than whites (or, shall we say, Americans), had a higher mortality rate, and were inevitably headed toward extinction (a bit of wishful thinking here, perhaps!). These characteristics, they asserted, were not due to any environmental condition or social deprivation, but rather to the Negro's inherent inferiority. Just about any statistic was twisted to suit this thesis. The low rate of suicide among blacks, for example, was interpreted as a reflection on blacks' limited intellect—the fact that they lived only for the moment, entirely in the present. True Americans, white-skinned and blue-blooded, lived for the future.

While most black physicians, in accordance with the expectations of the white establishment, stuck to clinical work among members of their own race, a few published in the late nineteenth- and early twentieth-century medical literature. The first Negro medical journal, *The Medical and Surgical Observer*, founded by Miles Vandahurst Lynk, appeared in December 1892, followed by *Hospital Herald* out of Charleston, South Carolina, in 1899, and *Journal of the National Medical Association* in 1909. Much of the material in these journals was technical, aimed at providing an alternative forum of shared learning and experience for black physicians, who, by and large, were excluded from membership in white professional organizations. Political issues, when broached at all, tended to be framed within the context of the need for black solidarity in an environment hostile to the participation of blacks. Black physicians viewed the establishment of their own professional organizations—segregated, separate from the mainstream, little known and often less recognized—as necessary in a racist society.

This view betokened a degree of toleration, if not acceptance, of the majority outlook. Similarly, black physicians remained more or less silent about the racial dogmas that flowed relentlessly into the social fabric out of the work of white scientists and physicians. For some, this publicly passive posture was a well-devised, carefully formulated strategy to assure professional self-preservation, comparable to that of blacks who avoided controversy in other walks of life. To have been outspoken, or even mildly critical, would have resulted in a professional backlash.

But, for others, the posture signified an acceptance of racial dogmas. These people suffered in silence, grasping for self-respect and dignity through the notion that somehow they were unique, different from most blacks. Some who were light-skinned attempted to blend into the white community, denying their heritage; one physician pleaded with the Alumni Office at his alma mater to strike any reference to his race, as he was "not regarded as a colored" by his clientele and did not want his origins revealed. Still others, also believing the dogmas, repeated and acted on them. This group sometimes became involved in work that assumed epidemiological stereotypes of blacks proposed by whites and that treated blacks as experimental subjects in ways that would never have been tolerated for whites. The various commissions on syphilis, hookworm, pellagra, and other "Negro" diseases set up by black professional organizations were motivated by the prevalence of these diseases in the black community, but they often fed into the notion of blacks as an inherently diseased race.

Thus, by the time Du Bois wrote *The Souls of Black Folk*, the myth of black inferiority was entrenched—and both victim and victimizer essentially subscribed to it. The racial thrust of science and medicine contrasted with Du Bois's positive image of African heritage. His was a lone (or lonely) voice crying in the wilderness. Yet even he did not challenge, in a consistent or forthright way, the scientific arguments for black inferiority. His commentary through *The Crisis* broaches a range of disciplines speaking to the condition of blacks, but he and other black intellectuals said surprisingly little about science.

Exceptions include Kelly Miller and C. V. Roman. Miller, a sociologist, studied and commented on the miscegenation issue, arguing "the brotherhood of man" against those who were terrified by the prospect of a nation of mulattoes. Roman, a physician whose technical expertise in these matters surpassed Miller's, asserted the biological equality of Negroes and whites in his book, *American Civilization and the Negro* (1916). "*The science of inequality is emphatically a science of white people,*" Roman stressed. "It is they who have invented it and set it agoing, who have maintained, cherished, and propagated it, thanks to *their* observations and *their* deductions." Roman concludes with a homily on science's potential for objective truth, minus the racial baggage: "Science builds no impassible walls between men with wide and narrow skulls, yellows and whites, tall and short men, those with thick and thin joints, those with small and large nostrils, those with straight and curved foreheads. . . . [L]ife passes above all these artificial partitions, and marches on their ruins towards unity."

In general, however, Du Bois's black contemporaries had little to be proud of, in the sense of reputation or self-worth, since they had been excoriated and stigmatized by the white scientific establishment as defective, deficient, inadequate. Even though many Americans may not have subscribed to Agassiz's notion of blacks as a biologically separate species, neither did they consider blacks to be "one of them." Blacks were in a different category of *Homo sapiens*—a different type of American, if an American at all. This view appeared to be substantiated by a cumulative, painstakingly acquired store of scientific and medical knowledge. While some conceded that blacks had the potential to assimilate, to become part of the American mainstream, such a move invariably required a repudiation of one's inherent "blackness." Tragically, it was not only whites who subscribed to this view. The image of self held by blacks during Du Bois's time was derived, by and large, from the image that others held of them.

Thus, being American and being black were antithetical concepts, poles apart. For no other group was the process of "Americanizing" so denied, or the American creed made so elusive. European immi-grants stood a chance for assimilation, while people of African descent did not.

Well into the twentieth century, science—or activities pursued in the name of science—continued to provide powerful reflectors in which blacks saw their cracked, imperfect image mirrored. Eugenics, carried on by American scientists such as Raymond Pearl, John C. Merriam, and C. B. Davenport as a reputable scientific movement, underscored the negative portrayal. Although their work was wide-ranging, its single connective tissue was a curiosity and fascination, bordering at times on the obsessive, with racial differences. The eugenics movement included geneticists, scientific popularizers, and social policy analysts. After the rediscovery in 1900 of Johann Gregor Mendel's seminal paper on genetics, and with the establishment of the Eugenics Records Office at Cold Spring Harbor, Long Island, in 1910, discussions of racial inferiority continued to be a legitimate question not only in science but in general social (even liberal) discourse as well.

Eugenics fed into socially disfunctional or regressive policies such as the anti-immigration movement, which drew its impetus from the atmosphere of jingoistic nationalism following World War I and its authority from eugenicists' data concerning "weak races." Eugenics also encouraged people to advocate coercive sterilization of blacks, who were viewed as a diseased, oversexed race. Such ideas permeated Amer-ican society, promoting racial fear on the part of whites and antipathy toward self on the part of many blacks. These ideas outlasted the eugenics movement, which slipped out of the mainstream of American science following its adoption as a key social policy by the Nazis in the 1930s.

Though muted and transformed, the legacy of craniometrists, eu-genicists, and others persisted. Examples are numerous. From 1932 to 1972, for instance, the United States Public Health Service carried on the Tuskegee Syphilis Experiment, using blacks as subjects (or objects) in a study of the long-term effects of syphilis. The project, backed mainly by the white medical profession, misled four hundred black "guinea pigs" about the nature of their illness (labeling it vaguely "bad blood") and withholding treatment from them in order to observe the progress of the disease. Then there was the segregation of blood in the armed services during World War II. The 1960s and 1970s saw the IQ work of Arthur Jensen, Richard Herrnstein, and William Shockley heralded (or challenged) in the scientific community and debated in public forums. Coming on the heels of the Black Power movement, when blacks were grappling to forge an identity that Du Bois could only have dreamed of, this work asserted that blacks were inherently less intelligent than whites. Shockley's proposals harked back to the days when sterilization was viewed, by American advocates of eugenics and by the framers of social policy in Germany, as a solution to society's ills. Since the 1980s, certain work in sociobiology, genetic engineering, and disciplines where there is an attempt to identify genes with behavioral traits has raised the possibility that eugenic views never really died out. In 1992, for example, the National Institutes of Health (NIH) provided funding for a conference on heredity and criminal behavior, but later suspended support when outside critics argued that linking genetics and crime in this way would add renewed authority to theories that blacks (represented disproportionately in U.S. crime statistics) are biologically inferior.

One might wonder how, with science generating such levels of race prejudice among whites and negative self-image among blacks, blacks could ever be drawn to careers in the field, or how they could revere science as a model of inspiration and a standard of achievement. Relatively few blacks have gone into science, but, ironically, the esteem for those who have done so—and succeeded—knows few bounds.

The Spingarn Medal, awarded every year since 1915 to the man or woman of "African descent" who performed "the foremost service to his race" was first given to a scientist: the biologist Ernest Everett Just. Other nominees for the honor in 1915 included representatives from the world of arts, journalism, commerce, politics, education, and athletics—fields more commonly associated with black accomplishment. But, by choosing a scientist, the NAACP aimed to do two things: establish the intellectual potential of blacks and place them in the mainstream of Western tradition. This was science as it was meant to be, the great universalizer knowing neither culture nor race. The award symbolized the Negro as a complete American. It was a rebuttal to generations of white scientists who, in denying the intellectual abilities of blacks, had betrayed their own scientific objectivity.

When Americans thought about black scientists, they thought of someone not like Just but like George Washington Carver. Carver, who worked at Tuskegee Institute alongside Booker T. Washington, espoused the traits of humility, diligence, and manual dexterity that whites appreciated in blacks and that many blacks accepted (by default or intent) as appropriate measures of fulfillment for themselves. Carver's work was inventive, rather than scientifically creative; product-oriented, rather than pressing to new theoretical heights; and carried out in the black community with few if any intrusions into the white. Carver, white scientists might have opined, "knew his place" and accepted it. Blacks in "pure" science were a relative rarity. Whites generally considered them as encroachers who were out of their depth.

The degree to which black scientists devoted themselves to this principle of "pure" science, untrammeled by extraneous considerations of race or culture, is quite remarkable. Not always with complete success, they insisted on being called "scientists," *never* "Negro scientists." The racial qualifier was to them an insidious, obfuscating element. It had its parallel in the broader concept of citizenry, of being (or not being) a full-fledged member of the society in which one lives and works. The term "Negro American," for example, also connoted a divided existence, a kind of provisional membership, a test case that might or might not work out. The term "American," on the other hand, connoted true acceptance, true participation.

As Du Bois published *The Souls of Black Folk* in 1903, three black scientists, all born in 1883, were about to embark on productive careers in science. William Augustus Hinton, a native of Chicago, went into bacteriology; Elmer Imes, born in Knoxville, Tennessee, became a physicist; and Ernest Everett Just, a native of Charleston, South Carolina, went into embryology. Each of these scientists sought to enter the mainstream of a white-dominated profession, carried out for the most part within white research centers and white institutions of higher learning. The training and content of this entity called "science" was supposedly not white at all but transparent, colorless. Science demanded abstract, objective approaches—unlike those for art, dance, music, literature, religion, or history—that precluded attention to cultural differences based on race or any other factor. Yet black scientists found it difficult to enter white scientific communities precisely *because* of their race. It was a confused, confusing predicament: how to follow through on a career where the work, while not usually biased per se, had tended to be carried out in a racially intolerant environment and had in certain instances fostered negative cultural stereotypes in the public psyche.

In grappling with this problem, some black scientists focused on the positive and submerged the negative. Just, for example, felt that science had much to offer the black community. Blacks, according to him, could benefit from science's "objective and cold blooded" approach as opposed to their typically emotional and intuitive outlook. They could gain insight into themselves—and into all the social forces that shaped and influenced their lives—if only they would lay out the facts and dissect them clinically, in microscopic detail. There was altogether too much emoting by blacks, Just felt, and that emoting was getting them nowhere. Only through rigorous scientific method could blacks hope to determine their own future: "Science could be a savior of black people, their road to an improved life."

Just never mentioned the use of science to argue black inferiority, even though the scientific and medical literature was replete with such arguments. It was not that he did not read the relevant journals. On the contrary, the journals to which he subscribed and in which he himself published contained racially oriented work. An article, for example, by J. E. Wodsedalek, which appeared in *Biological Bulletin* in 1916, suggested chromosomal differences between the black and white races and drew a specious analogy that "the Negro is fully as far removed from the white man as is the ass from the horse." This, coupled with comments like "unfortunately the mulatto is fertile," probably stung Just but he did not raise a fuss. Similarly, he never commented—either favorably or disparagingly—on the work of eugenicists, like Davenport, whom he knew through professional circles. Although he may not have been personally acquainted with Davenport (Just worked at the Marine Biological Laboratory at Woods Hole, Massachusetts, while Davenport was connected to the Cold Spring Harbor lab), they knew each other at least by reputation. Davenport's view of Just as a mediocre scientist, expressed to a foundation official, coincided conveniently with (and was probably colored by) the conclusions of his work: the inherent inequities between the races and the horrors of universal mongrelism.

Just avoided these issues because he considered them a distraction from the demands of his work. Also, becoming embroiled in such a controversy or confrontation would have highlighted the very thing —his race—that he was anxious to submerge, at least as it pertained to his professional life. A response to Wodsedalek would have made it more likely that he would be stuck with the qualifier term "Negro" appended to his preferred label, "scientist." Some white scientists with liberal leanings, such as Jacques Loeb, were able to express their outrage at Wodsedalek's remarks because the consequences for them were negligible. Just's response had to be more subtle, more covert; otherwise, he could not have survived, much less flourished, professionally. His response expressed itself in organic, fluid, not readily observable ways—the friends and colleagues, for example, toward whom he naturally gravitated. His time was spent not with Davenport or Wodsedalek, but with scientists like Franz Boas and Melville Herskovits, whose work demonstrated the possibility of a positive identity for blacks.

One of Just's close friends was Alain Locke, who helped galvanize a growing black intellectual consciousness in his book *The New Negro* (1924). Locke's work became an important impetus for the Harlem Renaissance, black nationalism, and other movements geared toward defining black identity in America, toward formulating a concept of what it meant (or might mean) to be a Negro American. But, while Locke and others had concluded that framing such a definition was a sensible and worthwhile effort, Just held firm to the principle that the term "Negro scientist" was vacuous, meaningless—except when intended, as Davenport had intended in his written appraisal of Just to the foundation, as a derogatory qualifier. Just demanded recognition "not as a Negro who works in biology, but as a biologist who is working in biology for his satisfaction and joy." Edwin R. Embree, president of the Julius Rosenwald Fund and one of Just's ardent white supporters, often remarked in public: "Dr. E. E. Just of Howard University is not a great Negro biologist, he is a great biologist." When seeking letters of recommendation in private, however, Embree wanted to be convinced. Was Just's work "really good," "first class . . . compared with any standard," or was it "simply unusual for a Negro"?

In his *An American Dilemma* (1944), Gunnar Myrdal points to the race label as a common problem for black professionals. Science (natural, not social), he believed, may have been an exception and Just a rare example of someone who eluded the racial stigma. This view appears reasonable, considering that the language and format of communication in science—characterized by spare formality—almost preclude racial qualifiers or identifiers in the course of normal discourse. When Just's work was cited by his peers, for example, it was simply by name, topic, or substance—no different than for any other scientist. Publications by other black scientists such as Moddie Taylor, Roger Arliner Young, Shiefflin Claytor, Henry C. McBay, Adolphus A.

Milligan, and Shirley Jackson give little or no clue as to the race of the author. Thus, in the printed record, they were able to sidestep a label designed, Myrdal says, "to discriminate individuals in the minds of the public."

White scientists who had never met Just, for example, would have had no way of telling from his work that he was black—except perhaps where his affiliation with Howard University was mentioned, and even that was no clear indicator, since Howard boasted many white scholars (including Herskovits at one point). Because the work was judged on merit alone, according to universally applied quantitative and objective norms, science had a built-in basis for equal opportunity that inevitably appealed to blacks aspiring to careers in the field. Black scientists could think of the scientific literature—and, for that matter, of their class-rooms and their laboratories—as asylums, worlds where racism held no sway and where only the laws of nature governed.

Nevertheless, many black scientists, Just included, noted a curious pattern over the course of their careers: that their work was cited more in European than American journals. This pattern defied the notion of science's neutrality. In the absence of mitigating "neutral" differences (number of journals, weighted emphasis on certain topics, etc.) between the scientific literatures on opposite sides of the Atlantic, black scientists were justified in suspecting that their relatively low rate of citation on one side had something to do with race. This is not to suggest that Europeans were more tolerant, simply that they had fewer ways than Americans of discerning race and therefore of acting on their prejudices. Further, Europeans often did not know black American scientists personally, nor were they aware of which insti-tutions might be predominantly black or black-affiliated.

In an ideal world, the term "Negro scientist" would have had no meaning beyond stating that the scientist in question happened to be a Negro. On the other hand, the notion of a Negro writer, dancer, musician, poet, lawyer, or historian carries with it certain connotations or assumptions about the individual's work. Some of these assumptions may be legitimate, others not. A cultural basis, perhaps an ethnic perspective may sometimes be discerned within the work of someone working in any of these fields. But, in the abstract, there can be no such entity as Negro science—no Negro physics, chemistry, or biology, no peculiarly Negro way of gathering and analyzing scientific data or of solving problems. "Negro scientist" is thus almost an oxymoronic expression. "It is not a meaningful exercise," Henry McBay asserts, "to classify oneself as, say, a black chemist. I'm not a black chemist, I'm a chemist. You know how that sounds when I say I don't want to be called a black man, but I don't. I want to be a member of the human enterprise."

Just confronted this problem throughout his career, as did other black scientists such as Elmer Imes, St. Elmo Brady, Percy L. Julian, and William Augustus Hinton. They resented having to explain the obvious. Chemistry and physics are about atoms, protons, and molecules; biology is about protoplasm and proteins. These phenomena know no color or religion, no national origin. The abstract, universal quality in science motivated black scientists. Relative to other blacks, their work is unique; their modes of conjecture, their methodologies, their conclusions are different from those of other black intellectuals. Rather than focusing on relatively small, some might even say provincial issues such as race relations, their sights are set on higher things, on the universal questions whose answers lie embedded in the natural world: where do we all, black and white, come from? where do we fit into the universe? While the viewpoint may appear arrogant, it has been in essence an assertion of self-worth and human equality.

Just never touched on scientific work dealing with race. He neither engaged in such work nor made reference to it in public forums or in private correspondence. The same can be said of the physicist Elmer Imes or the chemist Percy Julian. The work of some black scientists, Hinton for example, impinged on racial issues in oblique ways. Hinton's work, on syphilis, was in an area that medical authorities had always defined as being of special consequence to the black population.

Although not the only ones affected by syphilis, blacks were thought to be particularly prone to the disease. This view was based as much on nineteenth-century mythologies about the sexual prowess and proclivities of blacks as on solid scientific data. But Hinton's major published study, *Syphilis and Its Treatment* (1936), was about the etiology and clinical course of the disease, not about its impact on blacks. The only race-based reference was an explanation for the high rate of cardiovascular syphilis among Negroes, whose tertiary lesions, Hinton proposed, were large relative to whites because of heart and blood-vessel trauma resulting from physical labor. Although other black physicians knew of the Tuskegee Syphilis Experiment, Hinton most likely did not.

Nevertheless, Hinton was dogged by the specter of race. He declined several awards from black organizations out of fear that, if his race was revealed, the scientific world would take his work less seriously. "Although I am certain that most men interested in the field of syphilis are aware that I am a Negro," he once said, "I rather suspect that there are some persons as yet ignorant of this fact who might be unfavorably impressed were the racial issue brought up." Hinton did not see how he could "put the cards flat on the table" without "hinder[ing] the widespread use" of his work. He therefore declined the Spingarn Medal, as well as the Harmon Award (also an award given exclusively to blacks) and a distinguished service medal from the Manhattan Medical Society (a black professional organization). It was an agonizing position: producing brilliant scientific results and forgoing deserved accolades in the hope that, by so doing, his work would stand up better to scrutiny and "in the long run accomplish the very purpose for which we are all striving . . . a better recognition of merit, regardless of color."

A notable exception to this racial timidity, or caution, on the part of black scientists was the work of the pathologist Julian H. Lewis. Lewis's book, *Biology of the Negro* (1941), sought to present an unbiased treatment of a subject that generations of white anthropologists, biologists, and others had abused in their efforts to support theories of racial (especially black) inferiority. A review published in the *Journal of the National Medical Association* proclaimed Lewis's book "a fair, impartial, scientific and masterly study and analysis of racial characteristics, likenesses and differences, with special reference to the Negro." The reviewer noted that "the author has failed to discover any fundamental evidence to show that the Negro is biologically inferior to other groups of the genus homo." Lewis developed a reputation as an authority on race-science issues, which he was occasionally asked to write on for the *Journal of the American Medical Association*. Two of his pieces, on race crossing and on racial discrimination in the blood-banking system, were published in 1942. But this was an avocation for him; his full-time post was as a university faculty member and clinician.

The pursuit of science both removes blacks from their cultural background and constantly reminds them of their roots. It is a complicated, tension-filled phenomenon. As E. E. Just, Charles H. Turner, Percy Julian, and Walter Massey adopted scientific precepts and grew in professional stature, their world view was increasingly less able to accommodate a distinction between themselves and their white counterparts—between Negro scientists and scientists. It is not so much that they wanted not to be Negroes, but that they wanted to be scientists. Yet they could never quite escape the stigma that society placed on them for being of Negro heritage.

The professional world of science is split in its recognition of lure and loathing; it sways back and forth, blowing hot and cold, exuding mixed messages, often placing those who come in contact with it into turmoil, into a pressure cooker of divided allegiances and expectations. Science is objective, colorless. For blacks, as for anyone else, the work requires them to count, measure, record; they become faceless experimenters contributing to a cumulative body of knowledge; they scrupulously avoid the use of the personal pronoun "I"—in contrast, say, to an artist like Jessye Norman or Alvin Ailey; they take pride in contributing to an enterprise in which cultural or ethnic background is submerged, ideally irrelevant. The goal of black scientists is the objective search for truth, in which racial or ethnic or religious perspectives have no advantage—and essentially no meaning.

Yet, try as they might to submerge it, the issue of race intrudes on this peaceful, uncluttered scenario. The world of science constantly reminds black scientists of racial or ethnic factors, highlights their background, scrutinizes their origins, and points to their supposed inferiority. While black scientists strive for assimilation in a community that demands that they relinquish their heritage, that very community tells them they are different, part of a foreign or "other" culture. They may be "American," but, as Du Bois implied, they are separated from other Americans by a symbolic veil.

"In the Kingdom of Culture": Black Women and the Intersection of Race, Gender, and Class

Darlene Clark Hine

Black thinkers have pondered and agonized over questions of race, racism, and racial identity since the times of Phillis Wheatley. And even before Maria Stewart broke with convention and spoke before a mixed audience in 1831, black women wrestled with the complexities of constructing a racial identity that incorporated gender and class. From the outset black women encountered an America that denied their humanity, debased their femininity, and refused them self-possession. The acquisition of a measure of freedom and citizenship privileges would have to await a modern civil rights movement that they profoundly initiated and sustained.

When in 1903 W. E. B. Du Bois, the preeminent black scholar of his generation, wrote about racial identity in terms of "twoness" and "double-consciousness," he gave the term "Negro" a generic meaning:

Darlene Clark Hine has been John A. Hannah Professor of American History at Michigan State University since 1987. She has edited and written widely on African American history, particularly on black women in the nursing profession and in the Middle West. Her most recent book, *Black Women in White*, received several awards and was named Outstanding Book by the Gustavus Myers Center for the Study of Human Rights. Among Professor Hine's many honors are the 1988 Otto Wirth Alumni Award for Outstanding Scholarship from Roosevelt University and the 1991 Special Achievement Award from the Kent State University Alumni Association. At present, Hine is working to establish a unique Comparative Black History Ph.D. program at Michigan State University.

"It is a peculiar sensation, this double-consciousness, this sense of always looking at one's self through the eyes of others, of measuring one's soul by the tape of a world that looks on in amused contempt and pity." Du Bois's compelling prose in *The Souls of Black Folk* (1903) captured well his perception of the dichotomous nature of black identity struggles and the pressure to choose one or the other: "One ever feels his twoness—an American, a Negro; two souls, two thoughts, two unreconciled strivings; two warring ideals in one dark body, whose dogged strength alone keeps it from being torn asunder."

Had Du Bois specifically included the experiences and lives of black women in his lament he probably would have had to modify his prose. For Du Bois race was the master key to understanding American reality and the most potent factor shaping identity. Still, I suspect, had he considered the issue of gender, instead of writing "One ever feels his twoness," he would have mused about how one ever feels her "fiveness": Negro, American, woman, poor, black woman. An examination of the separate realities and complex identities of black women offers greater illumination of the power relations that operate along the interlocking grid of race, sex, and class in America. Du Bois's analysis dominated black thought for most of the twentieth century. As African American men and women of all classes, however, confront the twenty-first century there is a need for new thinking, and more inclusive and varied metaphors about black identity and the process of assimilation. The history of the American Negro is more than a history of efforts as Du Bois put it "to attain self-conscious manhood," it is simultaneously a story of the development and preservation of a dynamic, multiconscious black womanhood.

For the record, no such person as a generic Negro or a generic American exists. Inasmuch as we all experience life along axes of difference, each black or American is a person of some specific sex or sexual orientation. Each person has a certain class or social status and each belongs to what is called a "race." Here I must underscore that there is only one biological race and that is the human race. Today, when we use the term "race," we are actually talking about the social construction of differences. Race, class, and gender are not the only factors that shape identity, but they are, even more to the point, potent indicators of an individual's relation to power.

I will use the concepts of race, class, and gender in addition to those of region and profession as analytical tools to describe the process by which black women, too, became, in Du Bois's words, "co-worker(s) in the kingdom of culture." My own academic work focuses on the history of black women in the Middle West and in the nursing profession. I will return to these topics later in this essay, but first I want to focus attention on two crucial developments—the institution of slavery and the rise of women's clubs—that formed black women's identity and affected the extent of their assimilation in America.

I.

Fully to understand black women's identities requires that we push back the historical curtain to look yet again at the institution of slavery. My thinking about the multiple identities of black women and their adversarial relations with most of American society has led me to conclude that to the extent that assimilation depends upon, and is a reflection of, cultural values and material possession, black women are at once the most and the least assimilated Americans.

Slavery was the dominant economic and social system that shaped the experiences and lives of black women from the early seventeenth through the middle of the nineteenth century. Scholars have scrutinized and dissected this institution more than any other. But until the advent of black women's history, historians focused exclusively on male slaves, and even the new generation of revisionist scholars assumed little difference in the experiences of men and women slaves. The recent authentication of slave narratives written by captive women such as

Harriet Jacobs and Elizabeth Keckley, however, as well as the appearance of monographs such as Melton McLaurin's *Celia, A Slave* (1991) and Deborah Gray White's *Ar'n't I A Woman: Female Slaves in the Plantation South* (1985), point to a more inclusive scholarship in the future.

Slavery was many things, but it was first and foremost concerned with extracting the greatest amount of labor with the least amount of capital investment. While male slaves were highly valued for the work they were capable of doing, the whole institution rested most profoundly upon the backs of black women. Southern slavery developed a rigid political economy and social hierarchy with black women at the core. The very structure and organization of coerced labor depended upon the subordination and control of the women. Here I am suggesting that unraveling the interwoven systems of racial and sexual oppression and class exploitation in this society dictates a fundamental reconceptualization of African American, and indeed all of American history, from the perspective of black women. I am neither sanguine about the difficulty of such a project nor am I persuaded that this will be done soon, although important research and writing are presently underway.

As slavery became deeply entrenched in southern states, and the prospect of securing fresh Africans disappeared after 1807 with the official end of the slave trade, slave masters knew that control of the reproductive capacities of black women amounted to the only sure way of maintaining a viable slave-labor population. Regardless of the specificities of crop cultivation, or the myriad configurations of work assignments on farms and plantations, the need for new slaves steadily increased. The unending challenge therefore was to make black women envision their reproductive work as part of what it meant to be a woman, while insisting that their productive labor constituted a definition of what it meant to be a black. The master's objective was twofold, to enslave her mind as well as her body, to exploit both in order to maximize his economic profits.

But economic interests were actually only the most apparent concern. The effective management of slave women also meant appropriation of their sexuality. Slave masters, overseers, and other white men could and did rape slave women at will. Black women suffered direct white male sexual aggression, but the slave community as a whole was indirectly assaulted. No segment of the slave population possessed immunity from the psychological impact occasioned by white male sexual aggression against powerless women. The scholarly consensus is that at least 58 percent of all slave women between the ages of fifteen and thirty were sexually abused by white males. Rape had the added advantage of producing new slaves and thus enriching masters while satisfying white men's carnal desires. Perhaps the most daunting task confronting black women historians is to persuade students of slavery to see it as more than an economic institution. Slavery was also a sexual institution, and it was white male control of black women as sexual beings that shored up the patriarchal dimension of the system. Until gender becomes a central analytical concept in the writing of the history of slavery our appreciation of the complexities of the American past remains stillborn.

It would be a mistake to see black women solely as victims under slavery. It is equally undesirable, however, to create myths of the superheroic black woman who stoically met every obstacle, endured total debasement, only to rise above her tormentors and captors. Black women in all eras understood the multilayered realities of their oppression and exploitation and developed an array of survival strategies and functional identities. On plantations and farms of all sizes and purposes, black women developed networks with each other, and where feasible, they embraced their own form of Christianity, crafted a distinct moral code, and fashioned permeable family boundaries that freely made room for blood relatives and fictive kin. The extended, flexible, adaptable black family is as much black women's invention as it is an African retention. In other words, part of the requirements for survival dictated that black women, when necessary, reconfigured and reimagined families, communities, and themselves. Survival mandated that they develop private identities and inner worlds known only to their own.

Because of their separate realities and material conditions, black women created identities that remain ambiguous, and are seemingly contradictory. In tandem with their enslavement the dominant society fostered a host of negative ideas about black women's character, humanity, and sexuality. Ironically, in order to justify the multilayered oppression of black women, slave masters and apologists for slavery promoted distorted images that on the one hand blamed the victim and assuaged the guilt of white men in particular, creating the stereotypical image of the black woman as sexual wanton while at the same time maintained the image of the devoted house servant who loved her master's family more than she did her own. Few seemed disturbed by this paradox. Slavery was best served by ignoring or denying the existence of rebellious slave women who disguised their true feelings and deeds and attacked with arson, poison, or weapons when pushed too far.

Actually, most slave women cultivated or adopted a series of personas when appropriate. For the most part, slave women did the work assigned them, cared for their families, fought and resisted when they had to, and bit their tongues in order to minimize their hostility toward and discourse with whites. They practiced their religion and participated in the creation and dissemination of a unique culture that was by necessity woman-centered, because the guiding passion of slave masters intent on maximizing profits and their own security was to control and exploit the women who held the key to slavery's perpetuation. Women, like men, were often rendered submissive through brutal beatings. Although such violent attacks on women could impair their slave-bearing capacities and even destroy their lure as sex objects, virtually every slave narrative recounts an instance of the brutalization of a slave woman. Maintaining an atmosphere of terror, whether through violence or through threats of selling her away from her family, bolstered the master's efforts to defeminize and dehumanize the slave woman, to reduce her identity to property and to break her will to resist.

The lives and experiences of two of the most celebrated black women in antebellum America, the ex-slaves Sojourner Truth and Harriet Tubman, are critical to any discussion of identity formation. Both women used their considerable talents to actively oppose slavery, Truth through her participation in the abolition movement and as a fighter for women's rights, and Tubman as a fearless conductor of the Underground Railroad. Truth posited a new, inclusive definition of womanhood in her many speeches, while Tubman demonstrated what it meant to be a human being when she risked her life on dozens of trips to rescue hundreds of slaves along Maryland's eastern shore, and in her work as a spy and scout during the Civil War.

For both Truth and Tubman, freedom, and the unrelenting quest for freedom, was the mainstay of their identities. Their passionate embrace of freedom was born not of some abstract commitment to the Constitution or the noble sentiments embodied in the Declaration of Independence, but out of the reality of their enslavement and oppression. They knew firsthand what it meant to be owned by another, to be considered little more than a cow or a mule. Truth and Tubman also mastered the survival skills slavery and multiple oppression required. Slavery, and resistance to it, were the defining moment of the birth of black women's oppositional consciousness. The experiences of slavery and their acts of active and passive resistance deepened black women's understanding of the dynamics of patriarchy and the operation of racism. Out of these specific historical and material conditions black women developed a pattern of values, beliefs, customs, and behaviors that shaped their identities and comprised the heart of black culture.

The strength of the inner identities that black women forged and nurtured during slavery facilitated the transition to freedom. With dispatch black men and women reunited families, established separate churches, opened schools, and even attempted to exert some control over their economic lives by inventing the sharecropping system. In spite of these manifold efforts to give meaning to hard-won freedom, one thing, their economic subordination, remained fixed.

Notwithstanding the gradual rise of a black middle class, the vast majority of black women worked in domestic service and agriculture. The location of most of their jobs in white women's kitchens meant that at least some black women, even in freedom, remained vulnerable to white male sexual aggression. But the tenuous grip of black males on employment opportunities necessitated that married black women remain in the labor force. The intersection of race and gender constructions and relentless poverty consigned black women to the least desirable jobs, for which they receive negligible wages.

Black women's economic woes matched their low political status in a period that historian Rayford Logan called the nadir. Given the patriarchal nature of American society, it is not surprising that with few exceptions black men and women applauded, in 1870, the adoption of the Fifteenth Amendment to the U.S. Constitution. Inauspiciously, this amendment in some ways cemented a gender breach in black culture. While a large degree of sexual equality was manifested between slave men and women, the adoption of the Fifteenth Amendment created a fundamental inequality in their access to power. Once black men gained the right to vote, black women had no alternative but to negotiate with and convince their male relatives to use the ballot to advance group as opposed to individual interests. Black women dealt with questions of black political participation just as they appeared to acquiesce to their lack of visible positions of leadership in black churches. They worked to persuade men that their individual ballots were in reality their collective property.

I suspect that the most disturbing thing about the Fifteenth Amendment from a black woman's perspective was that it allowed black men the latitude to determine the public agenda in the struggle against racism. Black men embraced the ideology of integration. Few representative black leaders, despite advocacy of different tactics and strategies, questioned the rightness of the goal of full, unfettered assimilation. This is by no means intended to ignore the movement of the thousands of African Americans who left the South in the 1880s and established scores of all-black towns on the western frontiers. I am suggesting, however, that male leaders of the millions of blacks who remained in southern states and in some northern communities differed only as to the means by which assimilation and integration were to be achieved and over what time frame. Black men from Booker T. Washington to W. E. B. Du Bois viewed the establishment of autonomous, separate organizations and institutions essentially as a means to an end. Of course Marcus Garvey in the early twenties and Du Bois by the thirties had denounced integrationism. But when they did so they swam against mainstream black political thought.

As integrationism became the entrenched ideology and goal in the public-sphere debates, black women were increasingly silenced and overshadowed. Their desires for and efforts toward the creation of a network of separate autonomous community institutions as an end unto itself garnered less public regard. This does not mean that black women eschewed the fight for equal representation and full citizenship rights. Examples of their protest activities, from washerwomen strikes in Atlanta to civil suits against segregated trains throughout the South, readily disprove such notions.

In response to sexual repression within and without the Black community, black women developed a two-pronged attack. Some loudly proclaimed their allegiance to black men and insisted that the struggle for rights and opportunities had to be a unified one. Others looked to each other for the power they needed to change their lives. Many of the strategies that had enabled them to survive slavery were revised to meet contemporary exigencies. African American women combined work to advance the race as a whole with efforts to carve out psychic space for the development of a new collective black women's oppositional consciousness that was appropriate in the era of Jim Crow.

Black women's culture reached a new height of self-awareness in the closing decades of the nineteenth century. As they consolidated and formed national organizations, such as the National Association of Colored Women in 1896, black women defined the issues about which they would be concerned and the strategies they would employ. A direct line of activism extends from Harriet Tubman's work on the Underground Railroad to Ida B. Wells's antilynching crusade. Black women never abandoned their belief that the liberation and safety of black men was an inextricable component of the overall struggle, but they were acutely aware of gender concerns.

Within the confines of their separate realities, individual African American women had to create a patchwork of identities just to get through most days. Because the vast majority of them were poor, and therefore imprisoned in a horizontally segregated labor force, black women urgently yearned for middle-class respectability. Their legendary desire for respectability is reflected in a preoccupation with appearance—hair, dress, and skin color. Considering the singular wealth Madam C. J. Walker of Indianapolis, Indiana, amassed in the opening decades of the twentieth century, one could conclude that ambivalence existed in the American part of black women's identity. Is it possible to measure black women's assimilation in the Progressive Era not by the reform and social-welfare work they engaged in but by the extent to which they straightened their hair, wore socially accepted styles, and endeavored to lighten their complexions with cosmetics?

It is tempting to argue that black women made Madam C. J. Walker America's first self-made millionairess because she gave them the means to approximate whiteness by dispatching tightly curled hair with the straightening comb and miraculous hair tonics. But black women did not purchase beauty products and use skin-bleaching creams to obscure or to camouflage their blackness, their distinctiveness. Rather they used these technologies and products out of a desire for greater access to economic opportunities in a society that measured worth according to color and gender roles and material possessions. Cosmetics, dress, and hair styling became essential equipment in the unending work of black women to manipulate workable identities while shielding their inner lives from view. Black women desired what whiteness represented. They did not wish to be white, for to do so meant abandoning the culture and institutions they had created to ensure the survival and progress of their people.

Scholars of black women's history have invested an immense amount of research into the history of the rise of black women's clubs beginning in the late nineteenth century. Such concentration is warranted. The myriad organizations founded were more than a response to the insulting declarations of white newspaperman James T. Jacks that all black women were liars and prostitutes. Moreover, the clubs were not simply reactions to white women's denial of membership in their organizations. Rather club formation continued the organizing work of antebellum black women in the antislavery movement. Propitiously, coming together in clubs helped black women to accumulate information concerning the tribulations involved in migrating, and establish the networks needed to ease the stress of resettlement in regions such as the Middle West.

Through the vehicle of their clubs and organizations, which provided a measure of individual invisibility and protection, black women collectively addressed urban social problems by (re)creating an array of self-help institutions. This work on behalf of their communities reinforced their own self-constructed identities as respectable, moral race women and thus enabled them to be even more effective workers and leaders in "the kingdom of culture."

II.

In examining the culture and experiences of middle-western black women as a group or the life of individual black nurses, I seek to know what they believed, valued, and accomplished, and how they resisted the multiple oppressions that are constant forces in black women's existence. Black women are grounded in familial and friendship networks, and in larger social units that form communities. How these groups and communities define race, class, and gender roles and develop resistance strategies reflect the often invisible but nevertheless consequential work of black women. It is through their individual and collective work within families, friendship networks, and communities that a clear picture emerges of the contours of black women's identity, consciousness, and interdependence.

Any study of an individual black woman needs to place her in specific regional communities that possess a range of clubs, civic and religious organizations, and institutions. Black women's organizations nurtured and sustained the women, and empowered and supported black communities. Through voluntary organizations black women were able to develop by the turn of the century a substantial reform and race-uplift agenda. Specifically the club movement and the early entry of black women into key female professions, such as nursing, social work, librarianship, and teaching, afforded them the means and latitude to impose their own distinct visions and ideas, and to initiate a plethora of programs and projects. Black women's activism within the structure of clubs, organizations and institutions made possible greater sexual autonomy, encouraged economic development, and promoted racial progress, all without seeming to threaten or challenge male dominance.

In particular, the history of black women nurses provides ample illustration of how black women actually constructed positive identities and achieved greater self-awareness while permitting a glimpse of the abstractions and stereotypes that even now often diminish and caricature their lives and experiences. In the larger society, historically women's quest for personal achievement and self-fulfillment has been possible only through carefully prescribed channels. For black women, the range of roles permitted was even narrower, yet, on occasion, they forced reality to diverge from the so-called idealized construction of "women's sphere." Perhaps black women gained valuable breathing space when the larger society denied them membership in "the cult of true womanhood" characterized by piety, purity, submissiveness, and domesticity. It was within this breathing space that they subtly challenged the notions of "woman's sphere" and a "black's place."

In 1908 black nurses founded the National Association of Colored Graduate Nurses (NACGN). It became, under the dynamic leadership of Mabel Keaton Staupers in the 1940s, a powerful weapon in the struggle against discrimination and segregation in the nursing profession, and in the fight to abolish the quotas imposed by the U.S. Armed Forces Nurse Corps during World War II. Staupers, without trepidation, boldly attacked the racist policies of top military authorities and demanded that they dismantle Jim Crow quotas. Through the NACGN black women nurses acquired professional identity and the voice to articulate their grievances, and were able to develop more sophisticated connections with black communities that proved essential to the successful outcome of the overall quest for integration in nursing.

The white nursing profession held black nurses in low regard, frequently judging their skills and aptitude inferior to those of whites. Prior to the successes of the modern civil rights movement few white hospitals admitted black women into nurses' training, or hired black graduate nurses, or advanced them to supervisory positions in visiting-nurse agencies. As private-duty nurses black women received less pay and were often required to perform household chores in addition to nursing service. White nurses and white clients saw black nurses as little more than uniformed domestic servants.

In marked contrast, black communities held these same nurses in high esteem, according them the pride and dignity denied in their dealings with their white professional peers. Acting in their own best interests, black nurses grounded themselves within the communities that created and supported a nationwide network of clinics, hospitals, and training schools. The relationship black nurses enjoyed with black communities, therefore served as a powerful antidote to the racism, sexism, and elitism prevalent within the larger profession and throughout American society.

Black nurses were not the only ones who looked to community for a healthy sense of professional and personal identity. Midwestern black women, and I suspect the same is true for black women in all regions, developed an impressive array of clubs, and created autonomous organizations and institutions that first ensured racial survival, and second, facilitated selective adaptation and measured assimilation. Certainly the schools, hospitals, libraries, community centers, settlement houses, day-care centers, employment agencies that they erected and sustained had a strong "domestic" cast, but be not misled, for they were decidedly public in orientation. Again, these nurturing institutions cloaked black community women's individual and collective intent to erect bulwarks against the internalization of self-damaging norms, against beliefs that difference meant inferiority.

Not all black women successfully resisted assaults on their consciousness. Many succumbed to the forces that denigrated and marginalized their identities and experiences, filling them with self-loathing and self-abnegation. Not surprisingly then, some black women straddled, trying to adhere to the traditional cultural values and beliefs of the black community while embracing white ways in order to seize new opportunities. Had all abandoned their communities, families, and friends, there would be precious little to talk or to think about in black women's history. Cultural ambivalence notwithstanding, the founding of Provident Hospital and School of Nursing in Chicago united these disparate contexts and thus serves as a potent illustration of the way that race, access to resources, and gender roles forged black women's consciousness and activism.

When Emma Reynolds, the sister of a prominent black minister in Chicago, arrived in 1890 from Kansas City with hopes of attending nurses' training school, she quickly discovered the doors of the existing institutions closed. Denied admission into every nursing school in the city, Reynolds spoke to her brother, who in turn sought advice and assistance from physician Daniel Hale Williams. A group of black ministers, physicians, and businessmen approached white authorities but failed in their attempts to pry open the doors of the white nursing schools. Williams thereupon appealed for aid to the Reverend Jenkins Lloyd Jones, pastor of All Souls' Church, who placed the issue squarely before the members of his congregation. Fortuitously, the indefatigable black clubwoman and organizer Fannie Barrier Williams was in the congregation. With her usual verve, Williams, along with other black clubwomen, played a major role in mobilizing community support and raised money for the establishment of Provident Hospital and School of Nursing, thus ensuring that black women would have access to this profession, and that black patients would be treated with respect by their own physicians.

It is senseless to discuss the impact of racism on the formation of black identities without concomitant explorations into the ways in which race, a social construct of tremendous importance, nevertheless intersects with constructs of gender and class. Arguably, the history of black women in the United States provides the best available lens through which to illustrate the intersections of race, gender, and class across time. In other words, the ironies, contradictions, conflicts, and paradoxes of American history and culture are seen most graphically in the enigmatic black woman. An examination of this underside of American history requires an awareness of the relentless struggle black women have waged and continue to wage against sexual oppression, economic exploitation, social ridicule, and personal dehumanization.

FOR THE BEST IN PAPERBACKS, LOOK FOR THE 🐧

In every corner of the world, on every subject under the sun, Penguin represents quality and variety—the very best in publishing today.

For complete information about books available from Penguin—including Pelicans, Puffins, Peregrines, and Penguin Classics—and how to order them, write to us at the appropriate address below. Please note that for copyright reasons the selection of books varies from country to country.

In the United Kingdom: For a complete list of books available from Penguin in the U.K., please write to *Dept E.P., Penguin Books Ltd, Harmondsworth, Middlesex, UB7 0DA*.

In the United States: For a complete list of books available from Penguin in the U.S., please write to *Consumer Sales, Penguin USA, P.O. Box 999— Dept. 17109, Bergenfield, New Jersey 07621-0120*. VISA and MasterCard holders call 1-800-253-6476 to order all Penguin titles.

In Canada: For a complete list of books available from Penguin in Canada, please write to *Penguin Books Canada Ltd, 10 Alcorn Avenue, Suite 300, Toronto, Ontario, Canada M4V 3B2*.

In Australia: For a complete list of books available from Penguin in Australia, please write to the *Marketing Department, Penguin Books Ltd, P.O. Box 257, Ringwood, Victoria 3134*.

In New Zealand: For a complete list of books available from Penguin in New Zealand, please write to the *Marketing Department, Penguin Books (NZ) Ltd, Private Bag, Takapuna, Auckland 9*.

In India: For a complete list of books available from Penguin, please write to *Penguin Overseas Ltd, 706 Eros Apartments, 56 Nehru Place, New Delhi, 110019*.

In Holland: For a complete list of books available from Penguin in Holland, please write to *Penguin Books Nederland B.V., Postbus 195, NL-1380AD Weesp, Netherlands*.

In Germany: For a complete list of books available from Penguin, please write to *Penguin Books Ltd, Friedrichstrasse 10-12, D-6000 Frankfurt Main 1, Federal Republic of Germany*.

In Spain: For a complete list of books available from Penguin in Spain, please write to *Longman, Penguin España, Calle San Nicolas 15, E-28013 Madrid, Spain*.

In Japan: For a complete list of books available from Penguin in Japan, please write to *Longman Penguin Japan Co Ltd, Yamaguchi Building, 2-12-9 Kanda Jimbocho, Chiyoda-Ku, Tokyo 101, Japan*.